Jack London

THE CALL OF THE WILD
&
Other Stories

With ESSAYS IN CRITICISM

Annotated with Critical Introduction

by

Min, Kyung-taek

Shinasa

Signed photograph of Jack London, ca.1907-1908. Photo taken on board the Snark, the sailboat upon which he cruised the South Pacific for 27 months with his wife Charmian. (MSS 6240. Clifton Waller Barrett Library of American Literature. Image by Caroline Newcomb)

(http://smallnotes.library.virginia.edu/2013/09/23/l-is-for/)

(Posted on September 23, 2013 by Petrina Jackson)

CONTENTS

CRITICAL INTRODUCTION

THE TEXT

The Call of the Wild

Other Stories

ESSAYS IN CRITICISM

CRITICAL INTRODUCTION

1. Jack London의 생애

잭 런던(Jack London, 1876-1916)은 존 그리피쓰 체이니(John Griffith Chaney)라는 이름으로 1876년 1월 12일 샌프란시스코(San Francisco)에서 점성술가인 아버지 윌리엄 체이니(William H. Chaney)와 운하 건설기술자의 딸인 중류층 출신의 어머니 플로라 웰먼(Flora Wellman)의 사이에서 태어났다. 그의 어머니는 음악교사이며 심령주의자였는데 당시 떠돌이 점성술가였던 체이니와 법적으로 결혼했는지의 여부는 알려지지 않았지만 동거를 하였고 런던을 임신하게 된다. 체이니는 낙태할 것을 요구하였지만 플로라가 거부하자 체이니는 아이에 대한 책임을 부인하게 되고 플로라는 권총자살을 시도하지만 실패한다. 그녀는 심각한 부상은 피했지만 일시적인 정신착란에 빠졌으며 아이를 출산한 이후에 아이를 예전에 노예였었던 흑인여성인 버지니아 프렌티스(Virginia Prentiss)에게 맡기게 되며 그 후 프렌티스는 유모와 이미니의 역할을 대신하면서 런던에게 많은 영향을 주게 된다.

플로라는 1876년 9월에 남북전쟁의 상이군인이며 두 딸을 가진 홀아비인 존 런던(John London)과 결혼하면서 그녀의 아이를 데려옴으로써 그는 'John Griffith Chaney'에서 새로운 이름인 'Jack London'으로 불리게 된다. 존은 채소출하 농장에서 일하고 플로라는 음악을 가르치며 생계를 유지하지만 가난을 벗어나지 못한다. 런던은 초등학교에 다니면서 많은 책을 읽게 되며 특히 워싱턴 어빙(Washington Irving)과 위더(Ouida)의 작품에 감동을 받았다고 런던은 회상한다. 런던이 10세가 된 1886년에 존 런던은 가족들을 데리고 오클랜드(Oakland)로 이사를 가고 어린 런던은 나중에 계관시인이 된 아이나 쿨버쓰(Ina Coolbrith)의 안내로 오클랜드 공공 도서관에서 더 많은 책을 읽을 수 있는 기회를 얻게 되고 이것이 런던이 작가로 성장할 수 있는 밑거름이 되었다고 알려진다. 잭 런던은 서부 오클랜드(West Oakland)에 있는 '콜 중등학교'(Cole Grammar School)에 다니면서 신문을 배달하거나 통조림 공장에서 일을 하면서 생계에 도움을 준다.

1891년 15세가 된 런던은 콜 중등학교를 졸업하고 공장의 단조로운 일과 저임금에 환멸을 느껴 프렌티스로부터 돈을 빌려 범선을 구입해서 굴 해적질을 시작한다. 그는 유명한 선원이 되어 '굴 해적의 왕자'(Prince of the Oyster Pirates)로 알려지지만 해적생활에도 싫증을 느끼게 된다. 16세가 된 런던은 오히려 굴 해적질을 감시하는 '어업순찰대'(Fish Patrol)의 감시원이 되지만 이것도 그만두고 갱단에 가입하여 'Sailor Kid'로 불리며 부랑아 생활을 하게 된다. 1893년 17세의 런던은 7개월 동안 일본해와 베링해의 연안에서 이루어진 물개사냥 항해에 선원으로 참여한다. 그는 어머니의 권유로 에세이 콘테스트에 참가하여 이때의 경험을 "Story of a Typhoon off the Coast of Japan"이라는 글로 발표하여 수상함으로써 25달러를 받게 되고 이것은 런던이 작가로서의 기질을 서서히 발휘한 계기가 된다.

런던은 18세가 된 1894년에 광산에서 석탄을 채굴하는 광부로서 힘든 노동을 하면서 체력이 고갈되는 것을 느끼고 파업에 참여한다. 그는 제이콥 칵시(Jacob Coxey)가 이끄는 실업자 시위대의 워싱턴(Washington, D.C.) 행진에 가담한 후에 시카고에서 열린 '세계 콜롬비아 박람회'(World's Columbian Exposition)를 관람하고 이모인 메리 에버하드(Mary Everhard)와 함께 미시간의 세인트 조지프(St. Joseph)에서 보내면서 이모로부터 노동자에 관해 글을 써보도록 권유를 받게 된다. 그 후에 런던은 부랑아 생활을 하면서 뉴욕(New York) 주의 버펄로

(Buffalo)에서 체포되어 30일 동안 이어리 카운티(Erie County)의 구치소에 갇히기도 한다. 그는 보스턴(Boston)에서 뜨내기 지식인과 교육자들을 만나면서 다윈(Darwin)과 니체(Nietzsche) 그리고 마르크스(Marx) 등의 사상을 접하게 된다. 런던은 캘리포니아(California)의 사회주의자로 또한 철학자이며 천재적인 거리의 웅변가였던 프랭크 해밀턴(Frank Strawn Hamilton)을 만나면서 사회주의 사상에 영향을 받는다.

런던은 19세가 된 1895년에 오클랜드에 돌아와서 고등학교와 대학에 진학하려는 결심을 하게 된다. 그는 오클랜드 고등학교(Oakland High School)에서 공부하면서 그리고 학교 잡역부로서 아르바이트를 하면서도 틈틈이 학교의 문예잡지(literary magazine)인 '이지스'(*The Aegis*)에 글을 발표한다. 그는 'Henry Clay Debating Team'에 가입하여 사회주의 사상을 가진 많은 친구들과 나중에 첫 번째 아내가 된 베시 매던(Bessie Maddern)을 그곳에서 만나게 된다. 런던은 20세가 된 1896년 4월에 오클랜드의 사회노동당에 정식으로 가입한다. 그는 고등학교를 중퇴하고 대학예비학원에 들어가 베시와 다른 친구들의 도움으로 독학한 후에 UC 버클리(The University of California, Berkeley)에 합격하여 첫 학기를 마치고 사회주의 에세이와 간단한 여행의 글을 발표한다.

1897년 런던은 존 런던이 자신의 친부가 아니라는 것을 알게 되고 친부로 알려진 체이니(William Chaney)에게 확인하려고 하지만 그로부터 부자관계를 인정하지 않는 편지를 받고 더 큰 충격에 빠진다. 그는 이러한 충격의 여파와 학생들과 교수에게서 정치의 진지함을 느낄 수 없는 대학의 분위기에 절망하고 또한 경제적인 궁핍에 압박을 느껴서 대학을 중퇴한다. 그 후에 그는 세탁소에서 힘들게 일을 하면서 독서와 창작할 수 있는 시간을 갖지 못한다. 그는 이복누이의 매형인 제임스 셰퍼드(James Shepard)와 함께 알래스카 골드러시(Alaska Gold

Rush)에 참여하지만 매형은 중도에 포기하고 돌아가고 7월에 계부인 존 런던이 사망한다. 그러나 런던은 클론다이크(Klondike)의 오두막에서 겨울을 보내면서 추의와 사투를 벌이며 1년 정도 버티지만 금을 발견하지 못하고 괴혈병에 걸려 금 대신 글쓰기에 대한 많은 소재거리를 가지고 1898년 7월에 집으로 돌아온다. 가족들은 어머니의 연금으로 근근이 생활하지만 런던은 새로운 일자리를 찾는 데는 실패한다.

런던은 일자리를 포기하고 잡지에 글을 발표하기 시작하는데 *Overland Monthly*에 "To the Man on Trail"을 발표하여 5달러를 받게 된다. 그는 작가이면서 비평가인 클라우드슬레이 존스(Cloudsley Johns)와 교류하면서 본격적으로 글을 쓰기 시작한다. 그는 *Atlantic Monthly*에 "An Odyssey of the North"를 발표하여 40달러를 받는다. 런던은 24세인 1900년 4월 7일에 그의 첫 단편집 *A Son of the Wolf*를 출판하고 같은 날에 고교 친구인 베시 매던과 결혼한다. 1901년 딸 조운(Joan)이 태어나고 사회당원으로 오클랜드 시장에 출마하지만 실패한다. 그는 두 번째 단편집인 *The God of His Fathers & Other Stories*를 출판한다. 런던은 또 다른 단편 모음집인 *Children of the Frost*와 소설 *Cruize of the Dazzler*와 *A Daughter of the Snows*를 발표한다. 그의 둘째 딸 베키(Becky)가 태어나고 이듬 해인 1903년에는 시카고에 살고 있던 체이니(William Henry Chaney)가 사망한다. 1903년에 런던은 애너 스트런스키(Anna Strunsky)와 공동 집필한 *The Kempton-Wace Letters*를 발표하고 같은 해 그의 대표작인 *The Call of the Wild*를 발표함으로써 그는 세계적인 명성을 얻는 작가의 반열에 올라서게 된다.

그는 사진작가이면서 수필도 발표했던 신여성으로 자유분방한 성격의 차미언 키트리지(Charmian Kittredge)와 사랑에 빠지게 되고 베시와 별거를 시작한다. 그는 1903년에 런던에 수개월 동안 체류하면서 체험한 내용을 르뽀형식으로 엮은 *The People of the Abyss*를 발표하여 사회의 보고서가 하나의 장르소설이 되도록 하는데 기여하였다. 1904년에 28세의 런던은 러일전쟁을 취재하기 위하여 일본에 도착하여 당시 조선과 중국을 방문하게 된다. 런던은 왕성한 창작력으로 *Faith of Men & Other Stories*와 *The Sea Wolf*를 발표하지만 베시는 런던에게 가족을 방치한 것에 대해 이혼소송을 제기한다. 런던은 1905년에 오클랜드 시장에 다시 출마하지만 낙선하고 같은 해에 *War of the Classes*와 *The Game* 그리고 *Tales of the Fish Patrol* 등을 발표하고 글렌 엘렌(Glen Ellen)에 있는 129에이커의 거대한 힐 농장(Hill Ranch)을 구입하고 긴 바다여행을 계획한다. 그는 4개월 동안 사회주의 강연여행을 하면서 혁명을 강조하는 에세이를 계속 발표한다. 그는 베시와 마침내 이혼하고 차미언과 시카고에서 결혼하고 자메이카(Jamaica)와 쿠바(Cuba)로 신혼여행을 다녀온다.

1906년에 런던은 바다여행을 위해 대형 요트인 스나크(Snark)호를 건조하기 시작한다. 그는 샌프란시스코의 대지진에 대한 보고서인 "The Story of an Eye-Witness"를 발표하여 대중의 관심을 받는다. 그는 *Moon-Face & Other Stories*와 *The Call of the Wild*의 자매작으로 알려진 *White Fang*, 그리고 *Scorn of Women*을 연속적으로 발표한다. 1907년에 런던은 차미언과 함께 스나크호를 타고 7년 계획의 세계일주 여행을 떠나 자신의 모험이야기를 *The Road*의 책으로 발표한다. 그는 1908년에 사회주의 미래소설인 *The Iron Heel*을 발표하고 요트여행에서 질병으로 1909년에 캘리포니아로 되돌아오고 자전적 소설 *Martin Eden*을 발표한다. 런던은 1911년에 *South Seal Tales*와 1912년에 *Smoke Bellew*를 발표한다. 1913년에 그는 표면적으로는 세계에서 가장 성공한 돈 잘 버는 작가로 알려졌지만 사적인 삶에서는 딸들과의 단절과 전처인 베시와의 갈등, 농장 경영의 실패와 그의 사회주의 사상을 실현하기 위한 야심작인 울프 하우스(Wolf House)의 화재로 인한 소실 등으로 우울한 시기를 보냈으며 그해에 한 알콜중독자의 자전적인 소설인 *John Barleycorn*을 발표한다. 그는 1914년에 도시의 척박한 삶에서 자연의 삶으로 탈출을 묘사한 *The Valley of the Moon* 발표한다. 1915년 39세인 런던은 종군기자로 멕시코에 다녀왔으며 미국 내 감옥에서 벌어지는 가혹한 형벌에 대한 고발적인 환상소설인 *The Star Rover*를 발표한다. 1916년 11월 12일에 40세인 런던은 신장병으로 그가 가장 소중하게 생각했던 자신의 농장인 소노마 카운티(Sonoma-County)의 글렌 엘렌에 있는 '아름다운 농장'(Beauty-Ranch)에서 파란만장한 생을 마감한다.

2. Jack London의 작품세계

잭 런던은 스티븐 크레인(Stephen Crane, 1871-1900)과 프랭크 노리스(Frank Norris, 1870-1902)와 함께 초기 미국 자연주의 문학을 대표하는 소설가이다. 불우한 환경에서 잭 런던은 인간의 비극적인 운명의 원인을 냉혹한 자연환경과 무관심한 우주적 질서 또는 사회의 구조적인 모순과 부조리에서 찾으려고 하였다. 런던은 찰스 다윈(Charles Darwin)의 생물학적 진화론이나 칼 마르크스(Karl Marx)의 『자본론』(*Das Kapital*)과 같은 당시의 혁신적인 자연과학 이론뿐만 아니라 정치와 사회사상에 공감하면서 그러한 관점으로 인간의 삶을 분석하려고 시도하였다. 그는 19세기 말엽과 20세기 초엽의 세계와 미국의 정치, 경제, 사회의 흐름에 민감하였고 특히 실제로 사회당의 일원으로 정치에 참여하기도 하였다.

런던은 가난한 어린 시절부터 시작한 바다생활과 캐나다 북쪽의 클론다이크(Klondike)[1]의 골드러시에서 자신이 직접 경험한 사실을 바탕으로 동물들을 주인공으로 등장시키거나 작품의 소재로 활용하여 자신의 자연주의 사상을 많은 작품 속에 구현하고 있다. 비평가들은 일반적으로 런던의 자연주의를 약육강식, 자연도태, 적자생존 같은 생물학적 자연주의 사상이나 다윈의 진화론 또는 허버트 스펜서(Herbert Spencer)에 의해 표명되는 사회진화론(Social Darwinism)으로 설명하고 있다. 런던의 작품에서 배경으로 자주 등장하는 유콘(Yukon) 강의 자연환경은 법을 의미하는 '자연도태설'과 '적자생존론' 등이 끊임없이 재현되는 일종의 형이상학적인 상징적인 공간으로 간주되고 있다(Dickey 10). 런던의 자연주의 사상은 인간도 정글의 법칙이 적용되는 야생처럼 생존경쟁이 치열한 냉혹한 사회 환경 속에서 살아가고 있다는 것을 보여주는 것이다.

일반적으로 자연주의 작가들은 인간의 운명이 환경, 유전, 우연성에 의해 가장 많은 영향을 받는다고 생각한다. 그들은 우리 삶은 이미 비극적으로 결정되었고 인간의 의지는 제한적이라고 말하며 인간 사회의 부정적 요소와 부조리한 측면을 강조한다. 크레인은「무갑판선」("The Open Boat")에서 인간운명의 부조리성과 인간의 의지와는 무관한 냉혹한 자연과 우주의 법칙을 보여주었고, 노리스는『맥티그』(*Mcteague*)에서 물질에 노예가 된 인간과 자본화된 사회에서 인간의 비극적인 운명

1) 프랭클린 워커(Franklin Walker)의 연구에 따르면 어린 나이에 생계를 책임지고 있었던 런던은 가난을 벗어나기 위하여 1897년 7월에 캐나다 유콘(Yukon) 강 근처의 클론다이크에서 발견된 금을 채굴하여 돈을 벌어보려는 골드러시에 이복 매형과 함께 참여하지만 매형은 중도에 포기하고 런던은 1년 정도 버티지만 빈털터리로 돌아온다. 런던은 이곳에서 다윈의 사상을 심각하게 체험하게 되고 런던은 이러한 경험을 자신의 작품에 재현하게 된다(Wilcox 179).

을 그리고 있다. 반면에 런던은 인간 삶의 환경과 사회의 구조적인 측면에서 드러나는 모순과 악의 요소를 부각시키고 인간의 비극적인 조건을 강조하였다. 런던은 자신의 다양한 많은 작품에서 이러한 자연주의 사상을 표출함으로써 당시 문명에 대한 중요한 비판적인 시각을 드러내고 있는데, 이것은 그의 작품을 일관적으로 관통하는 주제라고 볼 수 있다.

3. *The Call of the Wild*

런던의 걸작인 『야성의 부름』(*The Call of the Wild*, 1903)은 세계 여러 나라에서 많은 다른 언어로 번역 출판되어 세계적인 인기를 얻은 베스트셀러이다. 이 작품은 그의 또 다른 소설인 『흰 어금니』(*White Fang*, 1906)와 자매작으로서 키플링(Rudyard Kipling)이 1894년에 발표하여 인기를 끌었던 늑대와 다른 동물들이 등장하는 아동소설인 『정글북』(*The Jungle Book*, 1894)처럼 늑대와 개가 주인공으로 등장한다는 점과 짧고 간결한 문장의 시적인 표현과 아름다운 생동감 있는 문체로 인하여 많은 사랑을 받았다.

런던은 『야성의 부름』에서 문명에 대한 비판적인 시각을 인간 사회와 자연과 야성의 대비적인 관점으로 잘 드러내고 있다. 즉 주인공 벅(Buck)은 따뜻한 남쪽의 인간의 집에서 편하게 지내다가 자신의 의지와는 전혀 무관하게 갑자기 납치되어 북쪽으로 팔려감으로써 모든 것이 달라지고 열악한 환경에서 썰매개로 살아가기 위하여 동물적인 본능과 야성에 의존하게 된다. 런던은 남쪽의 따뜻한 자연환경과 인간의 보호로부터 인간의 한계상황이 드러나는 북쪽의 추운 지방으로의 공간이동과 환경변화를 설정하고 벅의 생존에 대한 치열한 과정을 통하여 문명과 자연, 인간과 동물, 도덕과 본능, 야만과 사랑 등의 대조적인 가치들을 독자들로 하여금 반추해 보도록 함으로써 우리 삶의 궁극적인 진리를 조망하고 있다.

『야성의 부름』은 단순히 개의 모험이야기가 아니라 현대 인간의 존재에 대한 우화[2]라고 볼 수 있으며 인간의 물질에 대한 욕망과 자본주의에 대한 경고라고 볼 수 있다. 런던은 주인공인 개 벅을 의인화하여 자신의 견해가 투영된 동물의 시각으로 인간의 심리와 문명세계를 해부하고 있다. 런던은 작품의 도입부인 제1장 첫 문단부터 주인공인 개의 시각으로 볼 때 단지 "노란 금속"(43)에 불과한 금으로 상징화되는 인간의 물욕에 대해 냉소적인 견해를 드러낸다. 이 부분은 클론다이크의 골드러시에 참여했던 런던 자신의 알래스카에서의 개인적인 경험이 반영된 부분으로서 자본주의와 문명에 대한 비판적인 시각을 금의 가치를 전혀 알 수 없는 개의 눈을 통하여 보여주고 있다.

벅은 따뜻한 캘리포니아 남쪽의 산타클라라 계곡(Santa Clara Valley)에 있는 밀러(Miller) 판사의 대저택에서 "모든 기어 다니는 동물들에게 군림하는 왕처럼"(44) 살고 있으며 인간들에게 사랑받는 네 살 된 개다. 그는 혈통이 좋은 아비와 어미의 유전자를 물려받아 몸집이 거대하며 "당당한 귀족"(45)처럼 살아간다. 그러나 돈에 쪼들리며 마작을 좋아하는 주인집 정원사 조수인 매뉴엘(Manuel)에 의해 납치되어 50달러에 북쪽으로 팔려간다. 그는 자신의 의지와는 전혀 상관없이 샌프란시스코

---

2) 레이버와 레이츠(Earle Labor and Leitz)는 『야성의 부름, 흰 어금니, 그리고 기타 이야기들』(*The Call of the Wild, White Fang, and Other Stories*)에서 『야성의 부름』은 단순히 재미있고 쉽게 읽을 수 있는 책 이상으로서 세계의 위대한 동물 우화의 이야기들 중의 하나이며 이솝(Aesop)의 이야기들처럼 우리에게 교훈과 재미를 준다고 말한다. 그러나 단순한 동물 우화에서 벗어나 뛰어난 인간의 우화이며, 더 나아가 단순한 우화적인 의미를 뛰어넘어 상징적인 의미를 지닌다고 강조하였다(Introduction, xii-xiii 참조).

에서 시애틀을 거쳐 동토의 땅인 클론다이크로 강제로 끌려간다.

벅은 따뜻한 남쪽에서 추운 북쪽으로 이동하는데 남쪽은 문명을 상징하고 북쪽은 야성이 필요한 자연을 상징한다. 벅의 주거이동은 환경의 변화를 의미하며 벅은 실존의 고통과 적응의 시련을 경험하게 된다. 이 이동의 과정에서 벅은 다양한 사람의 주인을 만나게 되는데 특히 "빨간 스웨터"(49)를 입은 남자는 폭력적이며 잔인한 인간의 전형으로 반항하는 벅을 곤봉으로 매질하고 벅 또한 저항하는 과정에서 "빨간 눈의 악마"(49)로 변해간다. 그 후 벅의 머릿속에서 그 사람의 기억은 떠나지 않으며 곤봉을 가진 사람에게는 복종해야 한다는 교훈을 얻게 된다.

벅은 시애틀에서 다른 개들과 함께 "나월"(Narwhal)"이라는 배를 타고 북쪽으로 끌려가는데 그의 새로운 주인은 프랑스계 캐나다인인 페로우(Perrault)와 인디언과 혼혈인으로 역시 프랑스계 캐나다인인 프랑스와(Francois)이다. 그의 새 주인들은 썰매개를 이용하여 정부의 급송우편을 전달하는 사람들로 정의를 집행하는데 있어서 공정하고 조용하고 편견이 없는 사람들이다. 그러나 그들은 자신들에게 할당된 우편배달 업무를 신속하고 효율적으로 수행하기 위해 벅을 비롯한 썰매개들을 잘 활용하는데 더 집착함으로써 벅은 그들에게 애정은 생기지 않았지만 어느 정도경외심을 갖게 된다. 그들은 애정보다는 법의 권위를 이용하여 개를 다루는 전문가이며 엄정하고 냉정한 인간들의 표본이라고 볼 수 있다.

벅은 북부지방에서 처음 눈이 내리는 것을 보게 되며 추위에 어려움을 겪지만 빠르게 새로운 환경에 적응하게 된다. 북쪽의 황량한 자연환경은 스펜서가 이야기한 실증적인 논리로는 이해할 수 없고 상징적으로 또는 시적으로만 재현할 수 있는 '불가지물'이라고 볼 수 있다

(McClintock 83). 그는 문명의 심장부에서 원시적인 자연환경의 핵심으로 던져지게 되는데 그곳의 인간과 개들은 도시의 개와 인간과는 다른 반문명의 상태라고 묘사된다.

벅은 새로운 환경에 적응하고 살아가야 하는데 벅의 상황은 자본주의 시대의 현대인들이 자주 직면해야 할 환경변화의 상황과 유사하다. 벅은 장소의 이동을 통하여 정체성의 위기에 부딪치게 됨으로써 정체성 상실, 소외의 감정, 낯선 세계에 대한 믿음의 상실 등과 같은 문제에 대처하는 방법을 배워야 한다. 벅의 문제는 적대적인 세계에서 살아남는 방법을 배워야 하는 것이고 그것은 현대인이 직면해야할 실존적인 문제와 동일하다고 볼 수 있다(Spinner 234).

벅이 살아갈 북쪽 지방의 환경은 열악한 자연환경이며 그곳의 개와 사람을 포함한 모든 생명체들은 문명과는 거리가 먼 자연에 가까운 야만적인 상태의 존재들로 묘사된다. 벅은 다른 썰매개들과 함께 생존을 위해 치열한 무한경쟁에 몰리게 된다. 벅은 집안의 따뜻한 난롯가에서 자던 버릇을 버리고 다른 개들처럼 눈을 파서 구덩이를 만들어 눈 속에서 잠을 자는 방법을 터득하게 되며 살기 위해 먹이를 훔쳐 먹기도 한다. 그는 변화하는 환경에 빠르게 적응해 가는데 화자는 그것은 그의 "도덕적 본성의 쇠퇴"(62-63)이며 도덕은 생존의 무자비한 투쟁에서는 쓸모없으며 방해가 된다고 말한다. 또한 그는 사랑과 우정이 지배하는 남쪽지방에서는 개인의 재산과 감정을 존중하는 것이 충분히 가능하지만 "곤봉과 어금니의 법칙이 존재하는 북쪽지방"(63)에서는 그런 것을 고려하면 살아가기가 어렵다고 말한다.

즉 벅의 새로운 환경은 "도덕적 고려"(63)가 존재하지 않는 반문명적인 야만의 환경이라고 볼 수 있다. 런던은 벅이 그러한 환경에서 잘 적응하는 것을 "발달(또는 퇴화)"(63)이라고 설명함으로써 인간의 관점에서는 퇴화이지만 야생의 관점으로 보면 발달이라는 시각을 드러낸다. 벅은 점차로 튼튼한 근육과 원시의 늑대조상처럼 야생의 본능과 능력을 회복하게 된다. 그러나 아우어바흐(Auerbach)는 겉으로는 런던과 벅을 몰고 가는 가치와 본능의 두 개의 플롯이 존재하지만 훨씬 더 중요한 것은 완고한 다윈사상의 본능보다는 가치에 더 많이 관련되어 있고 내러티브를 제공하는 중심적인 역설은 벅이 야만적으로 변해야 한다는 것이라고 말한다(55). 즉 런던은 벅의 환경의 변화와 적응의 문제에도 불구하고 가치나 도덕의 문제에 항상 집착하고 있다는 것을 보여준다.

런던은 벅이 새로운 야만적인 환경에 적응해 가는 과정에서 냉혹한 자연의 질서를 강조하면서도 도덕과 가치의 문제를 버리지 않고 있다. 벅은 자신에게 할당된 먹이를 훔쳐가는 방식으로 그를 항상 괴롭히던 비열한 리더인 스피츠(Spitz)를 자신의 능력으로 싸워서 죽임으로써 썰매개의 새로운 강력한 리더가 된다. 그러나 화자는 벅이 스피츠가 없는 위대함의 자질 즉 "상상력"(79)을 소유함으로써 본능과 함께 머리를 가지고 생각하며 싸웠다고 말함으로써 벅의 차별성을 강조한다. 작가는 벅을 자연의 환경에 단순히 반응하는 생명체가 아니라 생각하는 능력을 소유한 인격의 주체로 승화시키고 있다.

그러나 벅은 도덕과 가치가 존중받기 어려운 환경에 끊임없이 노출됨으로써 그의 고통과 시련은 계속된다. 정부의 급송우편 썰매 일을 성공적으로 완수한 후에도 벅과 동료 썰매개들은 스코틀랜드 혼혈인에게 맡겨져 일반 우편썰매를 영하 50도의 강추위 속에서 쉬지도 잘 먹지도 못한 채 계속 끌면서 혹사당한다. 벅은 도슨(Dawson)시를 떠난 뒤 30일 만에 알래스카의 스캐그웨이(Skaguay)에 기력이 다 쇠진된 상태로 도착하지만 금광을 찾아가는 새로운 주인에게 다시 팔려간다.

새로운 주인은 한 가족으로 구성되었는데 중년의 찰스(Charles)와 19살에서 20살쯤 보이는 청년 핼(Hal)과 그의 누이며 찰스의 아내인 머시디즈(Mercedes) 등 세 명이다. 이들은 남쪽 출신의 사람들로 북쪽 지방에 산 경험이 전혀 없으며 썰매몰이에서 미숙함을 드러낸다.

그들은 문명을 상징하는 인물들로서 야생의 경험과 이해가 부족해서 결국 비극적인 최후를 맞이한다. 베노이트(Benoit)는 찰스, 핼, 머시디즈는 문명을 대변하는 인물들로서 허영을 버리고 자연의 교훈을 배우는데 실패했으며 런던은 지친 개들에게 문명의 짐들을 끌도록 강요하는 그들을 죽음으로 심판하고 있다고 말한다(Benoit 248). 그들이 썰매에 싣고 가려는 것들은 야생에서는 필요가 없는 문명의 이기들로 그들은 그것들을 썰매에 너무 많이 싣고 가려고 함으로써 오랜 썰매일로 체력이 떨어지고 지쳐버린 개들이 그 무게를 감당하지 못한다.

그들은 경험 많은 사람들의 충고로 짐을 줄이지만 머시디즈는 계속 썰매를 타고 감으로써 개들에게 부담을 가중시킨다. 그들은 지치고 굶주린 개들에게 휴식과 먹이를 충분히 주지 않고 내로 다스림으로써 개들은 주인에게 신뢰성을 갖지 못하며 개들은 식량 부족과 피로로 인하여 계속 죽게 된다. 쏜턴(John Thornton)의 캠프에 도착한 그들은 여행을 포기하라는 쏜턴의 충고를 듣지 않고 강을 무리하게 건너가던 과정에서 얼음이 깨져서 다른 개들과 함께 모두 익사한다. 쏜턴은 그들이 떠나기 전에 과로로 지쳐서 움직이지 못하던 벅을 잔인하게 매질하던 핼[3]과 결투하여 벅을 구해줌으로써 벅은 썰매개의 일에서 해방된다.

쏜턴은 벅의 마지막 주인으로 벅을 사랑으로 보살펴주고 휴식을 줌

3) 이 장면에서 핼은 개들의 건강과 체력을 전혀 고려하지 않고 얼음의 상태에 대한 판단부족과 자만심에 빠져서 썰매 여행을 강행하다가 결국 죽음을 맞이하는데 그의 이름은 지옥(hell)을 연상시킨다.

으로써 벅은 서서히 체력을 회복한다. 쏜턴의 친절과 관대함은 벅이 밀러 판사의 저택에서도 경험해보지 못했던 새로운 차원의 사랑이며, 벅은 새로운 주인에 대해 가슴 깊은 곳에서 진정한 사랑을 느꼈으며 강요가 아닌 자발적인 마음으로 열정적으로 숭배하게 된다. 벅에게 쏜턴은 지금까지의 주인과는 다른 종류의 사람이었다. 즉 그는 벅에게 폭력과 곤봉의 힘을 사용하지 않는 유일한 사랑의 신이었으며 개들을 친 자식처럼 대했고 매보다는 말로 대화를 나누었다. 벅의 지금까지 잃어버린 사랑의 감정은 쏜턴의 친절함에 다시 살아나고 주인에게 숭배로 충성을 보인다. 그러나 문명의 따뜻한 영향에도 불구하고 벅의 내부에는 북쪽지방에서 발산된 그의 원시적인 기질이 살아있었다. 화자는 일시적인 인간의 사랑으로도 벅의 되살아난 야성과 동물적인 본능은 사라지지 않았다는 것을 강조하면서 그가 경험한 세계는 약육강식과 적자생존의 법칙만 존재하는 무자비한 정글이라고 설명한다.

벅의 쏜턴에 대한 충성은 자기희생적인 사랑이며 이것은 문명의 세계에서도 찾기 어려운 이타적인 숭고한 사랑이라고 볼 수 있다. 벅은 쏜턴의 목숨을 여러 번 구해줌으로써 그의 명령에는 절대복종하게 된다. 벅은 자신의 갈비뼈가 부러지는 것도 아랑곳 하지 않고 물에 빠져 위험한 순간에서 주인을 급류에서 구해주었고 1000파운드의 썰매끌기의 내기에서 주인을 위해 사력을 다하여 돈을 벌게 해줌으로써 쏜턴에게 감동의 눈물을 흘리게 만든다. 그는 벅을 팔라는 제의를 일언지하에 거절함으로써 벅과 쏜턴의 관계는 벅이 야생으로 떠나고 싶은 본능을 억제하게 만드는 문명과의 마지막 긴밀한 끈으로 작용한다.

벅이 내기에서 벌어준 돈으로 빚을 청산한 쏜턴은 다시 금을 채굴하는데 성공하여 많은 돈을 벌지만 벅은 캠프에서 할 일이 없어지고 결국 숲속에서 들려오는 야생의 부름에 호응하게 된다. 벅은 늑대와

친해지고 캠프를 떠나서 며칠씩 야생을 돌아다니다가 쏜턴을 생각하고 마침내 돌아오곤 한다. 벅은 야생에서 더 많은 시간을 보냄으로써 살아있는 먹이를 사냥하는 사냥꾼의 습성을 갖게 되고 포식자로 변신하게 된다. 런던은 낭만주의 소설에 자주 등장하는 영웅들처럼 벅을 점차로 영웅 신화의 주인공으로 만들고 초월적 존재로 신격화하기 시작한다.

벅은 쏜턴이 이햇츠(Yeehats) 인디언들에게 살해되었을 때 이햇츠 인디언들을 포식자처럼 무자비하게 살육함으로써 복수를 한다. 쏜턴은 죽고 인간과 문명과의 마지막 관계가 끊어지고 "인간과 인간의 소유권은 그를 더 이상 구속하지 못함"(137)으로써 벅은 자유롭게 야생의 숲으로 돌아간다. 벅에게 쏜턴의 역할은 단지 안내자에 불과했으며 그런 주인의 죽음을 통하여 주인공 벅은 북쪽 지방의 두려운 유령의 개로 변모하는 과정을 완성하게 되는데, 이러한 과정은 바로 영원한 창조의 신비이며 그 생명력의 현현이라고 볼 수 있다(Labor and Leitz xiv). 그러니 화자는 작품 말미에서 벅은 이햇츠 인디언들에게 "유령의 개"(139)로 불리며 두려움의 전설이 되었지만 해마다 여름에 쏜턴이 금을 채굴하던 캠프가 있었던 계곡에 찾아와서 슬프게 울부짖다가 돌아간다고 묘사함으로써 벅의 내면에는 인간에 대한 따뜻한 사랑과 그리움이 남아 있음을 어느 정도 암시하고 있다.

런던의 사상을 지지하였던 오웰(Orwell)은 런던의 자연과 야성으로의 회귀의 과정은 잔인하지만 항상 일종의 기쁨이 존재하고 있으며 그것은 자연의 냉혹함을 인정하기보다는 오히려 자연은 그러한 것이라는 신비로운 믿음을 보여준다고 말한다(Dickey 11). 런던의 자연은 가면을 쓴 자연이며 실체를 정확하게 드러내지 않는다. 그러나 런던은 자연의 마스크를 파괴하여 진리에 도달하려는 멜빌(Melville)과는

달리 동물 진화의 두 가지 욕망 즉 동물적 생존과 자신을 재생산하려는 종의 욕구사이에는 도덕성이 내재되어 있음을 주장한다(Dickey 11). 즉 런던의 야성의 본능에는 문명의 중요한 상징인 도덕성이 연루되어 있기 때문에 완전한 개인주의와 독립적인 주체의 요구를 초월하고 있다. 즉 런던에게는 문명과 자연은 상호관련 되어 있으며 공유의 지점이 많다는 것을 보여준다.

런던이 바라보는 자연은 두 가지 얼굴을 가지고 있으며 그러한 두 가지 측면은 늑대의 이미지로 상징화된다. 늑대는 두 가지 속성을 가지고 있는데 하나는 외로운 남성적인 특성을 지닌 니체(Nietzsche)의 초인과 같은 특성이다. 다른 하나는 사교적이고 동료와 교감하려는 속성으로 이것은 우정을 추구하고 정의를 사랑하고 교육과 문명의 지적인 산물로서 무리지어 다니는 습성에서 나타난다. 런던의 본성의 두 가지 측면은 늑대의 상징에서 하나로 결합된다(Upton 193). 즉 벅에게는 늑대의 본성과 문명으로 길들여진 개의 두 가지 속성이 샴쌍둥이처럼 결합된 형태로 나타나고 있다.

자연에도 두 가지 얼굴이 있듯이 인간의 본성에도 선과 악처럼 항상 대립적인 가치들이 공존하고 있는 것이다. 런던은 주인공 벅이 그의 힘(권력)을 창조적으로 이용하여 문명을 버리고 무리의 지도자가 되는 과정에서 벅에게 니체의 복잡한 철학을 느슨하게 적용하고 있는 것처럼 보인다(Xiaofen 281). 그러나 『야성의 부름』은 "훌륭한 인간의 우화"(Labor 207)이며 런던이 문명을 비판적으로 그리고 있는 것이 사실이지만 니체처럼 개인의 온전한 잠재력의 실현을 방해한다는 이유로 민주주의, 현대문명, 종교, 그리고 서구의 도덕성을 거부하라고 강요하지는 않는다. 구리언(Gurian)이 말했듯이 『야성의 부름』은 생물학적으로 그리고 환경론적으로 결정되는 우주에 관한 완벽한 우화는

분명하지만, 동시에 『야성의 부름』은 완전히 자연주의적 우주에서 작동하는 완전한 자연주의적인 인간 영웅은 불가능하다는 진리를 암시하고 있다고 볼 수 있다(176-77). 즉 냉혹한 자연주의적인 세계의 질서에 살고 있는 것처럼 보이는 인간에게도 여전히 선과 악, 생각과 선택, 도덕과 의지와 같은 실존적인 문제가 남아있는 것이다.

잭 런던은 『야성의 부름』에서 문명과 자연 또는 문명과 야생의 대조적인 관계를 통하여 인간 삶의 진실한 모습을 드러내려고 하였다. 런던은 21세의 나이에 클론다이크 골드러시에 참여할 때 다윈의 『종의 기원』(*On the Origin of Species*)과 밀턴(John Milton)의 『실락원』(*Paradise Lost*) 그리고 마르크스의 『자본론』 등과 같은 책을 가지고 갔다고 할 정도로 다윈의 사상에 매료되었을 뿐만 아니라 자본주의에 대한 부정적인 견해와 함께 삶에 대한 비관주의적인 시각을 가지고 있었다. 런던은 1897년에 유콘(Yukon)강에 도착했을 때, 주로 사회학, 생물학, 철학 등의 분야에서 수백 권의 책과 기사를 이미 읽었다고 알려져 있다(Dickey 9). 일반적으로 『야성의 부름』은 런던이 다윈적인 그리고 스펜서적인 시각에 대한 잠재적인 가능성을 탐색한 힘차고 강렬한 모험이야기라고 할 수 있다(Wilcox 181).

런던은 『야성의 부름』에서 주인공 개인 벅을 등장시켜 문명에서 자연으로의 이동의 과정을 통하여 벅의 변화와 적응의 과정을 보여준다. 벅은 자신의 내부에 잠재되어 있던 원시적인 야성의 본능을 되살리며 자연의 질서에 적응하며 생존하게 된다. 런던은 이 작품에서 동물의 시각으로 인간의 세계를 해부하고 있기 때문에 이 책은 인간세계에 대한 우화라고 볼 수 있다. 따라서 벅은 열악한 환경에 내몰린 한 인간을 대변하고 있으며, 즉 인간세계도 적자생존의 냉혹한 정글의 법칙이 적용된다는 것을 보여주고 있다. 미국은 남북전쟁 이후 급속한 산업의 발달로 1870년대에서 1900년대까지 '도금시대'(The

Gilded Age)라고 일컬어질 정도로 당시의 사회와 정치에서 부정부패가 만연하고 있었고 자본주의의 폐해가 증가하고 있었다.

런던 자신도 여러 가지 직업에 전전했지만 가족을 부양하기에는 어려운 형편으로 항상 가난에 시달리다가 일확천금을 벌기 위해 클론다이크 골드러시에 참여하게 된다. 친 아버지로부터 버림받고 사생아로 태어난 런던은 어린 시절을 가난과 소외로 힘들게 보내면서 열악한 사회 환경에 내몰리게 된다. 런던은 인간사회도 적자생존이 적용되는 정글처럼 자본이나 권력과 같은 힘의 논리가 지배하는 약육강식의 세계이며 스펜서로 대변되는 사회진화론이 적용된다고 믿었다. 이런 측면에서 런던 자신의 자전적인 경험이 바탕이 된『야성의 부름』에서 저자가 이야기하고 있는 것은 그 밑에 깊게 내재되어 있는 진리이기 때문에 야성의 외침은 허구가 아니라 사실적인 이야기라고 볼 수 있다(Labor and Leitz x).

런던은 벅이 따뜻한 남쪽의 문명 세계에서 삶의 조건이 열악한 동토의 북쪽지방으로 이동해가면서 야생의 원시적인 본능으로 생존하듯이 인간세계도 환경에 적응하는 자만이 살아남는 치열한 실존경쟁의 세계임을 주장하고 있다. 그러나 다른 한편으로 런던은 인간 세계의 문명은 자기희생적인 도덕, 양심, 사랑 등을 강조하지만 이러한 숭고한 가치들이 자본주의의 발달과 함께 인간세계에서는 점차 사라지고 있다는 것을 벅의 우화를 통하여 교훈적으로 보여주고 있다. 따라서 런던은 "비관주의자이면서 동시에 인도주의자"(Cassuto 9)라고 일컬어지듯이 표면적으로는 자연주의적인 비관주의 시각을 가지고 있었지만, 내면적으로는 냉혹한 삶의 조건에서도 폭력이나 증오보다는 인간들의 따뜻한 사랑을 바탕으로 하는 조화로운 이상적인 세계를 추구한 작가로 볼 수 있다.

참고문헌

Auerbach, Jonathan. "'Congested Mails': Buck and Jack's 'Call'." *American Literature* 67.1 (1995): 51-76. Print.

Benoit, Raymond. "Notes: Jack London's '*The Call of the Wild*'." *American Quarterly* 20.2 (1968): 246-48. Print.

Cassuto, Leonard and Jeanne Campbell Reesman, ed. Introduction. *Rereading Jack London.* With an Afterword by Earle Labor. Stanford: Stanford UP, 1996. 1-9. Print.

Dickey, James. Introduction. *The Call of the Wild, White Fang, and Other Stories*. By Jack London. Ed. Andrew Sinclair. New York: Penguin Books, 1993. 7-18. Print.

Gurian, Jay. "The Romantic Necessity in Literary Naturalism: Jack London." *The Call of the Wild: A Casebook with Text, Background Sources, Reviews, Critical Essays, and Bibliography.* Compiled with an Introduction. Earl J. Wilcox. Chicago: Nelson-Hall, 1980. 174-77. Print.

Labor, Earle and Robert C. Leitz, Ⅲ. Introduction. *The Call of the Wild, White Fang, and Other Stories*. By Jack London. Ed. Earle Labor and Robert C. Leitz, Oxford: Oxford UP, 1998. ix-xxii. Print.

Labor, Earle. "Jack London's Mondo Cane: *The Call of the Wild and White Fang.*" *The Call of the Wild: A Casebook with Text, Background Sources, Reviews, Critical Essays, and Bibliography.* Compiled with an Introduction. Earl J. Wilcox. Chicago: Nelson-Hall, 1980. 202-16. Print.

London, Jack. *The Call of the Wild.* Ed. Andrew Sinclair. New York: Penguin Books, 1993. Print.

McClintock, James I. *Jack London's Strong Truths: A Study of His Short Stories.* Michigan: Michigan State UP, 1997. Print.

Spinner, Jonathan H. "A Syllabus for the 20th Century: Jack London's '*The Call of the Wild*'." *The Call of the Wild: A Casebook with Text,*

Background Sources, Reviews, Critical Essays, and Bibliography. Compiled with an Introduction. Earl J. Wilcox. Chicago: Nelson-Hall, 1980. 234-42. Print.

Upton, Ann. "The Wolf in London's Mirror." *The Call of the Wild: A Casebook with Text, Background Sources, Reviews, Critical Essays, and Bibliography.* Compiled with an Introduction. Earl J. Wilcox. Chicago: Nelson-Hall, 1980. 193-201. Print.

Wilcox, Earl J. "Jack London's Naturalism: The Example of *The Call of the Wild.*" *The Call of the Wild: A Casebook with Text, Background Sources, Reviews, Critical Essays, and Bibliography.* Compiled with an Introduction. Earl J. Wilcox. Chicago: Nelson-Hall, 1980. 178-92. Print.

Xiaofen Zhang. "Naturalism Presented in *The Call of the Wild.*" *Journal of Language Teaching and Research* 1.3 (2010): 278-81. Print.

4. Jack London 연보(Timeline)

Year of event	Age	Event	Historical/Sources
1876 January 12	0	Born as John Griffith Chaney in San Francisco, son of Astrologer William H. Chaney and Flora Wellman. William Chaney denies fathership and disappears. While Flora recuperates from difficulties of childbirth, the infant is suckled by Virginia Prentiss. The wet nurse, who is a former slave, remains close to Jack all of his life. Through Mrs. Prentiss, Flora meets John London.	Source: San Francisco Chronicle The U.S. war against the Indians of the Great Plains (Sioux, Cheyenne, Arapaho Nations) still being waged, General Custer and 200 soldiers die in the Battle of Little Big Horn Typewriters that work are developed but only type capital letters until 1878 Lewis Carroll writes poem "the Hunting of the Snark"

			Leo Tolstoy is writing "Ana Karenina" Mark Twain writes "Tom Sawyer"
1876 September 7	0 8mos	Flora Wellman Chaney marries Civil war Veteran John London. The infant John Griffith Chaney is renamed John Griffith London, henceforth known as Johnny then Jack.	Withdrawal of Federal troops ends post Civil War "Reconstruction" period in Southern U.S.
1877	1	John London's daughters, Eliza (age 10) and Ida (age 7) are removed from the orphanage and brought into the household.	Ku Klux Klan unleashes wave of terror against blacks to reassert white power in Southern U.S. Thomas Edison invents phonograph
1881	5	Jack attends school in Alameda. John works a truck farm, Flora teaches music and kindergarten.	U.S. President James Garfield assassinated Henry James publishes "Portrait of a Lady"
1882	6		Robert Louis Stevenson publishes "Treasure Island"
1883	7		Explosion of Krakatoa
1884	8		European powers continue to carve out colonies in Africa at the "Berlin Conference"
1885	9	John London purchases a farm in the Livermore Valley. Jack discovers the world of reading and in later years recalls the impact of Washington Irving's *The Alhambra* and Ouida's *Signa* on his young mind.	Livermore Valley. Jack discovers the world of reading and in later years recalls the impact of Washington Irving's THE ALHAMBRA and Ouida's SIGNA on his young mind. U.S. policy has left only about 2000 bison alive, the main staple of the economy of the Plains Indians, effectively forcing the surviving Indians onto reservations French Artist Henri Tolouse-Lautrec begins work in Paris
1886(?)	10	Eliza London, Jack's step-sister, marries captain James Shepard, a widower many years her senior.	Discovery of gold in Transvaal, South Africa Slavery abolished in Cuba

			Statue of Liberty, a gift from the French unveiled in New York
1886	10	John London purchases a home on east 17th Street near 23rd Avenue in Oakland. A succession of moves for the family. Jack discovers the wealth of reading available to him through the Oakland Public Library and the guidance of Librarian Ina Coolbrith (later Poet Laureate).	Robert Louis Stevenson publishes "Strange case of Dr. Jekyll and Mr. Hyde"
1887	11	Jack attends Cole Grammar School in West Oakland, befriends Frank Atherton, works as news paperboy	Sir Arthur Conan Doyle' first Sherlock Holmes story published Edison & Swan produce a household electric lamp French "union " of Indochina, colonizing Vietnam & Cambodia. Britain annexes Burma.
1888	12	Buys a small skiff and teaches himself to sail.	Slavery abolished in Brazil George Eastman produces roll film camera Edward Bellamy popularizes the ideal socialist utopia in his futuristic novel (set in 2000), "Looking Backwards" Vincent Van Gogh paints "Sunflowers" Robert Louis Stevensons sets sail for the South Seas
1890	14	Works in cannery, pressure of family's poverty leads Jack to frequently work overtime, 18-20 hours at a stretch.	Massacre of Sioux Indians at Wounded Knee by U.S. Cavalry.
1891	15	Graduates from Cole Grammar School (8th grade). Disgusted with factory drudgery and low wages, turns Oyster pirate; buys sloop "The Razzle Dazzle" with money borrowed from Virginia Prentiss. Becomes a master sailor on San Francisco Bay. Is known as the "Prince of the Oyster Pirates". Eventually becomes disillusioned with pirate life.	Britain claims East & Central Africa; Factory Act prohibits employment of children under age 11 in Britain French artist Paul Gauguin paints in Tahiti Famine in Russia follows crop failure. Construction on Trans-Siberian Railroad begins

1892	16	John London works as a watchman, the family is living at 971 West Street. Jack hired by Fish Patrol to stop the oyster pirates. Makes a suicide attempt when falls in deep water while drunk but changes his mind. Gives up Fish Patrol, joins a rough gang, is given the moniker "Sailor Kid" learns how to hobo as a "Road Kid".	French occupy Benin, West Africa Ellis Island in New York Harbor is opened by the U.S. government to process immigrants
1893 January 20 November 12	17	Family moves to 1321 22nd. Ave. Jack signs on as sailor on the three-masted schooner 'Sophia Sutherland', for a seven month sealing voyage along the coast of Japan and the Behring Sea. After returning to Oakland, works in jute mill for 10 cents per hour. At the urging of his mother, Flora, Jack enters a contest for a descriptive article. His essay: "Story of a Typhoon Off the Coast of Japan", wins first prize ($25.00) in the competition and is published in the San Francisco Call. His competitors include students from Stanford and the University of California. In addition to being his first time published, this is the first time Jack earns money by writing.	U.S. forces depose Queen Liliuokalani of Hawaii France annexes Laos, Ivory Coast becomes a French colony New Zealand becomes first country granting women the right to vote Czech composer Antonin Dvorak's "New World Symphony" performed in New York. Norwegian Artist Edvard Munch paints "The Scream"
1894 April	18	Works shoveling coal for street railway power plant. Discovers how exploited he has been by doing the work of two men. Joins Kelley's army, the western contingent of "Coxey's Industrial Army of the Unemployed", a group of the unemployed who marched on the capital in Washington D. C. Thousands of other have-nots from all over the United States participated in this trek. Coxey's contingent marched out of Massilon, Ohio (family home of Jack's mother, Flora) with 100 men. Jack keeps diary. Deserts and strikes out on his own. Visits Chicago to see the World's Columbian	(Source re JL :JL&HT) French military convicts Dreyfus, a Jewish French military officer, of treason; world wide protest and the efforts of many advocates leads to a new trial-eventually his name is cleared Rudyard Kipling publishes "The Jungle Book"

May		Exposition, collects mail and money sent by Flora. Spends time in St. Joseph, Michigan with Flora's sister, Mary Everhard who encourages his ideas about writing (later names protagonist of *The Iron Heel* after a cousin: Ernest Everhard). Roams as a tramp.	
June/July		Arrested for vagrancy in Buffalo, New York, spends 30 days in Erie County jail in violation of his legal rights. In Boston, encounters intellectual, educated hobos who introduce him to the modern world of ideas (Darwin/ Nietzsche/ Marx). Meets Frank Strawn-Hamilton. Learns to think of education as a means to social ascent and socialism as the promise of the future	
1895	19	Returns to Oakland determined to finish High School and go to University. In addition to attending Oakland High School, works as a janitor at the school. Publishes articles and essays in the Aegis, Oakland High School's literary magazine. Out of place among his fellow students "middle class boys and girls". Joins Henry Clay Debating Team. Embarks on intense regimen of self education; becomes friends with Oakland Public Library's Frederick Irons Bamford, Reference Librarian and Fred Jacobs. Bamford and Jack share an interest in socialism, Bamford exposes Jack to the writings of Ruskin, Carlyle, Arnold and Morris. Fred Jacobs while not a socialist, shares the similar experience of working his way through high school. Fred introduces Jack to Ted and Mabel Applegarth. Also to his fiancé, Bess Maddern who is going to night school in hopes of entering University. Bess Maddern would later become Jack's first wife. In addition to these new friends, spends time with British socialist Jim Whitaker who teaches him boxing and fencing.	(JL Source:JL&HT[1]) Jose Marti leads revolution against Spanish rule in Cuba H. G. Wells publishes "The Time Machine" French Lumiere brothers first showing of motion pictures

1896 April August	20	Officially joins the Oakland branch of the Socialist Labor Party. Frustrated and appalled at the idea of two more years of High School, borrows money from step-sister Eliza Shepard to enter "cramming" Academy (a college preparatory academy), but after completing the full two years worth in one semester, the extraordinary student is dismissed and his money refunded in full (he makes the other students look bad, which is bad for business). Begins "cramming" on his own, studies 19 hours a day in preparation for entrance exams at The University of California, Berkeley in August. Is tutored by Bess Maddern in mathematics and Fred Jacobs in physics. Takes and passes University entrance exams, enters University of California, Berkeley and completes first (Fall) semester. Writes first sociological essays, brief stories about his trip to Siberia.	(Source for JL: JL&HT) In response to ongoing Pogroms in Russia and the Dreyfus Affair, Political Zionism founded by Hungarian Theodore Herzl who calls for creation of a Jewish state Ethiopia's independence recognized by Italy
1897 February 4 February 12	21	From step relatives, learns to his shock that John London is not his father. Locates and corresponds with William Chaney who refuses to acknowledge his paternity, an even greater shock. Disillusioned with academia, the lack of political sincerity on the part of both the students and the professors, and feeling the pinch of poverty, quits the University. In a test case to challenge the constitutionality of a law which infringed upon free speech, Jack volunteers and is arrested for speaking in public without permission of the mayor.	(Source for JL :JL&HT) Apache groups continue to battle the U.S. government in resistance to forcible removal to reservations. Bram Stoker publishes Dracula. Mosquito as source of malaria identified by D. Ronald Ross.

<table>
<tr><td>July 25

October 14</td><td></td><td>Writes feverishly but unsuccessfully on a borrowed typewriter with only capital letters. Exhausting work in a steam laundry leaves no energy for reading or writing.

One of the first who follows the gold rush to Alaska "Grubstaked" (funded) and accompanied by his elderly brother-in- law, Captain James Shepard. Departs aboard the "SS Umatilla" for Port Townsend Washington, then aboard the "City of Topeka " for Juneau Alaska. Warned of the arduous journey ahead (such as the Chilkoot Pass), Shepard returns to Oakland.

Step-father John London dies.
Struggles to survive, spends winter in cabin in the Klondike, finds no gold, suffers from scurvy. Gains wealth of material for future writing.</td><td>The Klondike-Goldrush</td></tr>
<tr><td>1898
June

July</td><td>22</td><td>Travels by rough boat down the Yukon River, makes notes for future writing.

Works his way home as a coal stoker. Returns ill and broke to California. Unable to find work, briefly tries prospecting in the California Mountains. Begins writing about the "White Frontier" in the high north. Flora supplements family income of her small pension by teaching music, also takes Johnny Miller, son of John London's daughter, Ida, into her home where he is raised.

Jack's friend and Bess Maddern's fiancé, Fred Jacobs enlists and dies enroute to Manilla (Spanish American War)</td><td>Spanish American War, U. S. gains the Philippines, Guam, and Puerto Rico
Cuba wins independence from Spain, but is occupied by U.S. military
Britain & France claim Egypt
Pierre & Marie Curie discover radium</td></tr>
<tr><td>1899
January</td><td></td><td>"To the Man on Trail" published by the "Overland Monthly" for fee of $5.00

Is offered job at the Post Office but turns it down</td><td></td></tr>
</table>

July December	23	Begins correspondence with Cloudsley Johns, a writer, critic, and an early fan The "Atlantic Monthly", a leading U.S. magazine accepts "An Odyssey of the North" for publication in January 1900, fee of $40.00. Meets Anna Strunsky, a brilliant and charming Stanford University student of Russian Jewish descent. Their challenging relationship, stimulated by differing opinions, led to co-authorship.	Socialist Labor Party goes through factional disputes in these years Second trial of French officer Dreyfus sparks international protest Second Boer War begins Composer Jean Sibelius writes symphony "Finlandia"
1900 January April 7	24	"An Odyssey of the North" published in "Atlantic Monthly". Moves household (Flora London and Johnny Miller) to East 15th Street *A Son of the Wolf* published by Houghton Mifflin. This is London´s first book, a collection of his best short-stories, which is often called the "beginning of the modern American short-story". In a move which surprises many, but fits with his own plans, marries his friend and former tutor, Bessie Maddern on the same day his first book is published, April 7.	Turn of the century Boxer Rebellion in China Famine in India Paris, France: opening of the World Exhibition and the Paris Metro Kodak Brownie Box Camera available for $1.00K Sigmund Freud publishes "The Interpretation of Dreams"
1901 January 15 May	25	Birth of daughter Joan. Becomes member of the new "Socialist Party". Runs for mayor of Oakland on the Socialst balllot. *The God of his Fathers* & Other Stories published by McLure, Phillips, second collection of short-stories.	Formation of U.S. Socialist Party Commonwealth of Australia formed Britain's Queen Victoria dies Ashanti Kingdom in Africa annexed by the U.K. U.S. President McKinley assisinated, Theodore Roosevelt becomes president Russia occupies Manchuria Marconi sents first Morse code radio signals across Atlantic

1902 February September October October 20 July-October	26	Moves family to semi-rural Piedmont Hills *Children of the Frost*, another collection of short-stories published by Macmillan Publishes "Cruize of the Dazzler"(Century) and the novel *A Daughter of the Snows* (Lippincott) Daughter Bess (later known as Becky) born. Travels to London, one of the wealthest capitals on earth, initially hired as a war-correspondent to write about the Boer War in South-Africa, but the war ends prior to his arrival in London. So he decides to stay and investigates "under cover" the situation of *The People of the Abyss.*	Second Boer War ends Republic of Cuba declared Catastrophic eruption of Mount Pelee buries St. Pierre, Martinique, leaving as the only survivor, a prisoner in the city jail. French laws improve working conditions Italian tenor Enrique Caruso's 1st record sells one million copies Beatrix Potter publishes "The tale of Peter Rabbit"
1903 January 8 May July August October	27	William Henry Chaney dies in Chicago, Illinois *The Kempton-Wace Letters* co-authored by Anna Strunsky, published (Macmillan) *The Call of the Wild* published (Macmillan), London's all-time bestseller, an allegory in which a dog abandons civilization and returns to the origins of nature. Sells all rights to publisher for $2000.00 Falls in love with Charmian Kittredge and decides to separate from Bess. Jack moves into Frank Atherton's home in Oakland *The People of the Abyss published* (Macmillan) With this inflammatory book Jack London discovers the investigative social report as a new genre: Sociology narrated as a gripping account.	Panama gains independence Pogroms in Russia Turkish massacre Bulgarians ending Macedonian uprising Dutch government forces end to strike of railroad and dockworkers by calling in troops Attempting to limit immigration, U.S. imposes $2.00 per person tax on all immigrants Wright brothers invent a successful powered aircraft, first flight at Kitty Hawk, N.C. First Ford Model A automobile sold

1904 January- June April June October	28	Hired by Hearst to cover the Russo-Japanese war. Under adventurous circumstances, Jack London, the only Western reporter to do so, reaches the front of the Russian-Japanese war. *Faith of Men & Other Stories* published (Macmillan) Bessie M. London sues for divorce, on grounds of desertion, Anna Strunksky named in the case. *The Sea Wolf* published (Macmillan) and becomes book of the season in the US in the following year, 1905.	Russian expansion into Manchuria leads to Russo-Japanese war Helen Keller graduates with honors from Radcliffe College Theodore Roosevelt elected to 4 year U.S. Presidential term Russian physiologist Ivan Pavlov experiments with creating "conditioned reflex" in dogs J.M. Barrie's play "Peter Pan" performed
1905 April June September October November 18 November 19 December 27	29	Runs as Candidate for Mayor of Oakland on Socialist ticket receives 981 votes. *War of the Classes* published (Macmillan) revolutionary essays. *The Game* published (Macmillan), a novel about boxing. Spends summer at Wake Robin Lodge, Glen Ellen, Sonoma County "Tales of the Fish Patrol" published (Macmillan) Buys 129 acre Hill Ranch, Glen Ellen Starts thinking about long sea voyage Begins a four-month socialist lecture tour, where Jack London puts foward his essay "Revolution" again and again. In this essay he calls openly for a coup Divorce from Bessie M. London final. Marries Charmian Kittredge in Chicago, Illinois. Honeymoon in Jamaica and Cuba	Norway gains independence from Sweden Earthquake in India's Lahore province claims 10,000 lives Revolution begins in Russia but is crushed Sinn Fein Party founded in Ireland Albert Einstein formstheory of relativity Group of Expressionist artists, "Die Bruke" form in Germany "Les Fauves" artists Matisse, Braque, Derain, Vlamink and Dufy shock the Paris art world with their wild colors
1906		Begins to build the yacht "Snark" (named after a being in Lewis Carroll's *Alice in Wonderland*).	

April 18-19 May September October November	30	Reports on the San Francisco earthquake for Collier's Weekly "The Story of An Eye-Witness" published in May 5 edition. Because of the inflated cost of supplies and labor caused by the rebuilding of San Francisco after the earthquake, and the unscrupulousness of certain individuals, the cost of the project skyrockets, it becomes a media-event of high interest. The Londons take a brief vacation, horseback trip through Northern California. *Moon-Face & Other Stories* published (Macmillan) *White Fang* published (Macmillan) "Scorn of Women" published (Macmillan) In the background London writes his "great socialist novel" *The Iron Heel*.	Spain and France agree to share control of Morocco In France, Dreyfus declared innocent Devastating earthquake in San Francisco levels much of the City Film companies worldwide set up studios in New York City First (voice) radio broadcast
1907 April 23 May-October November	31	Leaving Charmian's aunt, Ninetta Eames, in charge of the ranch and business affairs the Londons depart for a proposed seven year voyage around the world. The Snark sets sail. Discovering that Charmian's Uncle, Sailing Master Roscoe Eames, is incompetent, London teaches himself navigation and arrives safely in Hawaii. Stay in Hawaiian Islands, Visits and writes of the leper colony of Molokai. "The Road" published (Macmillan) his wonderful account of adventures as a hobo, a colorful painting of his time.	Indian patriot Gandhi leads civil disobedience campaign supporting rights of Indians in South Africa U.S. supports revolution in Nicaragua New Zealand becomes a dominion of the British empire Spanish artist Pablo Picasso creates the first Cubist painting "Les Damoiselles d' Avignon"
1908	32	Stay in the south-sea, Hawaii, adventures with headhunters, visit of a leper's colony etc.	

1909	33	Return to California, enforced by disease. *Martin Eden*, autobiographical novel.	
1910	34	Enlarges his ranch to a model of modern agriculture.	
1911	35	*South Seal Tales*	
1912	36	dito; *Smoke Bellew*, written only for the market but very successful and enjoyable return of the Alaska-Theme. Journey on a four-mast vessel round Cape Horn (Basics for "The Mutiny of the Elsinore").	Sinking of the Titanic
1913	37	On the surface the most successful year. Jack London´s - best money making author of the world -, in his private life a year of catastrophes: alienation form his daughters, troubles with bess, loss of unborn children by Charmian, failures in agricultures, Wolf House burns down. weiter. *John Barleycorn*, the bible of the Prohibition movement-written by a notorious drinker.	
1914	38	a.o. *The Valley of the Moon*, a sentimental eulogy of the landlife as escape from proletarian drudgery.	World War I
1915	39	War correspondent in Mexico. *The Star Rover*, Novel about re-incarnation and a harsh pillory of punishment in state prisons.	
1916	40	22.11. dies on kidneys failure after 14 hours of agony on his Beauty-Ranch at Glen Ellen, Sonoma-County.	

출처(http://www.jack-london.org/timeline.htm)

THE CALL OF THE WILD
&
Other Stories

Chapter I
Into the Primitive

"Old longings nomadic[1] leap,
Chafing at[2] custom's chain;
Again from its brumal sleep[3]
Wakens the ferine strain.[4]"

Buck[5] did not read the newspapers, or he would have known

※이 제사(epigraph)에서 런던은 1902년에 발표된 오해러(John Myers O'Hara)의 시 "격세유전(Atavism)"의 첫 부분을 그대로 인용하고 있는데 이 내용은 작품의 중요한 주제 중 하나를 담고 있다.

1) nomadic: 방랑의, 유목의

2) Chafing at: ~에 안달하다, ~에 짜증내다

3) brumal sleep: 겨울잠

4) ferine strain; 야생의 기질

5) Buck: 이 작품의 주인공인 개의 이름인데 작가는 이솝우화(Aesop's Fables) 같은 다른 동물들을 주인공으로 한 작품들처럼 동물을 의인화해서 표현하고 있다.

that trouble was brewing, not alone for himself, but for every tide-water[6] dog, strong of muscle and with warm, long hair, from Puget Sound[7] to San Diego[8]. Because men, groping in the Arctic darkness, had found a yellow metal[9], and because steamship and transportation companies were booming the find, thousands of men were rushing into the Northland. These men wanted dogs, and the dogs they wanted were heavy dogs, with strong muscles by which to toil, and furry coats to protect them from the frost.

Buck lived at a big house in the sun-kissed[10] Santa Clara Valley[11]. Judge Miller's place, it was called. It stood back from the road, half hidden among the trees, through which glimpses could be caught of the wide cool veranda that ran around its four sides. The house was approached by gravelled driveways which wound about through[12] wide-spreading lawns and under the interlacing boughs[13] of tall poplars. At the rear things were on even a more spacious scale than at the front. There were great stables, where a dozen grooms and boys held forth[14], rows of vine-clad servants' cottages, an endless and orderly array of outhouses[15], long grape arbors, green pastures, orchards, and berry patches. Then there was the pumping plant for the artesian

6) tide-water: 해안지대

7) Puget Sound: 워싱턴 주 북서부의 만

8) San Diego: 미국 California주 남부의 항구 도시

9) a yellow metal: gold, 금을 상징

10) sun-kissed: 햇볕이 밝은

11) Santa Clara Valley: San Francisco의 남쪽 도시

12) wound about through: ~통해 구부러져 있는

13) interlacing boughs: 서로 엉켜있는 나뭇가지들

14) held forth: 떠들었다, 장황하게 이야기하다

15) outhouses: 별채

well[16], and the big cement tank where Judge Miller's boys took their morning plunge and kept cool in the hot afternoon.

And over this great demesne[17] Buck ruled. Here he was born, and here he had lived the four years of his life. It was true, there were other dogs, There could not but be other dogs on so vast a place, but they did not count[18]. They came and went, resided in the populous kennels[19], or lived obscurely in the recesses of the house after the fashion of Toots, the Japanese pug[20], or Ysabel, the Mexican hairless[21],—strange creatures that rarely put nose out of doors or set foot to ground. On the other hand, there were the fox terriers, a score of them at least, who yelped fearful promises at Toots and Ysabel looking out of the windows at them and protected by a legion of[22] housemaids armed with brooms and mops.

But Buck was neither house-dog nor kennel-dog. The whole realm was his. He plunged into the swimming tank or went hunting with the Judge's sons; he escorted Mollie and Alice, the Judge's daughters, on long twilight or early morning rambles; on wintry nights he lay at the Judge's feet before the roaring library fire; he carried the Judge's grandsons on his back, or rolled them in the grass, and guarded their footsteps through wild adventures down to the fountain in the stable yard, and even beyond, where the paddocks were, and the berry patches. Among the terriers he

---

16) artesian well: 파내려간 우물《지하수의 압력으로 물을 뿜음》, 분수(噴水) 우물

17) demesne: 점유지, 영역

18) count: 여기서는 자동사로 '중요한 가치가 있다'의 의미

19) kennel: 개집

20) Toots: the Japanese pug와 동격, 일본산 발바리의 일종

21) Ysabel: the Mexican hairless와 동격, 멕시코산 털 없는 개의 일종

22) a legion of: a lot of

stalked imperiously, and Toots and Ysabel he utterly ignored, for he was king,—king over all creeping, crawling, flying things of Judge Miller's place, humans included.

His father, Elmo, a huge St. Bernard[23], had been the Judge's inseparable companion, and Buck bid fair to[24] follow in the way of his father. He was not so large,—he weighed only one hundred and forty pounds,—for his mother, Shep, had been a Scotch shepherd dog. Nevertheless, one hundred and forty pounds, to which was added the dignity that comes of good living and universal respect, enabled him to carry himself in right royal fashion. During the four years since his puppyhood he had lived the life of a sated aristocrat; he had a fine pride in himself, was even a trifle egotistical, as country gentlemen sometimes become because of their insular[25] situation. But he had saved himself by not becoming a mere pampered[26] house-dog. Hunting and kindred outdoor delights had kept down the fat and hardened his muscles; and to him, as to the cold-tubbing races[27], the love of water had been a tonic and a health preserver.

And this was the manner of dog Buck was in the fall of 1897, when the Klondike[28] strike dragged men from all the world into the frozen North. But Buck did not read the newspapers, and he did not know that Manuel, one of the gardener's helpers,

---

23) St. Bernard: 세인트버나드(몸집이 크고 튼튼한 개. 스위스가 원산지로 원래 눈 속에서 실종된 사람들을 찾는 데 이용되었음), Alps의 St. Bernard에 있는 수도원에서 사육했던 구명용 개에서 유래.

24) bid fair to: ~할 가망이 있다

25) insular: 섬의, 고립된, 편협한

26) pampered: 응석받이로 자란, 방종한

27) the cold-tubbing races: 냉수목욕을 좋아하는 종족처럼

28) Klondike: 클론다이크(캐나다 Yukon강 유역; 골드러시(1897-98)의 중심적 금산지)

was an undesirable acquaintance. Manuel had one besetting sin. He loved to play Chinese lottery. Also, in his gambling, he had one besetting[29] weakness—faith in a system; and this made his damnation certain. For to play a system requires money, while the wages of a gardener's helper do not lap over[30] the needs of a wife and numerous progeny[31].

The Judge was at a meeting of the Raisin Growers' Association, and the boys were busy organizing an athletic club, on the memorable night of Manuel's treachery. No one saw him and Buck go off through the orchard on what Buck imagined was merely a stroll. And with the exception of a solitary man, no one saw them arrive at the little flag station known as College Park. This man talked with Manuel, and money chinked[32] between them.

"You might wrap up the goods before you deliver 'm,[33]" the stranger said gruffly, and Manuel doubled a piece of stout rope around Buck's neck under the collar.

"Twist it, an' you'll choke 'm plentee,[34]" said Manuel, and the stranger grunted a ready affirmative.

Buck had accepted the rope with quiet dignity. To be sure, it was an unwonted[35] performance: but he had learned to trust in men he knew, and to give them credit for a wisdom that outreached[36] his own. But when the ends of the rope were

---

29) besetting: 성가시게 따라다니는, 괴롭히는

30) lap over: ~을 감당하다, ~을 충족시키다,

31) progeny: 자손, 자식들

32) chinked: 돈이 쨍그랑 소리를 내었다, 돈이 오고갔다는 의미

33) 'm: him의 약칭, Buck을 의미

34) plentee: plenty, 충분히

35) unwonted: 이례적인, 드문, 특이한; 《고어》 익숙지 않은

36) outreached: ~보다 멀리 미치다, ~의 밖에까지 퍼지다, 넘다; ~보다 낫다; (손 · 팔

placed in the stranger's hands, he growled menacingly. He had merely intimated his displeasure, in his pride believing that to intimate was to command. But to his surprise the rope tightened around his neck, shutting off his breath. In quick rage he sprang at the man, who met him halfway, grappled him close by the throat, and with a deft[37] twist threw him over on his back. Then the rope tightened mercilessly, while Buck struggled in a fury, his tongue lolling out of his mouth and his great chest panting futilely. Never in all his life had he been so vilely treated, and never in all his life had he been so angry. But his strength ebbed, his eyes glazed, and he knew nothing when the train was flagged[38] and the two men threw him into the baggage car.

The next he knew, he was dimly aware that his tongue was hurting and that he was being jolted[39] along in some kind of a conveyance. The hoarse shriek of a locomotive whistling a crossing told him where he was. He had travelled too often with the Judge not to know the sensation of riding in a baggage car. He opened his eyes, and into them came the unbridled anger of a kidnapped king. The man sprang for his throat, but Buck was too quick for him. His jaws closed on the hand, nor did they relax till his senses were choked out of him once more.

"Yep, has fits[40]," the man said, hiding his mangled[41] hand from the baggageman, who had been attracted by the sounds of

---

을) 앞으로 내밀다; ~을 속이다

37) deft: 솜씨가 좋은, 능란한, 능숙한(skillful)

38) was flagged: 정지했다, [사람 · 탈것에] (기 · 손으로) 정지 신호[경고]를 보내다 [down]; ~을 기로 알리다

39) jolted: 덜걱덜걱 흔들리면서 가다, 덜컹거리다

40) has fits: 발작을 일으키다

41) mangled: 찢어진

struggle. "I'm takin' 'm up for the boss to 'Frisco. A crack[42] dog-doctor there thinks that he can cure 'm."

Concerning that night's ride, the man spoke most eloquently for himself, in a little shed back of a saloon on the San Francisco water front.

"All I get is fifty for it," he grumbled; "an' I wouldn't do it over for a thousand, cold cash[43]."

His hand was wrapped in a bloody handkerchief, and the right trouser leg was ripped from knee to ankle.

"How much did the other mug[44] get?" the saloon-keeper demanded.

"A hundred," was the reply. "Wouldn't take a sou less, so help me."[45]

"That makes a hundred and fifty," the saloon-keeper calculated; "and he's worth it, or I'm a squarehead[46]."

The kidnapper undid the bloody wrappings and looked at his lacerated[47] hand. "If I don't get the hydrophoby[48]—"

"It'll be because you was born to hang," laughed the saloon-keeper. "Here, lend me a hand before you pull your freight," he added.

Dazed, suffering intolerable pain from throat and tongue, with

---

42) crack: 일류의

43) cold cash: 현금

44) mug: 얼간이, 바보

45) "Wouldn't take a sou less, so help me.": "한 푼도 덜 받으려고 하지 않았어. 그러니 나 좀 도와주게."

46) squarehead: 바보, 멍청이

47) lacerated: 찢긴

48) hydrophoby: hydrophobia, 공수병, 광견병

the life half throttled[49] out of him, Buck attempted to face his tormentors. But he was thrown down and choked repeatedly, till they succeeded in filing the heavy brass collar from off his neck. Then the rope was removed, and he was flung into a cagelike crate.[50]

There he lay for the remainder of the weary night, nursing his wrath and wounded pride. He could not understand what it all meant. What did they want with him, these strange men? Why were they keeping him pent up in this narrow crate? He did not know why, but he felt oppressed by the vague sense of impending calamity. Several times during the night he sprang to his feet when the shed door rattled open, expecting to see the Judge, or the boys at least. But each time it was the bulging face of the saloon-keeper that peered in at him by the sickly light of a tallow candle. And each time the joyful bark that trembled[51] in Buck's throat was twisted into a savage growl.

But the saloon-keeper let him alone, and in the morning four men entered and picked up the crate. More tormentors, Buck decided, for they were evil-looking creatures, ragged and unkempt[52]; and he stormed and raged at them through the bars. They only laughed and poked sticks at him, which he promptly assailed with his teeth till he realized that that was what they wanted. Whereupon[53] he lay down sullenly and allowed the crate to be lifted into a wagon. Then he, and the crate in which he

---

49) throttled: ~의 목을 조르다, 질식시키다

50) crate: 나무틀 상자, 큰 용기

51) trembled: 떨다, 진동하다

52) unkempt: 거친, 난잡한

53) Whereupon: 그래서, 그 때문에, 그 결과, 그 후에

was imprisoned, began a passage through many hands. Clerks in the express office took charge of him; he was carted about in another wagon; a truck carried him, with an assortment of[54] boxes and parcels, upon a ferry steamer; he was trucked off the steamer into a great railway depot, and finally he was deposited in an express car.

For two days and nights this express car was dragged along at the tail of shrieking locomotives; and for two days and nights Buck neither ate nor drank. In his anger he had met the first advances of the express messengers with growls, and they had retaliated[55] by teasing him. When he flung himself against the bars, quivering and frothing[56], they laughed at him and taunted him. They growled and barked like detestable dogs, mewed, and flapped their arms and crowed. It was all very silly, he knew; but therefore the more outrage to his dignity, and his anger waxed and waxed. He did not mind the hunger so much, but the lack of water caused him severe suffering and fanned his wrath to fever-pitch[57]. For that matter, high-strung[58] and finely sensitive, the ill treatment had flung him into a fever, which was fed by the inflammation[59] of his parched and swollen throat and tongue.

He was glad for one thing: the rope was off his neck. That had given them an unfair advantage; but now that it was off, he would show them. They would never get another rope around

---

54) an assortment of: 여러 가지의, 여러 종류의

55) retaliated: 보복하다, 앙갚음하다

56) frothing: 거품을 내다

57) fever-pitch: 병적 흥분, 열광

58) high-strung: 신경질적인, 흥분하기 쉬운, 극도로 긴장한, 줄을 팽팽하게 한

59) inflammation: 격노, 흥분, 염증, 점화

his neck. Upon that he was resolved. For two days and nights he neither ate nor drank, and during those two days and nights of torment, he accumulated a fund of wrath that boded ill for whoever first fell foul of him. His eyes turned blood-shot, and he was metamorphosed into a raging fiend. So changed was he that the Judge himself would not have recognized him; and the express messengers breathed with relief when they bundled him off the train at Seattle.

Four men gingerly[60] carried the crate from the wagon into a small, high-walled back yard. A stout man, with a red sweater[61] that sagged generously at the neck, came out and signed the book for the driver. That was the man, Buck divined[62], the next tormentor, and he hurled himself savagely against the bars. The man smiled grimly, and brought a hatchet and a club[63].

"You ain't going to take him out now?" the driver asked.

"Sure," the man replied, driving the hatchet into the crate for a pry.

There was an instantaneous scattering of the four men who had carried it in, and from safe perches on top the wall they prepared to watch the performance.

Buck rushed at the splintering wood, sinking his teeth into it, surging and wrestling with it. Wherever the hatchet fell on the outside, he was there on the inside, snarling and growling, as furiously anxious to get out as the man in the red sweater was

60) gingerly: 극히 조심스레, 주의 깊게, 신중히

61) A stout man, with a red sweater: Buck에게 최초로 폭력을 행사한 '목 부분이 축 늘어진 빨간 스웨터를 입은 억세게 생긴 남자'

62) divined: 알아채다

63) a hatchet and a club: 손도끼와 곤봉

calmly intent on getting him out.

"Now, you red-eyed devil[64]," he said, when he had made an opening sufficient for the passage of Buck's body. At the same time he dropped the hatchet and shifted the club to his right hand.

And Buck was truly a red-eyed devil, as he drew himself together for the spring, hair bristling, mouth foaming, a mad glitter in his blood-shot eyes. Straight at the man he launched his one hundred and forty pounds of fury, surcharged with the pent passion of two days and nights. In mid air, just as his jaws were about to close on the man, he received a shock that checked his body and brought his teeth together with an agonizing clip. He whirled over, fetching the ground on his back and side. He had never been struck by a club in his life, and did not understand. With a snarl that was part bark and more scream he was again on his feet and launched into the air. And again the shock came and he was brought crushingly to the ground. This time he was aware that it was the club, but his madness knew no caution. A dozen times he charged[65], and as often the club broke the charge and smashed him down.

After a particularly fierce blow, he crawled to his feet, too dazed to rush. He staggered limply about, the blood flowing from nose and mouth and ears, his beautiful coat sprayed and flecked with bloody slaver. Then the man advanced and deliberately dealt him a frightful blow on the nose. All the pain he had endured was as nothing compared with the exquisite agony[66] of this. With a roar that was almost lionlike

---

64) red-eyed devil: 빨간 눈의 악마, Buck을 지칭하는 말

65) charged: 공격하다, 돌격하다

66) exquisite agony: 엄청난 고통

in its ferocity, he again hurled himself at the man. But the man, shifting the club from right to left, coolly caught him by the under jaw, at the same time wrenching downward and backward. Buck described a complete circle in the air, and half of another, then crashed to the ground on his head and chest.

For the last time he rushed. The man struck the shrewd blow he had purposely withheld for so long, and Buck crumpled up[67] and went down, knocked utterly senseless.

"He's no slouch at dog-breakin', that's wot I say,"[68] one of the men on the wall cried enthusiastically.

"Druther break cayuses any day, and twice on Sundays,"[69] was the reply of the driver, as he climbed on the wagon and started the horses.

Buck's senses came back to him, but not his strength. He lay where he had fallen, and from there he watched the man in the red sweater.

"'Answers to the name of Buck,'" the man soliloquized, quoting from the saloon-keeper's letter which had announced the consignment[70] of the crate and contents. "Well, Buck, my boy," he went on in a genial voice, "we've had our little ruction[71], and the best thing we can do is to let it go at that. You've learned your place, and I know mine. Be a good dog and all 'll go well and the goose hang high. Be a bad dog, and I'll whale the

---

67) crumpled up: 완전히 굴복하다, 풀이 죽다

68) "He's no slouch at dog-breakin', that's wot I say,": "내가 뭐라고 했어. 그는 개를 다루는데 일가견이 있는 사람이야"

69) "Druther break cayuses any day, and twice on Sundays,": "아무리 생각해 봐도 조랑말을 길들이는 것이 낫겠어. 일요일마다 두 번씩이라도"

70) consignment: 위탁, 탁송

71) ruction: 소동, 소란

stuffin' outa you.[72] Understand?"

As he spoke he fearlessly patted the head he had so mercilessly pounded, and though Buck's hair involuntarily bristled at touch of the hand, he endured it without protest. When the man brought him water he drank eagerly, and later bolted a generous meal of raw meat, chunk by chunk, from the man's hand.

He was beaten (he knew that); but he was not broken. He saw, once for all[73], that he stood no chance against a man with a club. He had learned the lesson, and in all his after life he never forgot it. That club was a revelation. It was his introduction to the reign of primitive law[74], and he met the introduction halfway. The facts of life took on a fiercer aspect; and while he faced that aspect uncowed, he faced it with all the latent cunning of his nature aroused. As the days went by, other dogs came, in crates and at the ends of ropes, some docilely[75], and some raging and roaring as he had come; and, one and all, he watched them pass under the dominion of the man in the red sweater. Again and again, as he looked at each brutal performance, the lesson was driven home to Buck: a man with a club was a lawgiver, a master to be obeyed, though not necessarily conciliated. Of this last Buck was never guilty, though he did see beaten dogs that fawned upon the man, and wagged their tails, and licked his hand. Also he saw one dog, that would neither conciliate nor obey, finally killed in the struggle for mastery.

---

72) I'll whale the stuffin' outa you.: 내가 너를 흠씬 두들겨 때려서 혼내줄 거다.

73) once for all: 끝으로 한번만 더, 최종적으로, 한 번에

74) the reign of primitive law: 원시 법의 지배에

75) docilely: 유순하게

Now and again men came, strangers, who talked excitedly, wheedlingly, and in all kinds of fashions to the man in the red sweater. And at such times that money passed between them the strangers took one or more of the dogs away with them. Buck wondered where they went, for they never came back; but the fear of the future was strong upon him, and he was glad each time when he was not selected.

Yet his time came, in the end, in the form of a little weazened[76] man who spat broken English and many strange and uncouth exclamations which Buck could not understand.

"Sacredam!"[77] he cried, when his eyes lit upon Buck. "Dat one dam bully dog! Eh? How moch?"

"Three hundred, and a present at that," was the prompt reply of the man in the red sweater. "And seem' it's government money, you ain't got no kick coming, eh, Perrault?"

Perrault grinned. Considering that the price of dogs had been boomed skyward by the unwonted demand, it was not an unfair sum for so fine an animal. The Canadian Government would be no loser, nor would its despatches travel the slower. Perrault knew dogs, and when he looked at Buck he knew that he was one in a thousand—" One in ten t'ousand," he commented mentally.

Buck saw money pass between them, and was not surprised when Curly, a good-natured Newfoundland, and he were led away by the little weazened man. That was the last he saw of the man in the red sweater, and as Curly and he looked at receding Seattle from the deck of the Narwhal[78], it was the

76) weazened: 시든, (사람 · 얼굴 등이) 몹시 여윈

77) "Sacredam!": Sacre dame, Goddamn!

78) Narwhal: 일각과(科)의 고래, 여기서는 Buck이 팔려서 북쪽으로 갈 때 실려 간

last he saw of the warm Southland. Curly and he were taken below by Perrault and turned over to a black-faced giant called Francois. Perrault was a French-Canadian, and swarthy[79]; but Francois was a French-Canadian half-breed[80], and twice as swarthy. They were a new kind of men to Buck (of which he was destined to see many more), and while he developed no affection for them, he none the less grew honestly to respect them. He speedily learned that Perrault and Francois were fair men, calm and impartial in administering justice, and too wise in the way of dogs to be fooled by dogs.

In the 'tween-decks of the Narwhal, Buck and Curly joined two other dogs. One of them was a big, snow-white fellow from Spitzbergen who had been brought away by a whaling captain, and who had later accompanied a Geological Survey into the Barrens. He was friendly, in a treacherous sort of way, smiling into one's face the while he meditated some underhand trick, as, for instance, when he stole from Buck's food at the first meal. As Buck sprang to punish him, the lash of Francois's whip sang through the air, reaching the culprit first; and nothing remained to Buck but to recover the bone. That was fair of Francois, he decided, and the half-breed began his rise in Buck's estimation.

The other dog made no advances, nor received any; also, he did not attempt to steal from the newcomers. He was a gloomy, morose[81] fellow, and he showed Curly plainly that all he desired was to be left alone, and further, that there would be trouble if

---

배의 이름

79) swarthy: (피부 등이) 거무스레한, 가무잡잡한

80) half-breed: 혼혈인

81) morose: 시무룩한, 뚱한, 기분이 언짢은

he were not left alone. "Dave" he was called, and he ate and slept, or yawned between times, and took interest in nothing, not even when the Narwhal crossed Queen Charlotte Sound[82] and rolled and pitched and bucked like a thing possessed.[83] When Buck and Curly grew excited, half wild with fear, he raised his head as though annoyed, favored them with an incurious glance, yawned, and went to sleep again.

Day and night the ship throbbed to the tireless pulse of the propeller, and though one day was very like another, it was apparent to Buck that the weather was steadily growing colder. At last, one morning, the propeller was quiet, and the Narwhal was pervaded with an atmosphere of excitement. He felt it, as did the other dogs, and knew that a change was at hand. Francois leashed them and brought them on deck. At the first step upon the cold surface, Buck's feet sank into a white mushy[84] something very like mud. He sprang back with a snort. More of this white stuff was falling through the air. He shook himself, but more of it fell upon him. He sniffed it curiously, then licked some up on his tongue. It bit like fire, and the next instant was gone. This puzzled him. He tried it again, with the same result. The onlookers laughed uproariously,[85] and he felt ashamed, he knew not why, for it was his first snow.

---

82) Queen Charlotte Sound: part of the Inside Passage shipping route. It is a sound of the Pacific Ocean in British Columbia, Canada, between Vancouver Island in the south and Haida Gwaii (formerly Queen Charlotte Islands) in the north. It merges with Hecate Strait in the north and Queen Charlotte Strait in the south.

83) rolled and pitched and bucked like a thing possessed: (배가) 신들린 것처럼 좌우와 앞뒤로 흔들리고 갑자기 덜커덕 움직일 때도 (Dave는 관심을 보이지 않았다).

84) mushy: 죽 같은, 흐늘흐늘한; (기능이) 고르지 못한

85) The onlookers laughed uproariously: 구경꾼들은 깔깔대며 웃었다.

Chapter II
The Law of Club and Fang

Buck's first day on the Dyea beach was like a nightmare. Every hour was filled with shock and surprise. He had been suddenly jerked from the heart of civilization and flung into the heart of things primordial[1]. No lazy, sun-kissed life was this, with nothing to do but loaf and be bored. Here was neither peace, nor rest, nor a moment's safety. All was confusion and action, and every moment life and limb[2] were in peril. There was imperative need to be constantly alert; for these dogs and men were not town dogs and men. They were savages, all of them, who knew no law but the law of club and fang[3].

He had never seen dogs fight as these wolfish creatures fought, and his first experience taught him an unforgetable lesson. It is true, it was a vicarious[4] experience, else he would not have lived to profit by it. Curly was the victim. They were camped near the log store, where she, in her friendly way, made advances to a husky dog[5] the size of a full-grown wolf, though not half so large as she. There was no warning, only a leap in like a flash, a metallic clip of teeth, a leap out equally swift, and Curly's face was ripped open from eye to jaw.

---

1) primordial: 원시(시대부터)의; 최초의; [생물] 초생의; 근본적인

2) life and limb: 사지, 온몸

3) the law of club and fang: 곤봉과 어금니의 법칙, 약육강식, 적자생존 등 다윈의 사상 연관

4) vicarious: 대리의

5) husky dog: 억세고 튼튼한 에스키모인의 개

It was the wolf manner of fighting, to strike and leap away; but there was more to it than this. Thirty or forty huskies ran to the spot and surrounded the combatants in an intent and silent circle. Buck did not comprehend that silent intentness, nor the eager way with which they were licking their chops. Curly rushed her antagonist, who struck again and leaped aside. He met her next rush with his chest, in a peculiar fashion that tumbled her off her feet. She never regained them, This was what the onlooking huskies had waited for. They closed in upon her, snarling and yelping, and she was buried, screaming with agony, beneath the bristling mass of bodies.

So sudden was it, and so unexpected, that Buck was taken aback. He saw Spitz run out his scarlet tongue in a way he had of laughing; and he saw Francois, swinging an axe, spring into the mess of dogs. Three men with clubs were helping him to scatter them. It did not take long. Two minutes from the time Curly went down, the last of her assailants were clubbed off. But she lay there limp and lifeless in the bloody, trampled snow, almost literally torn to pieces, the swart half-breed standing over her and cursing horribly. The scene often came back to Buck to trouble him in his sleep. So that was the way[6]. No fair play[7]. Once down, that was the end of you. Well, he would see to it that he never went down. Spitz ran out his tongue and laughed again, and from that moment Buck hated him with a bitter and deathless hatred.

Before he had recovered from the shock caused by the tragic passing of Curly, he received another shock. Francois

---

6) So that was the way: 그래서 그것은 그곳의 방식이었다.

7) No fair play: 정당한 게임은 없었다. 북쪽의 삶의 방식은 정글의 법칙이 적용되는 공간이라는 의미.

fastened upon him an arrangement of straps and buckles. It was a harness, such as he had seen the grooms put on the horses at home. And as he had seen horses work, so he was set to work, hauling Francois on a sled to the forest that fringed the valley, and returning with a load of firewood. Though his dignity was sorely hurt by thus being made a draught animal, he was too wise to rebel. He buckled down with a will and did his best, though it was all new and strange. Francois was stern, demanding instant obedience, and by virtue of his whip receiving instant obedience; while Dave, who was an experienced wheeler, nipped Buck's hind quarters[8] whenever he was in error. Spitz was the leader, likewise experienced, and while he could not always get at Buck, he growled sharp reproof now and again, or cunningly threw his weight in the traces to jerk Buck into the way he should go. Buck learned easily, and under the combined tuition of his two mates and Francois made remarkable progress. Ere they returned to camp he knew enough to stop at "ho," to go ahead at "mush,"[9] to swing wide on the bends, and to keep clear of the wheeler when the loaded sled shot downhill at their heels.

"T'ree vair' good dogs," Francois told Perrault. "Dat Buck, heem pool lak hell. I tich heem queek as anyt'ing." [10]

By afternoon, Perrault, who was in a hurry to be on the trail with his despatches, returned with two more dogs. "Billee" and

---

8) hind quarters: (짐승의) 뒤 4반부 고기; (pl.) (짐승의) 궁둥이와 뒷다리

9) to stop at "ho," to go ahead at "mush,": 썰매를 끄는 개에게 멈추게 할 때 "호"라고 외치고, 가게 할 때는 "머쉬"라고 소리친다.

10) "Dat Buck, heem pool lak hell. I tich heem queek as anyt'ing.": "저 벅은 끄는 힘이 엄청나. 그는 다른 무엇보다도 빠르게 배우고 있어."

"Joe" he called them, two brothers, and true huskies both. Sons of the one mother though they were, they were as different as day and night. Billee's one fault was his excessive good nature, while Joe was the very opposite, sour and introspective,[11] with a perpetual snarl and a malignant eye. Buck received them in comradely fashion, Dave ignored them, while Spitz proceeded to thrash first one and then the other. Billee wagged his tail appeasingly,[12] turned to run when he saw that appeasement was of no avail, and cried (still appeasingly) when Spitz's sharp teeth scored his flank[13]. But no matter how Spitz circled, Joe whirled around on his heels to face him, mane bristling, ears laid back, lips writhing and snarling, jaws clipping together as fast as he could snap, and eyes diabolically[14] gleaming—the incarnation of belligerent fear. So terrible was his appearance that Spitz was forced to forego disciplining him; but to cover his own discomfiture[15] he turned upon the inoffensive[16] and wailing Billee and drove him to the confines of the camp.

By evening Perrault secured another dog, an old husky, long and lean and gaunt, with a battle-scarred face and a single eye which flashed a warning of prowess that commanded respect. He was called Sol-leks, which means the Angry One. Like Dave, he asked nothing, gave nothing, expected nothing; and when he marched slowly and deliberately into their midst, even

---

11) sour and introspective: 찌무룩하고 내성적인

12) appeasingly: 달래려는 듯이, 진정시키려는 듯이

13) flank: 옆구리

14) diabolically: 극악무도하게, 지독하게

15) discomfiture: 실패, 당황, 패배

16) inoffensive: 해가 되지 않는, (사람·행위가) 악의가 없는, (말 따위가) 거슬리지 않는, 불쾌감을 주지 않는, 싫지 않은

Spitz left him alone. He had one peculiarity which Buck was unlucky enough to discover. He did not like to be approached on his blind side. Of this offence Buck was unwittingly[17] guilty, and the first knowledge he had of his indiscretion[18] was when Solleks whirled upon him and slashed his shoulder to the bone for three inches up and down. Forever after Buck avoided his blind side, and to the last of their comradeship had no more trouble. His only apparent ambition, like Dave's, was to be left alone; though, as Buck was afterward to learn, each of them possessed one other and even more vital ambition.

That night Buck faced the great problem of sleeping. The tent, illumined by a candle, glowed warmly in the midst of the white plain; and when he, as a matter of course, entered it, both Perrault and Francois bombarded him with curses and cooking utensils, till he recovered from his consternation[19] and fled ignominiously[20] into the outer cold. A chill wind was blowing that nipped him sharply[21] and bit with especial venom into his wounded shoulder. He lay down on the snow and attempted to sleep, but the frost soon drove him shivering to his feet. Miserable and disconsolate,[22] he wandered about among the many tents, only to find that one place was as cold as another. Here and there savage dogs rushed upon him, but he bristled his neck-hair and snarled (for he was learning fast), and they let him go

---

17) unwittingly: 뜻하지 않게, 부지중에

18) indiscretion: 경솔함, 무분별함

19) consternation: 섬뜩 놀람, 소스라침, 당황

20) ignominiously: 비열하게, 수치스럽게

21) nipped him sharply: 날카롭게 그의 살을 에이다

22) disconsolate: 쓸쓸한, 위안이 없는, 수심에 잠긴, 슬픈

his way unmolested.[23]

Finally an idea came to him. He would return and see how his own team-mates were making out. To his astonishment[24], they had disappeared. Again he wandered about through the great camp, looking for them, and again he returned. Were they in the tent? No, that could not be, else he would not have been driven out. Then where could they possibly be? With drooping tail and shivering body, very forlorn indeed, he aimlessly circled the tent. Suddenly the snow gave way beneath his fore legs and he sank down. Something wriggled[25] under his feet. He sprang back, bristling and snarling, fearful of the unseen and unknown. But a friendly little yelp reassured him, and he went back to investigate. A whiff of warm air ascended to his nostrils, and there, curled up under the snow in a snug ball, lay Billee. He whined placatingly[26], squirmed and wriggled to show his good will and intentions, and even ventured, as a bribe for peace, to lick Buck's face with his warm wet tongue.

Another lesson. So that was the way they did it, eh? Buck confidently selected a spot, and with much fuss and waste effort proceeded to dig a hole for himself. In a trice the heat from his body filled the confined space and he was asleep. The day had been long and arduous, and he slept soundly and comfortably, though he growled and barked and wrestled with bad dreams.

Nor did he open his eyes till roused by the noises of the waking camp. At first he did not know where he was. It had

---

23) unmolested: 방해되지(시달리지) 않은, 괴로움을 겪지 않은; 평온한

24) To his astonishment: 그가 깜작 놀랍게도

25) wriggled: 꿈틀거리다

26) placatingly: 달래는 듯이, 부드럽게

snowed during the night and he was completely buried. The snow walls pressed him on every side, and a great surge of fear swept through him—the fear of the wild thing for the trap. It was a token that he was harking back through his own life to the lives of his forebears[27]; for he was a civilized dog, an unduly civilized dog[28], and of his own experience knew no trap and so could not of himself fear it. The muscles of his whole body contracted spasmodically and instinctively, the hair on his neck and shoulders stood on end, and with a ferocious snarl he bounded straight up into the blinding day, the snow flying about him in a flashing cloud. Ere he landed on his feet, he saw the white camp spread out before him and knew where he was and remembered all that had passed from the time he went for a stroll with Manuel to the hole he had dug for himself the night bcforc.

A shout from Francois hailed his appearance. "Wot I say?" the dog-driver cried to Perrault. "Dat Buck for sure learn queek as anyt'ing."

Perrault nodded gravely. As courier for thc Canadian Government, bearing important despatches, he was anxious to secure the best dogs, and he was particularly gladdened by the possession of Buck.

Three more huskies were added to the team inside an hour, making a total of nine, and before another quarter of an hour had passed they were in harness and swinging up the trail toward the Dyea Canon[29]. Buck was glad to be gone, and though

27) forebears: 선조, 조상

28) an unduly civilized dog: 매우 문명화 된 개(벅은 남쪽에서 인간의 손에 의해 심하게 길들여진 개라는 의미)

29) Dyea Canon: 다이어 협곡, 알래스카에 속한 캐나다 변경과 접한 도시, Klondike

the work was hard he found he did not particularly despise it. He was surprised at the eagerness which animated the whole team and which was communicated to him; but still more surprising was the change wrought in Dave and Sol-leks. They were new dogs, utterly transformed by the harness. All passiveness and unconcern had dropped from them. They were alert and active, anxious that the work should go well, and fiercely irritable with whatever, by delay or confusion, retarded[30] that work. The toil of the traces seemed the supreme expression of their being, and all that they lived for and the only thing in which they took delight.

Dave was wheeler or sled dog, pulling in front of him was Buck, then came Sol-leks; the rest of the team was strung out ahead, single file, to the leader, which position was filled by Spitz.

Buck had been purposely placed between Dave and Sol-leks so that he might receive instruction. Apt scholar that he was, they were equally apt teachers, never allowing him to linger long in error, and enforcing their teaching with their sharp teeth. Dave was fair and very wise. He never nipped Buck without cause, and he never failed to nip him when he stood in need of it. As Francois's whip backed him up, Buck found it to be cheaper to mend his ways than to retaliate. Once, during a brief halt, when he got tangled in the traces and delayed the start, both Dave and Solleks flew at him and administered a sound trouncing[31]. The resulting tangle was even worse, but Buck took good care to keep the traces clear thereafter; and ere the day was done, so well had he mastered his work, his mates about ceased

---

Gold Rush 때 채굴업자들의 중요한 기착지

30) retard: 속력을 늦추다; 늦어지게 하다, 지체시키다

31) a sound trouncing: 심하게 공격하기, 심하게 혼내주기, 호되게 패주기

nagging him. Francois's whip snapped less frequently, and Perrault even honored Buck by lifting up his feet and carefully examining them.

It was a hard day's run, up the Canon, through Sheep Camp, past the Scales and the timber line, across glaciers and snowdrifts hundreds of feet deep, and over the great Chilcoot Divide[32], which stands between the salt water and the fresh and guards forbiddingly the sad and lonely North. They made good time down the chain of lakes which fills the craters of extinct volcanoes, and late that night pulled into the huge camp at the head of Lake Bennett[33], where thousands of goldseekers were building boats against the break-up of the ice in the spring. Buck made his hole in the snow and slept the sleep of the exhausted just, but all too early was routed out in the cold darkness and harnessed with his mates to the sled.

That day they made forty miles, the trail being packed; but the next day, and for many days to follow, they broke their own trail, worked harder, and made poorer time. As a rule, Perrault travelled ahead of the team, packing the snow with webbed shoes to make it easier for them. Francois, guiding the sled at the gee-pole[34], sometimes exchanged places with him, but not often. Perrault was in a hurry, and he prided himself on his knowledge of ice, which knowledge was indispensable, for the fall ice was very thin, and

32) Chilcoot Divide: The Chilkoot Trail was long a route used by the Tlingit for trade. During the Klondike Gold Rush of the late 19th century, it was used by prospectors and packers to get through the mountains.

33) Lake Bennett: It is a lake in the Province of British Columbia and Yukon Territory in northwestern Canada.[1] It is just north of the border with the United States state of Alaska, near the Alaskan port of Skagway.

34) gee-pole: 개(가 끄는) 썰매의 채

where there was swift water, there was no ice at all.

Day after day, for days unending, Buck toiled in the traces. Always, they broke camp in the dark, and the first gray of dawn found them hitting the trail with fresh miles reeled off behind them. And always they pitched camp after dark, eating their bit of fish, and crawling to sleep into the snow. Buck was ravenous[35]. The pound and a half of sun-dried salmon, which was his ration for each day, seemed to go nowhere. He never had enough, and suffered from perpetual hunger pangs. Yet the other dogs, because they weighed less and were born to the life, received a pound only of the fish and managed to keep in good condition.

He swiftly lost the fastidiousness[36] which had characterized his old life. A dainty eater, he found that his mates, finishing first, robbed him of his unfinished ration. There was no defending it. While he was fighting off two or three, it was disappearing down the throats of the others. To remedy this, he ate as fast as they; and, so greatly did hunger compel him, he was not above taking what did not belong to him. He watched and learned. When he saw Pike, one of the new dogs, a clever malingerer[37] and thief, slyly steal a slice of bacon when Perrault's back was turned, he duplicated the performance the following day, getting away with the whole chunk. A great uproar was raised, but he was unsuspected; while Dub, an awkward blunderer who was always getting caught, was punished for Buck's misdeed.

This first theft marked Buck as fit to survive in the hostile

---

35) ravenous: 게걸스럽게 먹는; 몹시 굶주린, 탐욕스러운

36) fastidiousness: 세심함, 꼼꼼함, 까다로움

37) malingerer: 꾀병을 부리는 자

Northland environment. It marked his adaptability[38], his capacity to adjust himself to changing conditions, the lack of which would have meant swift and terrible death. It marked, further, the decay or going to pieces of his moral nature, a vain thing and a handicap in the ruthless struggle for existence. It was all well enough in the Southland, under the law of love and fellowship, to respect private property and personal feelings; but in the Northland, under the law of club and fang, whoso[39] took such things into account was a fool, and in so far as he observed them he would fail to prosper.

Not that Buck reasoned it out. He was fit, that was all, and unconsciously he accommodated himself to the new mode of life. All his days, no matter what the odds, he had never run from a fight. But the club of the man in the red sweater had beaten into him a more fundamental and primitive code. Civilized, he could have died for a moral consideration, say the defence of Judge Miller's riding-whip; but the completeness of his decivilization[40] was now evidenced by his ability to flee from the defence of a moral consideration and so save his hide. He did not steal for joy of it, but because of the clamor of his stomach. He did not rob openly, but stole secretly and cunningly, out of respect for club and fang. In short, the things he did were done because it was easier to do them than not to do them.

His development (or retrogression[41]) was rapid. His muscles

38) adaptability: 순응성, 적응성, 융통성

39) whoso: 《고어》 =whoever

40) decivilization: 반문명화, 야만

41) retrogression: 역행, 퇴보, 후퇴; [생물] 퇴화, [천문] (행성의) 역행

※ 벅이 북쪽 지방의 견디기 어려운 추위와 열악한 자연환경에 점차 적응하는 것을

became hard as iron, and he grew callous[42] to all ordinary pain. He achieved an internal as well as external economy. He could eat anything, no matter how loathsome[43] or indigestible[44]; and, once eaten, the juices of his stomach extracted the last least particle of nutriment[45]; and his blood carried it to the farthest reaches of his body, building it into the toughest and stoutest of tissues. Sight and scent became remarkably keen, while his hearing developed such acuteness that in his sleep he heard the faintest sound and knew whether it heralded peace or peril. He learned to bite the ice out with his teeth when it collected between his toes; and when he was thirsty and there was a thick scum of ice over the water hole, he would break it by rearing and striking it with stiff fore legs. His most conspicuous trait was an ability to scent the wind and forecast it a night in advance. No matter how breathless the air when he dug his nest by tree or bank, the wind that later blew inevitably found him to leeward[46], sheltered and snug.

And not only did he learn by experience, but instincts long dead became alive again. The domesticated generations fell from him. In vague ways he remembered back to the youth of the breed, to the time the wild dogs ranged in packs through

---

화자는 발전 또는 퇴화의 견해로 다를 수 있지만 벅의 근육과 신체는 더욱 강해졌다는 의미이다. 다윈의 적자생존과 자연도태의 이론이 적용되는 대목이다.

42) callous: (피부가) 굳은, 못이 박힌, 경결(硬結)한, 무감각한(insensible), 무정한, 냉담한

43) loathsome: 싫은, 지긋지긋한, 불쾌한(disgusting), 역겨운(sickening)

44) indigestible: 소화되지 않는, 삭이기 어려운, 이해하기 어려운, 받아들이기 어려운, 참을 수 없는, 불쾌한

45) nutriment: 영양물, 음식물, 영양소, 성장을 돕는 것

46) to leeward: 바람이 불어가는 쪽을 향하여

the primeval forest and killed their meat as they ran it down. It was no task for him to learn to fight with cut and slash and the quick wolf snap. In this manner had fought forgotten ancestors. They quickened the old life within him, and the old tricks which they had stamped into the heredity of the breed were his tricks. They came to him without effort or discovery, as though they had been his always. And when, on the still cold nights, he pointed his nose at a star and howled long and wolflike, it was his ancestors, dead and dust, pointing nose at star and howling down through the centuries and through him. And his cadences[47] were their cadences, the cadences which voiced their woe and what to them was the meaning of the stiffness, and the cold, and dark.

Thus, as token of[48] what a puppet thing life is, the ancient song surged through him and he came into his own again; and he came because men had found a yellow metal in the North, and because Manuel was a gardener's helper whose wages did not lap over[49] the needs of his wife and divers small copies of himself.[50]

---

47) cadences: 박자, 목소리의 내림조, 억양

48) as token of: ~의 증거로, ~의 표시로

49) lap over: ~을 충족시키다, ~을 (감싸듯이) 둘러싸다

50) divers small copies of himself: 자신의 몇몇 조그만 복사물들, 즉 그의 조그만 자식들을 의미

Chapter III
The Dominant Primordial Beast

The dominant primordial beast[1] was strong in Buck, and under the fierce conditions of trail life it grew and grew. Yet it was a secret growth. His newborn cunning gave him poise[2] and control. He was too busy adjusting himself to the new life to feel at ease, and not only did he not pick fights, but he avoided them whenever possible. A certain deliberateness characterized his attitude. He was not prone to rashness and precipitate[3] action; and in the bitter hatred between him and Spitz he betrayed no impatience, shunned all offensive acts.

On the other hand, possibly because he divined in Buck a dangerous rival, Spitz never lost an opportunity of showing his teeth. He even went out of his way to bully Buck, striving constantly to start the fight which could end only in the death of one or the other. Early in the trip this might have taken place had it not been for an unwonted[4] accident. At the end of this day they made a bleak and miserable camp on the shore of Lake Le Barge[5]. Driving snow, a wind that cut like a white-hot knife, and darkness had forced them to grope for a camping place. They could hardly have fared worse. At their backs rose

---

1) dominant primordial beast: 지배적인 원시의 야수적 본능

2) poise: 평형, 균형

3) precipitate: 재촉하다, 촉진시키다, 몰아대다, (어떤 상태에) 갑자기 빠뜨리다

4) unwonted: 이례적인, 드문, 특이한, 《고어》익숙지 않은

5) Lake Le Barge: It is a widening of the Yukon River north of Whitehorse, Yukon in Canada.

a perpendicular[6] wall of rock, and Perrault and Francois were compelled to make their fire and spread their sleeping robes on the ice of the lake itself. The tent they had discarded at Dyea in order to travel light. A few sticks of driftwood furnished them with a fire that thawed down through the ice and left them to eat supper in the dark.

Close in under the sheltering rock Buck made his nest. So snug and warm was it, that he was loath to leave it when Francois distributed the fish which he had first thawed[7] over the fire. But when Buck finished his ration and returned, he found his nest occupied. A warning snarl told him that the trespasser[8] was Spitz. Till now Buck had avoided trouble with his enemy, but this was too much. The beast in him roared. He sprang upon Spitz with a fury which surprised them both, and Spitz particularly, for his whole experience with Buck had gone to teach him that his rival was an unusually timid dog, who managed to hold his own only because of his great weight and size.

Francois was surprised, too, when they shot out in a tangle from the disrupted nest and he divined the cause of the trouble. "A-a-ah!" he cried to Buck. "Gif it to heem, by Gar! Gif it to heem, the dirty t'eef![9]"

Spitz was equally willing. He was crying with sheer rage and eagerness as he circled back and forth for a chance to spring in. Buck was no less eager, and no less cautious, as he likewise

---

6) perpendicular: 수직 의, 직립한, 수직선, 급경사면면

7) thawed: 녹았다

8) trespasser: 침입자, 방해자

9) Gif it to heem, the dirty t'eef!: 그 더러운 도둑놈을 혼내줘라!

circled back and forth for the advantage. But it was then that the unexpected happened, the thing which projected their struggle for supremacy far into the future, past many a weary mile of trail and toil.

An oath from Perrault, the resounding impact of a club upon a bony frame, and a shrill yelp of pain, heralded the breaking forth of pandemonium[10]. The camp was suddenly discovered to be alive with skulking[11] furry forms,—starving huskies, four or five score of them, who had scented the camp from some Indian village. They had crept in while Buck and Spitz were fighting, and when the two men sprang among them with stout clubs they showed their teeth and fought back. They were crazed by the smell of the food. Perrault found one with head buried in the grub-box[12]. His club landed heavily on the gaunt ribs, and the grub-box was capsized on the ground. On the instant a score of the famished brutes were scrambling for the bread and bacon. The clubs fell upon them unheeded. They yelped and howled under the rain of blows, but struggled none the less madly till the last crumb had been devoured.

In the meantime the astonished team-dogs had burst out of their nests only to be set upon by the fierce invaders. Never had Buck seen such dogs. It seemed as though their bones would burst through their skins. They were mere skeletons, draped loosely in draggled hides[13], with blazing eyes and

---

10) pandemonium: 악마전(殿), 복마전, 지옥, 아수라장, 대혼란(의 곳)

11) skulking: 슬그머니 숨다, 잠복하다, 몸을 안전한 곳에 두다, 살금살금 걷다, 살금살금 ~하다, 몰래[가만히, 슬그머니] 달아나다(sneak)

12) grub-box: 음식물 상자, 음식 보관 상자

13) draggled hides: 말라서 늘어난 가죽들

slavered fangs[14]. But the hunger-madness made them terrifying, irresistible. There was no opposing them. The team-dogs were swept back against the cliff at the first onset. Buck was beset by three huskies, and in a trice his head and shoulders were ripped and slashed. The din was frightful. Billee was crying as usual. Dave and Sol-leks, dripping blood from a score of wounds, were fighting bravely side by side. Joe was snapping like a demon. Once, his teeth closed on the fore leg of a husky, and he crunched down through the bone. Pike, the malingerer, leaped upon the crippled animal, breaking its neck with a quick flash of teeth and a jerk, Buck got a frothing adversary[15] by the throat, and was sprayed with blood when his teeth sank through the jugular[16]. The warm taste of it in his mouth goaded him to greater fierceness. He flung himself upon another, and at the same time felt teeth sink into his own throat. It was Spitz, treacherously attacking from the side.

Perrault and Francois, having cleaned out their part of the camp, hurried to save their sled-dogs. The wild wave of famished beasts rolled back before them, and Buck shook himself free. But it was only for a moment. The two men were compelled to run back to save the grub, upon which the huskies returned to the attack on the team. Billee, terrified into bravery, sprang through the savage circle and fled away over the ice. Pike and Dub followed on his heels, with the rest of the team behind. As Buck drew himself together to spring after them, out of the tail of his eye he saw Spitz rush upon him with the evident intention

---

14) slavered fangs: 침 흘리는 송곳니니

15) frothing adversary: 게거품을 내며 달려드는 대항자

16) jugular: 경정맥(= ~ vèin), (적의) 최대의 약점, 급소

of overthrowing him. Once off his feet and under that mass of huskies, there was no hope for him. But he braced himself to the shock of Spitz's charge, then joined the flight out on the lake.

Later, the nine team-dogs gathered together and sought shelter in the forest. Though unpursued, they were in a sorry plight. There was not one who was not wounded in four or five places, while some were wounded grievously[17]. Dub was badly injured in a hind leg; Dolly, the last husky added to the team at Dyea, had a badly torn throat; Joe had lost an eye; while Billee, the good-natured, with an ear chewed and rent to ribbons, cried and whimpered[18] throughout the night. At daybreak they limped warily back to camp, to find the marauders[19] gone and the two men in bad tempers. Fully half their grub supply was gone. The huskies had chewed through the sled lashings and canvas coverings. In fact, nothing, no matter how remotely eatable, had escaped them. They had eaten a pair of Perrault's moose-hide moccasins, chunks out of the leather traces, and even two feet of lash from the end of Francois's whip. He broke from a mournful contemplation of it to look over his wounded dogs.

"Ah, my frien's," he said softly, "mebbe it mek you mad dog, dose many bites. Mebbe all mad dog, sacredam! Wot you t'ink, eh, Perrault?"

The courier shook his head dubiously. With four hundred miles of trail still between him and Dawson[20], he could ill

---

17) grievously: 슬프게도, 몹시

18) whimpered: 호소하듯, 처량하게)울다, 훌쩍이다, 울먹이다, 애처로이 하소연하다, 투덜거리다, (바람, 시내 등) 낮고 구슬픈 소리를 내다.

19) marauders: 약탈자들, 습격자들

20) Dawson: It is a town in Yukon, Canada. It is inseparably linked to the Klondike

afford to have madness break out among his dogs. Two hours of cursing and exertion got the harnesses into shape, and the wound-stiffened team was under way, struggling painfully over the hardest part of the trail they had yet encountered, and for that matter, the hardest between them and Dawson.

The Thirty Mile River[21] was wide open. Its wild water defied the frost, and it was in the eddies only and in the quiet places that the ice held at all. Six days of exhausting toil were required to cover those thirty terrible miles. And terrible they were, for every foot of them was accomplished at the risk of life to dog and man. A dozen times, Perrault, nosing the way broke through the ice bridges, being saved by the long pole he carried, which he so held that it fell each time across the hole made by his body. But a cold snap was on, the thermometer registering fifty below zero[22], and each time he broke through he was compelled for very life to build a fire and dry his garments.

Nothing daunted him. It was because nothing daunted him that he had been chosen for government courier. He took all manner of risks, resolutely thrusting his little weazened[23] face into the frost and struggling on from dim dawn to dark. He skirted the frowning shores on rim ice that bent and crackled under foot and upon which they dared not halt. Once, the sled broke

Gold Rush (1896-99).

21) The Thirty Mile River: It is The Yukon River is one of the grandest in the world. It flows almost two thousand miles from Marsh Lake to the Bering Sea. One of the gems in the entire Yukon River system - a section only thirty miles long - is now Canadian Heritage river.

22) the thermometer registering fifty below zero: 온도계가 영하 50도를 기록하고 있었고 (북쪽의 추위가 인간의 한계상황을 보여주고 있음)

23) weazened: =wíz·en(ed), wéa·zen(ed) a. 시든, (사람·얼굴 등이) 몹시 여윈.

through, with Dave and Buck, and they were half-frozen and all but drowned by the time they were dragged out. The usual fire was necessary to save them. They were coated solidly with ice, and the two men kept them on the run around the fire, sweating and thawing, so close that they were singed by the flames.

At another time Spitz went through, dragging the whole team after him up to Buck, who strained backward with all his strength, his fore paws on the slippery edge and the ice quivering and snapping all around. But behind him was Dave, likewise straining backward, and behind the sled was Francois, pulling till his tendons cracked[24].

Again, the rim ice broke away before and behind, and there was no escape except up the cliff. Perrault scaled it by a miracle, while Francois prayed for just that miracle; and with every thong and sled lashing and the last bit of harness rove into a long rope, the dogs were hoisted, one by one, to the cliff crest. Francois came up last, after the sled and load. Then came the search for a place to descend, which descent was ultimately made by the aid of the rope, and night found them back on the river with a quarter of a mile to the day's credit.

By the time they made the Hootalinqua[25] and good ice, Buck was played out. The rest of the dogs were in like condition; but Perrault, to make up lost time, pushed them late and early. The first day they covered thirty-five miles to the Big Salmon;

---

24) till his tendons cracked: 그의 힘줄이 우두둑 금이 갈 때까지

25) Hootalinqua: It is the name Hootalinqua is from the Northern Tutchone word Hudinlin, meaning "running against the mountain." Hootalinqua was a popular gathering site for trade and visiting between the Tlingit, Southern Tutchone and Northern Tutchone people.

the next day thirty-five more to the Little Salmon; the third day forty miles, which brought them well up toward the Five Fingers[26].

Buck's feet were not so compact and hard as the feet of the huskies. His had softened during the many generations since the day his last wild ancestor was tamed by a cave-dweller[27] or river man. All day long he limped in agony, and camp once made, lay down like a dead dog. Hungry as he was, he would not move to receive his ration of fish, which Francois had to bring to him. Also, the dog-driver[28] rubbed Buck's feet for half an hour each night after supper, and sacrificed the tops of his own moccasins[29] to make four moccasins for Buck. This was a great relief, and Buck caused even the weazened face of Perrault to twist itself into a grin one morning, when Francois forgot the moccasins and Buck lay on his back, his four feet waving appealingly in the air, and refused to budge without them. Later his feet grew hard to the trail, and the worn-out foot-gear was thrown away.

At the Pelly one morning, as they were harnessing up, Dolly, who had never been conspicuous for anything, went suddenly mad. She announced her condition by a long, heartbreaking wolf howl that sent every dog bristling with fear, then sprang straight for Buck. He had never seen a dog go mad, nor did he have any

---

26) Five Fingers: The Five Finger Rapids is one of the obstacles on the journey along the Yukon River to Dawson. Four islands at the Rapids force the swift and turbulent currents to divide in five narrow channels, making the journey very dangerous.

27) cave-dweller: (특히 선사 시대의) 동굴 주거인, 원시인

28) dog-driver: 개몰이꾼

29) moccasins: 북아메리카 원주민의 뒤축 없는 신, (그와 비슷한) 신의 일종, 독사의 일종

reason to fear madness; yet he knew that here was horror, and fled away from it in a panic. Straight away he raced, with Dolly, panting and frothing[30], one leap behind; nor could she gain on him, so great was his terror, nor could he leave her, so great was her madness. He plunged through the wooded breast of the island, flew down to the lower end, crossed a back channel filled with rough ice to another island, gained a third island, curved back to the main river, and in desperation started to cross it. And all the time, though he did not look, he could hear her snarling just one leap behind. Francois called to him a quarter of a mile away and he doubled back, still one leap ahead, gasping painfully for air and putting all his faith in that Francois would save him. The dog-driver held the axe poised in his hand, and as Buck shot past him the axe crashed down upon mad Dolly's head.

Buck staggered over against the sled, exhausted, sobbing for breath, helpless. This was Spitz's opportunity. He sprang upon Buck, and twice his teeth sank into his unresisting foe and ripped and tore the flesh to the bone. Then Francois's lash descended, and Buck had the satisfaction of watching Spitz receive the worst whipping as yet administered to any of the teams.

"One devil, dat Spitz," remarked Perrault. "Some dam day heem keel dat Buck."

"Dat Buck two devils," was Francois's rejoinder. "All de tam I watch dat Buck I know for sure. Lissen: some dam fine day heem get mad lak hell an' den heem chew dat Spitz all up an' spit heem out on de snow. Sure. I know."

From then on it was war between them. Spitz, as lead-dog and acknowledged master of the team, felt his supremacy threatened

---

30) panting and frothing: 헐떡이며 거품을 뿜고 있는

by this strange Southland dog. And strange Buck was to him, for of the many Southland dogs he had known, not one had shown up worthily in camp and on trail. They were all too soft, dying under the toil, the frost, and starvation. Buck was the exception. He alone endured and prospered, matching the husky in strength, savagery, and cunning. Then he was a masterful[31] dog, and what made him dangerous was the fact that the club of the man in the red sweater had knocked all blind pluck and rashness out of his desire for mastery. He was preeminently cunning, and could bide his time with a patience that was nothing less than primitive.

It was inevitable that the clash for leadership should come. Buck wanted it. He wanted it because it was his nature, because he had been gripped tight by that nameless, incomprehensible pride of the trail and trace—that pride which holds dogs in the toil to the last gasp, which lures them to die joyfully in the harness, and breaks their hearts if they are cut out of the harness. This was the pride of Dave as wheel-dog[32], of Sol-leks as he pulled with all his strength; the pride that laid hold of them at break of camp, transforming them from sour and sullen brutes into straining, eager, ambitious creatures; the pride that spurred them on all day and dropped them at pitch of camp at night, letting them fall back into gloomy unrest and uncontent. This was the pride that bore up Spitz and made him thrash the sled-dogs who blundered and shirked[33] in the traces or hid away at

---

31) masterful: 건방진, 오만한(domineering), 주인티를 내는, 솜씨가 능숙한, 노련한, 교묘한

32) wheel-dog: one of the dogs directly in front of the sled that take most of the force. 썰매의 앞 부분을 끌고가는 개, 중요한 역할을 수행하는 썰매개, (미 속어) 실력자, 거물

33) shirked: (책임 등을) 회피하다, 기피하다

harness-up time in the morning. Likewise it was this pride that made him fear Buck as a possible lead-dog. And this was Buck's pride, too.

He openly threatened the other's leadership. He came between him and the shirks he should have punished. And he did it deliberately. One night there was a heavy snowfall, and in the morning Pike, the malingerer, did not appear. He was securely hidden in his nest under a foot of snow. Francois called him and sought him in vain. Spitz was wild with wrath. He raged through the camp, smelling and digging in every likely place, snarling so frightfully that Pike heard and shivered in his hiding-place.

But when he was at last unearthed[34], and Spitz flew at him to punish him, Buck flew, with equal rage, in between. So unexpected was it, and so shrewdly managed, that Spitz was hurled backward and off his feet. Pike, who had been trembling abjectly, took heart at this open mutiny, and sprang upon his overthrown leader. Buck, to whom fair play was a forgotten code, likewise sprang upon Spitz. But Francois, chuckling at the incident while unswerving[35] in the administration of justice, brought his lash down upon Buck with all his might. This failed to drive Buck from his prostrate[36] rival, and the butt of the whip was brought into play. Half-stunned by the blow, Buck was knocked backward and the lash laid upon him again and again, while Spitz soundly punished the many times offending Pike.

---

34) unearthed: (땅 속에서) 발굴하다, 파내다, (여우 따위를) 굴에서 몰아내다, 발견하다(discover), (음모 따위를) 밝혀내다, 폭로하다, 적발하다

35) unswerving: 빗나가지〔벗어나지〕 않는, 갈팡질팡하지 않는, 부동의, 확고한

36) prostrate: 엎어진, 엎드린, 부복(俯伏)한, 패배한, 항복한

In the days that followed, as Dawson grew closer and closer, Buck still continued to interfere between Spitz and the culprits; but he did it craftily, when Francois was not around, With the covert mutiny[37] of Buck, a general insubordination[38] sprang up and increased. Dave and Sol-leks were unaffected, but the rest of the team went from bad to worse. Things no longer went right. There was continual bickering and jangling[39]. Trouble was always afoot, and at the bottom of it was Buck. He kept Francois busy, for the dog-driver was in constant apprehension of the life-and-death[40] struggle between the two which he knew must take place sooner or later; and on more than one night the sounds of quarrelling and strife among the other dogs turned him out of his sleeping robe, fearful that Buck and Spitz were at it.

But the opportunity did not present itself, and they pulled into Dawson one dreary afternoon with the great fight still to come. Here were many men, and countless dogs, and Buck found them all at work. It seemed the ordained order of things that dogs should work. All day they swung up and down the main street in long teams, and in the night their jingling bells still went by. They hauled cabin logs and firewood, freighted up to the mines, and did all manner of work that horses did in the Santa Clara Valley. Here and there Buck met Southland dogs, but in the main they were the wild wolf husky breed. Every night, regularly, at nine, at twelve, at three, they lifted a nocturnal[41]

---

37) mutiny: (특히 군인 · 수병 등의) 폭동, 반란, 하극상

38) insubordination: 불순종, 반항

39) bickering and jangling: 계속 다투고 으르렁거리는

40) life-and-death: 사활이 걸린, 극히 중대한

41) nocturnal: 밤의, 야간의

song, a weird and eerie chant[42], in which it was Buck's delight to join.

With the aurora borealis[43] flaming coldly overhead, or the stars leaping in the frost dance, and the land numb and frozen under its pall[44] of snow, this song of the huskies might have been the defiance of life, only it was pitched in minor key, with long-drawn wailings and half-sobs, and was more the pleading of life, the articulate travail of existence. It was an old song, old as the breed itself—one of the first songs of the younger world in a day when songs were sad. It was invested with the woe of unnumbered generations, this plaint by which Buck was so strangely stirred. When he moaned and sobbed, it was with the pain of living that was of old the pain of his wild fathers, and the fear and mystery of the cold and dark that was to them fear and mystery. And that he should be stirred by it marked the completeness with which he harked back through the ages of fire and roof to the raw beginnings of life in the howling ages.

Seven days from the time they pulled into Dawson, they dropped down the steep bank by the Barracks to the Yukon Trail, and pulled for Dyea and Salt Water. Perrault was carrying despatches if anything more urgent than those he had brought in; also, the travel pride had gripped him, and he purposed to make the record trip of the year. Several things favored him in this. The week's rest had recuperated[45] the dogs and put them in thorough trim. The trail they had broken into the country was

---

42) a weird and eerie chant: 불가사의하고 섬뜩한 울음소리

43) aurora borealis: 북극광(the northern lights)

44) pall: 장막, 덮개, 휘장

45) recuperated: (건강 따위를) 회복하다, (손실 따위를) 만회하다

packed hard by later journeyers. And further, the police had arranged in two or three places deposits of grub for dog and man, and he was travelling light.

They made Sixty Mile, which is a fifty-mile run, on the first day; and the second day saw them booming up the Yukon well on their way to Pelly. But such splendid running was achieved not without great trouble and vexation on the part of Francois. The insidious[46] revolt led by Buck had destroyed the solidarity of the team. It no longer was as one dog leaping in the traces. The encouragement Buck gave the rebels led them into all kinds of petty misdemeanors[47]. No more was Spitz a leader greatly to be feared. The old awe departed, and they grew equal to challenging his authority. Pike robbed him of half a fish one night, and gulped it down under the protection of Buck. Another night Dub and Joe fought Spitz and made him forego the punishment they deserved. And even Billee, the good-natured, was less good-natured, and whined not half so placatingly as in former days. Buck never came near Spitz without snarling and bristling menacingly[48]. In fact, his conduct approached that of a bully, and he was given to swaggering[49] up and down before Spitz's very nose.

The breaking down of discipline likewise affected the dogs in their relations with one another. They quarrelled and bickered more than ever among themselves, till at times the camp was

---

46) insidious: 틈을 엿보는, 음험한, 교활한, 방심할 수 없는(treacherous), (병 등이) 모르는 사이에 진행하는, 잠행성(潛行性)의

47) misdemeanors: 경범죄(cf. felony), 비행, 행실(품행)이 나쁨.

48) menacingly: 위협하듯. 험악하게, 절박하게

49) was given to swaggering: 뽐내며 걷는데 열중했다

a howling bedlam[50]. Dave and Sol-leks alone were unaltered, though they were made irritable by the unending squabbling[51]. Francois swore strange barbarous oaths, and stamped the snow in futile rage, and tore his hair. His lash was always singing among the dogs, but it was of small avail. Directly his back was turned they were at it again. He backed up Spitz with his whip, while Buck backed up the remainder of the team. Francois knew he was behind all the trouble, and Buck knew he knew; but Buck was too clever ever again to be caught red-handed. He worked faithfully in the harness, for the toil had become a delight to him; yet it was a greater delight slyly to precipitate a fight amongst his mates and tangle the traces.

At the mouth of the Tahkeena[52], one night after supper, Dub turned up a snowshoe rabbit, blundered it, and missed. In a second the whole team was in full cry. A hundred yards away was a camp of the Northwest Police, with fifty dogs, huskies all, who joined the chase. The rabbit sped down the river, turned off into a small creek, up the frozen bed of which it held steadily. It ran lightly on the surface of the snow, while the dogs ploughed through[53] by main strength. Buck led the pack, sixty strong, around bend after bend, but he could not gain. He lay down low to the race, whining eagerly, his splendid body flashing forward, leap by leap, in the wan white moonlight. And leap by leap, like

---

50) bedlam: 소란한 장소, 대혼란, 수라장, 정신 병원(madhouse); (B-) 런던의 St. Mary of Bethlehem 정신 병원

51) squabbling: 시시한 언쟁, 말다툼.

52) Tahkeena: It is also known as “Takhini”. The Tahkeena River is a part of the Yukon River system. There were Police Quarters here during the time of the Gold Rush.

53) ploughed through: 헤치고 나아가다, (어려움을) 뚫고 달려가다

some pale frost wraith, the snowshoe rabbit flashed on ahead.

All that stirring of old instincts which at stated periods drives men out from the sounding cities to forest and plain to kill things by chemically propelled leaden pellets[54], the blood lust, the joy to kill—all this was Buck's, only it was infinitely more intimate. He was ranging at the head of the pack, running the wild thing down, the living meat, to kill with his own teeth and wash his muzzle[55] to the eyes in warm blood.

There is an ecstasy that marks the summit of life, and beyond which life cannot rise. And such is the paradox of living, this ecstasy comes when one is most alive, and it comes as a complete forgetfulness that one is alive. This ecstasy, this forgetfulness of living, comes to the artist, caught up and out of himself in a sheet of flame; it comes to the soldier, war-mad on a stricken field and refusing quarter; and it came to Buck, leading the pack, sounding the old wolf-cry, straining after the food that was alive and that fled swiftly before him through the moonlight. He was sounding the deeps of his nature, and of the parts of his nature that were deeper than he, going back into the womb of Time. He was mastered by the sheer surging of life, the tidal wave of being, the perfect joy of each separate muscle, joint, and sinew[56] in that it was everything that was not death, that it was aglow and rampant[57], expressing itself in movement, flying exultantly under the stars and over the face of dead matter that did not move.

54) leaden pellets: 납 탄알들

55) muzzle: (동물의) 입 · 코 부분, 부리, 주둥이

56) sinew: 힘줄, 근육, 체력, 정력

57) rampant: (사람, 짐승이) 과격한, 사나운, 광포한, 날뛰는

But Spitz, cold and calculating even in his supreme moods, left the pack and cut across a narrow neck of land where the creek made a long bend around. Buck did not know of this, and as he rounded the bend, the frost wraith of a rabbit still flitting before him, he saw another and larger frost wraith leap from the overhanging bank into the immediate path of the rabbit. It was Spitz. The rabbit could not turn, and as the white teeth broke its back in mid air it shrieked as loudly as a stricken man may shriek. At sound of this, the cry of Life plunging down from Life's apex in the grip of Death, the fall pack at Buck's heels raised a hell's chorus of delight.

Buck did not cry out. He did not check himself, but drove in upon Spitz, shoulder to shoulder, so hard that he missed the throat. They rolled over and over in the powdery snow. Spitz gained his feet almost as though he had not been overthrown, slashing Buck down the shoulder and leaping clear. Twice his teeth clipped together, like the steel jaws of a trap, as he backed away for better footing, with lean and lifting lips that writhed and snarled.

In a flash[58] Buck knew it. The time had come. It was to the death. As they circled about, snarling, ears laid back, keenly watchful for the advantage, the scene came to Buck with a sense of familiarity. He seemed to remember it all,—the white woods, and earth, and moonlight, and the thrill of battle. Over the whiteness and silence brooded a ghostly calm. There was not the faintest whisper of air—nothing moved, not a leaf quivered, the visible breaths of the dogs rising slowly and lingering in the frosty air. They had made short work of the snowshoe rabbit,

---

58) In a flash: =like a ~ 대번에, 즉시

these dogs that were ill-tamed wolves; and they were now drawn up in an expectant circle. They, too, were silent, their eyes only gleaming and their breaths drifting slowly upward. To Buck it was nothing new or strange, this scene of old time. It was as though it had always been, the wonted way of things.

Spitz was a practised fighter. From Spitzbergen through the Arctic, and across Canada and the Barrens, he had held his own with all manner of dogs and achieved to mastery over them. Bitter rage was his, but never blind rage. In passion to rend and destroy, he never forgot that his enemy was in like passion to rend and destroy. He never rushed till he was prepared to receive a rush; never attacked till he had first defended that attack.

In vain Buck strove to sink his teeth in the neck of the big white dog. Wherever his fangs struck for the softer flesh, they were countered by the fangs of Spitz. Fang clashed fang[59], and lips were cut and bleeding, but Buck could not penetrate his enemy's guard. Then he warmed up and enveloped Spitz in a whirlwind of rushes. Time and time again he tried for the snow-white throat, where life bubbled near to the surface, and each time and every time Spitz slashed him and got away. Then Buck took to rushing, as though for the throat, when, suddenly drawing back his head and curving in from the side, he would drive his shoulder at the shoulder of Spitz, as a ram by which to overthrow him. But instead, Buck's shoulder was slashed down each time as Spitz leaped lightly away.

Spitz was untouched, while Buck was streaming with blood and panting hard. The fight was growing desperate. And all the while the silent and wolfish circle waited to finish off whichever

---

59) Fang clashed fang: 어금니와 어금니가 소리를 내며 충돌하였다

dog went down. As Buck grew winded, Spitz took to rushing, and he kept him staggering for footing. Once Buck went over, and the whole circle of sixty dogs started up; but he recovered himself, almost in mid air, and the circle sank down again and waited.

But Buck possessed a quality that made for greatness—imagination. He fought by instinct, but he could fight by head as well. He rushed, as though attempting the old shoulder trick, but at the last instant swept low to the snow and in. His teeth closed on Spitz's left fore leg. There was a crunch[60] of breaking bone, and the white dog faced him on three legs. Thrice he tried to knock him over, then repeated the trick and broke the right fore leg. Despite the pain and helplessness, Spitz struggled madly to keep up. He saw the silent circle, with gleaming eyes, lolling tongues[61], and silvery breaths drifting upward, closing in upon him as he had seen similar circles close in upon beaten antagonists in the past. Only this time he was the one who was beaten.

There was no hope for him. Buck was inexorable[62]. Mercy was a thing reserved for gentler climes. He manoeuvred for the final rush. The circle had tightened till he could feel the breaths of the huskies on his flanks. He could see them, beyond Spitz and to either side, half crouching for the spring, their eyes fixed upon him. A pause seemed to fall. Every animal was motionless as though turned to stone. Only Spitz quivered and bristled as

---

60) crunch: 부서지는 소리

61) lolling tongues: 축 늘어진 혀

62) inexorable: 무정한, 냉혹한, (아무의 간청을) 들어주지 않는, 굽힐 수 없는, 움직일 수 없는

he staggered back and forth, snarling with horrible menace, as though to frighten off impending death. Then Buck sprang in and out; but while he was in, shoulder had at last squarely met shoulder[63]. The dark circle became a dot on the moon-flooded snow as Spitz disappeared from view. Buck stood and looked on, the successful champion, the dominant primordial beast[64] who had made his kill and found it good.

---

63) shoulder had at last squarely met shoulder: 마침내 어깨와 어깨가 정면으로 부딪쳤다

64) dominant primordial beast: 강력한 원시적 짐승(Buck이 Spitz와의 리더 싸움 경쟁에서 Spitz를 죽임으로써 승리함)

Chapter IV
Who Has Won to Mastership

"Eh? Wot I say?[1] I spik true w'en I say dat Buck two devils.[2]" This was Francois's speech next morning when he discovered Spitz missing and Buck covered with wounds. He drew him to the fire and by its light pointed them out.

"Dat Spitz fight lak hell," said Perrault, as he surveyed the gaping rips and cuts[3].

"An' dat Buck fight lak two hells," was Francois's answer. "An' now we make good time. No more Spitz, no more trouble, sure."

While Perrault packed the camp outfit and loaded the sled, the dog-driver proceeded to harness the dogs. Buck trotted up to the place Spitz would have occupied as leader; but Francois, not noticing him, brought Sol-leks to the coveted position. In his judgment, Sol-leks was the best lead-dog left. Buck sprang upon Sol-leks in a fury, driving him back and standing in his place.

"Eh? eh?" Francois cried, slapping his thighs gleefully. "Look at dat Buck. Heem keel dat Spitz, heem t'ink to take de job."

"Go 'way, Chook![4]" he cried, but Buck refused to budge.

He took Buck by the scruff of the neck, and though the dog growled threateningly, dragged him to one side and replaced Sol-leks. The old dog did not like it, and showed plainly that he

---

1) Wot I say?: 내가 뭐라고 말했어?

2) I spik true w'en I say dat Buck two devils.: 내가 벅은 악마가 둘은 붙은 것 같다고 말했지.

3) rips and cuts: 찢어지고 베인 상처

4) Go 'way, Chook!: 어서 꺼져!

was afraid of Buck. Francois was obdurate, but when he turned his back Buck again displaced Sol-leks, who was not at all unwilling to go.

Francois was angry. "Now, by Gar, I feex you![5]" he cried, coming back with a heavy club in his hand.

Buck remembered the man in the red sweater, and retreated slowly; nor did he attempt to charge in when Sol-leks was once more brought forward. But he circled just beyond the range of the club, snarling with bitterness and rage; and while he circled he watched the club so as to dodge it if thrown by Francois, for he was become wise in the way of clubs. The driver went about his work, and he called to Buck when he was ready to put him in his old place in front of Dave. Buck retreated two or three steps. Francois followed him up, whereupon he again retreated. After some time of this, Francois threw down the club, thinking that Buck feared a thrashing[6]. But Buck was in open revolt. He wanted, not to escape a clubbing, but to have the leadership. It was his by right. He had earned it, and he would not be content with less.

Perrault took a hand.[7] Between them they ran him about for the better part of an hour. They threw clubs at him. He dodged. They cursed him, and his fathers and mothers before him, and all his seed to come after him down to the remotest generation, and every hair on his body and drop of blood in his veins; and he answered curse with snarl and kept out of their reach. He did not try to run away, but retreated around and around the camp,

---

5) Now, by Gar, I feex you. 지금 바로 너를 반드시 혼내주겠다

6) thrashing: 채찍질

7) Perrault took a hand.: 페로가 거들었다.

advertising plainly that when his desire was met, he would come in and be good.

Francois sat down and scratched his head. Perrault looked at his watch and swore. Time was flying, and they should have been on the trail an hour gone. Francois scratched his head again. He shook it and grinned sheepishly at the courier, who shrugged his shoulders in sign that they were beaten. Then Francois went up to where Sol-leks stood and called to Buck. Buck laughed, as dogs laugh, yet kept his distance. Francois unfastened Sol-leks's traces and put him back in his old place. The team stood harnessed to the sled in an unbroken line, ready for the trail. There was no place for Buck save at the front. Once more Francois called, and once more Buck laughed and kept away.

"T'row down de club," Perrault commanded.

Francois complied, whereupon Buck trotted in, laughing triumphantly, and swung around into position at the head of the team. His traces were fastened, the sled broken out, and with both men running they dashed out on to the river trail.

Highly as the dog-driver had forevalued[8] Buck, with his two devils, he found, while the day was yet young, that he had undervalued. At a bound Buck took up the duties of leadership; and where judgment was required, and quick thinking and quick acting, he showed himself the superior even of Spitz, of whom Francois had never seen an equal.

But it was in giving the law and making his mates live up to it, that Buck excelled. Dave and Sol-leks did not mind the change in leadership. It was none of their business. Their

8) forevalued: 미리 평가하였다

business was to toil, and toil mightily, in the traces. So long as that were not interfered with, they did not care what happened. Billee, the good-natured[9], could lead for all they cared, so long as he kept order. The rest of the team, however, had grown unruly during the last days of Spitz, and their surprise was great now that Buck proceeded to lick them into shape.

Pike, who pulled at Buck's heels, and who never put an ounce more of his weight against the breast-band[10] than he was compelled to do, was swiftly and repeatedly shaken for loafing; and ere the first day was done he was pulling more than ever before in his life. The first night in camp, Joe, the sour one, was punished roundly—a thing that Spitz had never succeeded in doing. Buck simply smothered[11] him by virtue of superior weight, and cut him up till he ceased snapping and began to whine for mercy.

The general tone of the team picked up immediately. It recovered its old-time solidarity, and once more the dogs leaped as one dog in the traces. At the Rink Rapids two native huskies, Teek and Koona, were added; and the celerity with which Buck broke them in took away Francois's breath.

"Nevaire such a dog as dat Buck!"[12] he cried. "No, nevaire! Heem worth one t'ousan' dollair, by Gar! Eh? Wot you say, Perrault?"[13]

---

9) good-natured: (마음씨가) 착한, 온후한, 친절한

10) breast-band: 가슴걸이

11) smothered: ~에게 숨막히게 하다, 숨차게 하다; 질식(사)시키다; ~의 성장(발전)을 저지하다

12) "Nevaire such a dog as dat Buck!" : 저 벅과 같은 개는 본적이 없어!

13) Heem worth one t'ousan' dollair, by Gar! Eh? Wot you say, Perrault?" : 어림잡아 1000달러의 가치는 나갈거야, 응? 페로, 너는 어떻게 생각해?

And Perrault nodded. He was ahead of the record then, and gaining day by day. The trail was in excellent condition, well packed and hard, and there was no new-fallen snow with which to contend. It was not too cold. The temperature dropped to fifty below zero and remained there the whole trip. The men rode and ran by turn, and the dogs were kept on the jump, with but infrequent stoppages.

The Thirty Mile River was comparatively coated with ice, and they covered in one day going out what had taken them ten days coming in. In one run they made a sixty-mile dash from the foot of Lake Le Barge[14] to the White Horse Rapids[15]. Across Marsh, Tagish[16], and Bennett (seventy miles of lakes), they flew so fast that the man whose turn it was to run towed behind the sled at the end of a rope. And on the last night of the second week they topped White Pass[17] and dropped down the sea slope with the lights of Skaguay[18] and of the shipping at their feet.

It was a record run. Each day for fourteen days they had

---

14) Lake Le Barge: It is a widening of the Yukon River north of Whitehorse, Yukon in Canada. It is fifty kilometres long and ranges from two to five kilometres wide. Its water is always very cold, and its weather often harsh and suddenly variable.

15) White Horse Rapids: They were rapids on the Yukon River in Canada's Yukon Territory, named for their supposed resemblance to the mane of a charging white horse.

16) Tagish: Tagish is an unincorporated community in Yukon, Canada. It is 30 kilometres (19 mi) east of Carcross, Yukon on the Tagish Road at the northern end of Tagish Lake.

17) White Pass: 50 miles west of Yakima and 110 miles east of Tacoma, Washington, White Pass Ski Area is just 12 miles southeast of Mt. Rainer National Park in the Washington Cascades.

18) Skaguay: It is a first-class borough in Alaska on the Alaska Panhandle.

averaged forty miles. For three days Perrault and Francois threw chests up and down the main street of Skaguay and were deluged with invitations to drink, while the team was the constant centre of a worshipful crowd of dog-busters[19] and mushers. Then three or four western bad men aspired to clean out the town, were riddled like pepper-boxes[20] for their pains, and public interest turned to other idols. Next came official orders. Francois called Buck to him, threw his arms around him, wept over him. And that was the last of Francois and Perrault. Like other men, they passed out of Buck's life for good.

A Scotch half-breed took charge of him and his mates, and in company with a dozen other dog-teams he started back over the weary trail to Dawson. It was no light running now, nor record time, but heavy toil each day, with a heavy load behind; for this was the mail train, carrying word from the world to the men who sought gold under the shadow of the Pole.

Buck did not like it, but he bore up well to the work, taking pride in it after the manner of Dave and Sol-leks, and seeing that his mates, whether they prided in it or not, did their fair share. It was a monotonous life, operating with machine-like regularity. One day was very like another. At a certain time each morning the cooks turned out, fires were built, and breakfast was eaten. Then, while some broke camp, others harnessed the dogs, and they were under way an hour or so before the darkness fell which gave warning of dawn. At night, camp was made. Some pitched the flies, others cut firewood and pine boughs for the beds, and still others carried water or ice for the cooks. Also,

---

19) dog-busters: 개 조련사

20) pepper-boxes: 후춧가루 통, (후춧가루통 비슷한) 작은 탑, 성급한 사람

the dogs were fed. To them, this was the one feature of the day, though it was good to loaf around, after the fish was eaten, for an hour or so with the other dogs, of which there were fivescore and odd.[21] There were fierce fighters among them, but three battles with the fiercest brought Buck to mastery, so that when he bristled and showed his teeth they got out of his way.

Best of all, perhaps, he loved to lie near the fire, hind legs crouched under him, fore legs stretched out in front, head raised, and eyes blinking dreamily at the flames. Sometimes he thought of Judge Miller's big house in the sun-kissed Santa Clara Valley, and of the cement swimming-tank, and Ysabel, the Mexican hairless, and Toots, the Japanese pug; but oftener he remembered the man in the red sweater, the death of Curly, the great fight with Spitz, and the good things he had eaten or would like to eat. He was not homesick. The Sunland was very dim and distant, and such memories had no power over him. Far more potent were the memories of his heredity that gave things he had never seen before a seeming familiarity;[22] the instincts (which were but the memories of his ancestors become habits) which had lapsed in later days, and still later, in him, quickened and become alive again.

Sometimes as he crouched there, blinking dreamily at the flames, it seemed that the flames were of another fire, and that as he crouched by this other fire he saw another and different man from the half-breed cook before him. This other man was shorter of leg and longer of arm, with muscles that were stringy

---

21) fivescore and odd: 100 남짓

22) familiarity: 친밀, 친숙, 친교, 친밀한 사이

and knotty rather than rounded and swelling[23]. The hair of this man was long and matted, and his head slanted back under it from the eyes. He uttered strange sounds, and seemed very much afraid of the darkness, into which he peered continually, clutching in his hand, which hung midway between knee and foot, a stick with a heavy stone made fast to the end. He was all but naked, a ragged and fire-scorched[24] skin hanging part way down his back, but on his body there was much hair. In some places, across the chest and shoulders and down the outside of the arms and thighs, it was matted into almost a thick fur. He did not stand erect, but with trunk inclined forward from the hips, on legs that bent at the knees. About his body there was a peculiar springiness, or resiliency, almost catlike, and a quick alertness as of one who lived in perpetual fear of things seen and unseen.

At other times this hairy man squatted by the fire with head between his legs and slept. On such occasions his elbows were on his knees, his hands clasped above his head as though to shed rain by the hairy arms. And beyond that fire, in the circling darkness, Buck could see many gleaming coals, two by two, always two by two, which he knew to be the eyes of great beasts of prey. And he could hear the crashing of their bodies through the undergrowth, and the noises they made in the night. And dreaming there by the Yukon bank, with lazy eyes blinking at the fire, these sounds and sights of another world would make the hair to rise along his back and stand on end

---

23) stringy and knotty rather than rounded and swelling: 둥글고 부풀 어 오른 것보다는 심줄과 옹이가 많은

24) fire-scorched: 불로 그슬린

across his shoulders and up his neck, till he whimpered low and suppressedly, or growled softly, and the half-breed cook shouted at him, "Hey, you Buck, wake up!" Whereupon[25] the other world would vanish and the real world come into his eyes, and he would get up and yawn and stretch as though he had been asleep.

It was a hard trip, with the mail behind them, and the heavy work wore them down. They were short of weight and in poor condition when they made Dawson, and should have had a ten days' or a week's rest at least. But in two days' time they dropped down the Yukon bank from the Barracks, loaded with letters for the outside. The dogs were tired, the drivers grumbling, and to make matters worse, it snowed every day. This meant a soft trail, greater friction on the runners, and heavier pulling for the dogs; yet the drivers were fair through it all, and did their best for the animals.

Each night the dogs were attended to first. They ate before the drivers ate, and no man sought his sleeping-robe till he had seen to the feet of the dogs he drove. Still, their strength went down. Since the beginning of the winter they had travelled eighteen hundred miles, dragging sleds the whole weary distance; and eighteen hundred miles will tell upon life of the toughest. Buck stood it, keeping his mates up to their work and maintaining discipline, though he, too, was very tired. Billee cried and whimpered regularly in his sleep each night. Joe was sourer than ever, and Sol-leks was unapproachable[26], blind side or other side.

---

25) Whereupon: 그래서, 그 때문에, 그 결과, 그 후에, 그 위에, 게다가

26) unapproachable: 접근하기 어려운(inaccessible), 먼, (태도 따위가) 쌀쌀한, 가까이하기 어려운, 따를 수 없는, 무비(無比)의, 무적의

But it was Dave who suffered most of all. Something had gone wrong with him. He became more morose and irritable, and when camp was pitched at once made his nest, where his driver fed him. Once out of the harness and down, he did not get on his feet again till harness-up time in the morning[27]. Sometimes, in the traces, when jerked by a sudden stoppage of the sled, or by straining to start it, he would cry out with pain. The driver examined him, but could find nothing. All the drivers became interested in his case. They talked it over at meal-time, and over their last pipes before going to bed, and one night they held a consultation[28]. He was brought from his nest to the fire and was pressed and prodded till he cried out many times. Something was wrong inside, but they could locate no broken bones, could not make it out.

By the time Cassiar Bar[29] was reached, he was so weak that he was falling repeatedly in the traces. The Scotch half-breed called a halt and took him out of the team, making the next dog, Sol-leks, fast to the sled. His intention was to rest Dave, letting him run free behind the sled. Sick as he was, Dave resented being taken out, grunting and growling while the traces were unfastened, and whimpering broken-heartedly when he saw Sol-leks in the position he had held and served so long. For the pride of trace and trail was his, and, sick unto death, he could not bear

27) he did not get on his feet again till harness-up time in the morning.: 그는 아침에 마구장치를 맬 시간까지 다시 일어서지 않았다.

28) consultation: 상담, 의논, 협의, 자문, 진찰

29) Cassiar Bar: The Cassiar Land District is one of the two northernmost of the province's Land Districts, the other being the Peace River Land District to its east, which covers the northeastern portion of the province adjacent to the Northwest Territories and Alberta.

that another dog should do his work.

When the sled started, he floundered[30] in the soft snow alongside the beaten trail, attacking Sol-leks with his teeth, rushing against him and trying to thrust him off into the soft snow on the other side, striving to leap inside his traces and get between him and the sled, and all the while whining and yelping and crying with grief and pain. The half-breed tried to drive him away with the whip; but he paid no heed to the stinging lash, and the man had not the heart to strike harder. Dave refused to run quietly on the trail behind the sled, where the going was easy, but continued to flounder alongside in the soft snow, where the going was most difficult, till exhausted. Then he fell, and lay where he fell, howling lugubriously[31] as the long train of sleds churned by.[32]

With the last remnant of his strength he managed to stagger along behind till the train made another stop, when he floundered past the sleds to his own, where he stood alongside Sol-leks. His driver lingered a moment to get a light for his pipe from the man behind. Then he returned and started his dogs. They swung out on the trail with remarkable lack of exertion, turned their heads uneasily, and stopped in surprise. The driver was surprised, too; the sled had not moved. He called his comrades to witness the sight. Dave had bitten through both of Sol-leks's traces, and was standing directly in front of the sled in his proper place.

He pleaded with his eyes to remain there. The driver was perplexed. His comrades talked of how a dog could break its

30) floundered: (흙 · 진창 속에서) 버둥거리다, 몸부림치다, 허위적 거리며 나아가다

31) howling lugubriously: 애처롭게 길 게 소리지르며

32) churned by: 거품을 일으키며 나아가다

heart through being denied the work that killed it, and recalled instances they had known, where dogs, too old for the toil, or injured, had died because they were cut out of the traces. Also, they held it a mercy, since Dave was to die anyway, that he should die in the traces[33], heart-easy and content. So he was harnessed in again, and proudly he pulled as of old, though more than once he cried out involuntarily[34] from the bite of his inward hurt. Several times he fell down and was dragged in the traces, and once the sled ran upon him so that he limped thereafter in one of his hind legs.

But he held out till camp was reached, when his driver made a place for him by the fire. Morning found him too weak to travel. At harness-up time he tried to crawl to his driver. By convulsive efforts he got on his feet, staggered, and fell. Then he wormed his way forward slowly toward where the harnesses were being put on his mates. He would advance his fore legs and drag up his body with a sort of hitching movement, when he would advance his fore legs and hitch[35] ahead again for a few more inches. His strength left him, and the last his mates saw of him he lay gasping in the snow and yearning toward them. But they could hear him mournfully howling till they passed out of sight behind a belt of river timber.

Here the train was halted.[36] The Scotch half-breed slowly

---

33) he should die in the traces: 그는 봇 줄(개를 썰매에 매는 가죽 줄)에 매인 상태에서 죽어야 한다(썰매개로서의 썰매를 끌다가 죽는 것이 썰매개의 자존심이라는 의미).

34) involuntarily: 부지불식간에, 본의 아니게, 무심결에

35) hitch: 와락 잡아당기다

36) Here the train was halted.: 여기서 그 행렬은 멈췄다.

retraced his steps to the camp they had left. The men ceased talking. A revolver-shot rang out. The man came back hurriedly. The whips snapped, the bells tinkled merrily,[37] the sleds churned along the trail; but Buck knew, and every dog knew, what had taken place behind the belt of river trees.

37) tinkled merrily: 즐겁게 울려 퍼지다

Chapter V
The Toil of Trace and Trail

Thirty days from the time it left Dawson, the Salt Water Mail, with Buck and his mates at the fore, arrived at Skaguay. They were in a wretched state, worn out and worn down. Buck's one hundred and forty pounds had dwindled to one hundred and fifteen. The rest of his mates, though lighter dogs, had relatively lost more weight than he. Pike, the malingerer, who, in his lifetime of deceit, had often successfully feigned a hurt leg, was now limping in earnest. Sol-leks was limping, and Dub was suffering from a wrenched shoulder-blade.

They were all terribly footsore[1]. No spring or rebound was left in them. Their feet fell heavily on the trail, jarring their bodies and doubling the fatigue of a day's travel. There was nothing the matter with them except that they were dead tired. It was not the dead-tiredness[2] that comes through brief and excessive effort, from which recovery is a matter of hours; but it was the dead-tiredness that comes through the slow and prolonged strength drainage[3] of months of toil. There was no power of recuperation left, no reserve strength to call upon. It had been all used, the last least bit of it. Every muscle, every fibre, every cell, was tired, dead tired. And there was reason for it. In less than five months they had travelled twenty-five hundred miles, during the last eighteen hundred of which they had had but five days' rest.

---

1) footsore: 발병난, 신발에 쓸려 상처가 난

2) dead-tiredness: 죽음 같은 피곤함, 심각한 피로감

3) prolonged strength drainage: 장기간 의 힘의 방출

When they arrived at Skaguay they were apparently on their last legs. They could barely keep the traces taut, and on the down grades just managed to keep out of the way of the sled.

"Mush on, poor sore feets," the driver encouraged them as they tottered down the main street of Skaguay. "Dis is de las'. Den we get one long res'.[4] Eh? For sure. One bully long res'."

The drivers confidently expected a long stopover[5]. Themselves, they had covered twelve hundred miles with two days' rest, and in the nature of reason and common justice they deserved an interval of loafing. But so many were the men who had rushed into the Klondike, and so many were the sweethearts, wives, and kin that had not rushed in, that the congested mail was taking on Alpine proportions[6]; also, there were official orders. Fresh batches[7] of Hudson Bay dogs were to take the places of those worthless for the trail. The worthless ones were to be got rid of, and, since dogs count for little against dollars, they were to be sold.

Three days passed, by which time Buck and his mates found how really tired and weak they were. Then, on the morning of the fourth day, two men from the States came along and bought them, harness and all, for a song. The men addressed each other as "Hal" and "Charles." Charles was a middle-aged, lightish-colored man, with weak and watery eyes and a mustache that

---

4) Dis is de las'. Den we get one long res'.: 이번이 마지막이고 그 후엔 긴 휴식을 가질 거다.

5) stopover: (여행 중의) 단기 체재(지), 도중하차(하선)(지), 잠깐 들르는 곳

6) the congested mail was taking on Alpine proportions: 밀린 메일이 알프스 크기(산더미처럼 많이)처럼 쌓이고 있었다.

7) batches: [사람·물건의] 한 묶음[다발, 무리], 일단[of ~]

twisted fiercely and vigorously up, giving the lie to the limply drooping lip it concealed. Hal was a youngster of nineteen or twenty, with a big Colt's revolver and a hunting-knife strapped about him on a belt that fairly bristled with cartridges. This belt was the most salient thing about him. It advertised his callowness[8]—a callowness sheer and unutterable. Both men were manifestly out of place, and why such as they should adventure the North is part of the mystery of things that passes understanding.

Buck heard the chaffering[9], saw the money pass between the man and the Government agent, and knew that the Scotch half-breed and the mail-train drivers were passing out of his life on the heels of Perrault and Francois and the others who had gone before. When driven with his mates to the new owners' camp, Buck saw a slipshod[10] and slovenly[11] affair, tent half stretched, dishes unwashed, everything in disorder; also, he saw a woman. "Mercedes" the men called her. She was Charles's wife and Hal's sister—a nice family party.

Buck watched them apprehensively as they proceeded to take down the tent and load the sled. There was a great deal of effort about their manner, but no businesslike method. The tent was rolled into an awkward bundle three times as large as it should have been. The tin dishes were packed away unwashed. Mercedes continually fluttered in the way of her men and kept

---

8) callowness: 미숙함, 풋내기임

9) chaffering: 흥정

10) slipshod: 뒤축이 닳아빠진 구두〔슬리퍼〕를 신은, 다리를 질질 끄는(shuffling), 초라한, (입은 옷, 언동 따위가) 단정치 못한(slovenly), 되는 대로의, 부주의한

11) slovenly: 단정치 못한, 되는대로, 추접스러운, untidy

up an unbroken chattering of remonstrance[12] and advice. When they put a clothes-sack on the front of the sled, she suggested it should go on the back; and when they had put it on the back, and covered it over with a couple of other bundles, she discovered overlooked articles which could abide nowhere else but in that very sack, and they unloaded again.

Three men from a neighboring tent came out and looked on, grinning and winking at one another.

"You've got a right smart load as it is," said one of them; "and it's not me should tell you your business, but I wouldn't tote[13] that tent along if I was you."

"Undreamed of!"[14] cried Mercedes, throwing up her hands in dainty dismay. "However in the world could I manage without a tent?"

"It's springtime, and you won't get any more cold weather," the man replied.

She shook her head decidedly, and Charles and Hal put the last odds and ends on top the mountainous load.

"Think it'll ride?" one of the men asked.

"Why shouldn't it?" Charles demanded rather shortly.

"Oh, that's all right, that's all right," the man hastened meekly to say. "I was just a-wonderin', that is all. It seemed a mite top-heavy."

Charles turned his back and drew the lashings down as well as he could, which was not in the least well.

"An' of course the dogs can hike along all day with that

---

12) remonstrance: 충고, 타이름, 진정서, 항의

13) tote: 나르다, 짊어지다

14) "Undreamed of!": 생각지도 않은, 전혀 뜻밖의, 의외의

contraption[15] behind them," affirmed a second of the men.

"Certainly," said Hal, with freezing politeness, taking hold of the gee-pole with one hand and swinging his whip from the other. "Mush!" he shouted. "Mush on there!"

The dogs sprang against the breast-bands, strained hard for a few moments, then relaxed. They were unable to move the sled.

"The lazy brutes, I'll show them," he cried, preparing to lash out at them with the whip.

But Mercedes interfered, crying, "Oh, Hal, you mustn't," as she caught hold of the whip and wrenched it from him. "The poor dears! Now you must promise you won't be harsh with them for the rest of the trip, or I won't go a step."

"Precious lot[16] you know about dogs," her brother sneered; "and I wish you'd leave me alone. They're lazy, I tell you, and you've got to whip them to get anything out of them. That's their way. You ask any one. Ask one of those men."

Mercedes looked at them imploringly, untold repugnance at sight of pain written in her pretty face.

"They're weak as water, if you want to know," came the reply from one of the men. "Plum tuckered out,[17] that's what's the matter. They need a rest."

"Rest be blanked," said Hal, with his beardless lips; and Mercedes said, "Oh!" in pain and sorrow at the oath.

But she was a clannish[18] creature, and rushed at once to the defence of her brother. "Never mind that man," she said

15) contraption: 진기한 장치, 신안, 고안물, 기계장치

16) Precious lot: 굉장히 많은

17) Plum tuckered out: 완전히 지치다

18) clannish: 당파적인; 배타적인; 씨족의

pointedly. "You're driving our dogs, and you do what you think best with them."

Again Hal's whip fell upon the dogs. They threw themselves against the breast-bands, dug their feet into the packed snow, got down low to it, and put forth all their strength. The sled held as though it were an anchor. After two efforts, they stood still, panting. The whip was whistling savagely, when once more Mercedes interfered. She dropped on her knees before Buck, with tears in her eyes, and put her arms around his neck.

"You poor, poor dears," she cried sympathetically, "why don't you pull hard?—then you wouldn't be whipped." Buck did not like her, but he was feeling too miserable to resist her, taking it as part of the day's miserable work.

One of the onlookers, who had been clenching his teeth to suppress hot speech, now spoke up:—

"It's not that I care a whoop what becomes of you, but for the dogs' sakes I just want to tell you, you can help them a mighty lot by breaking out that sled. The runners[19] are froze fast. Throw your weight against the gee-pole[20], right and left, and break it out."

A third time the attempt was made, but this time, following the advice, Hal broke out the runners which had been frozen to the snow. The overloaded and unwieldy sled forged ahead, Buck and his mates struggling frantically under the rain of blows. A hundred yards ahead the path turned and sloped steeply into the main street. It would have required an experienced man to keep the top-heavy sled upright, and Hal was not such a man.

---

19) runners: (스케이트, 썰매 따위의) 활주부(滑走部)

20) gee-pole: 개(가 끄는) 썰매의 채

As they swung on the turn the sled went over, spilling half its load through the loose lashings. The dogs never stopped. The lightened sled bounded on its side behind them. They were angry because of the ill treatment they had received and the unjust load. Buck was raging. He broke into a run, the team following his lead. Hal cried "Whoa! whoa!"[21] but they gave no heed. He tripped and was pulled off his feet. The capsized sled ground over him, and the dogs dashed on up the street, adding to the gayety[22] of Skaguay as they scattered the remainder of the outfit along its chief thoroughfare[23].

Kind-hearted citizens caught the dogs and gathered up the scattered belongings. Also, they gave advice. Half the load and twice the dogs, if they ever expected to reach Dawson, was what was said. Hal and his sister and brother-in-law listened unwillingly, pitched tent, and overhauled the outfit. Canned goods were turned out that made men laugh, for canned goods on the Long Trail is a thing to dream about. "Blankets for a hotel" quoth one of the men who laughed and helped. "Half as many is too much; get rid of them. Throw away that tent, and all those dishes,—who's going to wash them, anyway? Good Lord, do you think you're travelling on a Pullman[24]?"

And so it went, the inexorable elimination of the superfluous.[25] Mercedes cried when her clothes-bags were dumped on the

---

21) "Whoa! whoa!" : 워, 우어, 기다려(말 등을 멈추게 할 때)

22) gayety: 유쾌. 들뜬 기분

23) along its chief thoroughfare: 주요 도로를 따라

24) Pullman: [철도] 풀먼 차량: 쾌적한 설비를 갖춘 침대차·객차

25) And so it went, the inexorable elimination of the superfluous. : 그래서 일은 그렇게 진행되었고 (불필요한) 잉여물건들은 냉혹하게 제거되었다.

ground and article after article was thrown out. She cried in general, and she cried in particular over each discarded thing. She clasped hands about knees, rocking back and forth broken-heartedly. She averred she would not go an inch, not for a dozen Charleses[26]. She appealed to everybody and to everything, finally wiping her eyes and proceeding to cast out even articles of apparel that were imperative necessaries. And in her zeal, when she had finished with her own, she attacked the belongings of her men and went through them like a tornado.

This accomplished, the outfit, though cut in half, was still a formidable bulk. Charles and Hal went out in the evening and bought six Outside dogs. These, added to the six of the original team, and Teek and Koona, the huskies obtained at the Rink Rapids on the record trip, brought the team up to fourteen. But the Outside dogs, though practically broken in since their landing, did not amount to much. Three were short-haired pointers, one was a Newfoundland, and the other two were mongrels of indeterminate breed[27]. They did not seem to know anything, these newcomers. Buck and his comrades looked upon them with disgust, and though he speedily taught them their places and what not to do, he could not teach them what to do. They did not take kindly to trace and trail. With the exception of the two mongrels, they were bewildered and spirit-broken by the strange savage environment in which they found themselves and by the ill treatment they had received. The two mongrels were without spirit at all; bones were the only things breakable about them.

---

26) not for a dozen Charleses: 12명의 Charles가 온다고 해도 조금도 움직이지 않겠다

27) mongrels of indeterminate breed: 불명확한 혈통의 잡종개

With the newcomers hopeless and forlorn, and the old team worn out by twenty-five hundred miles of continuous trail, the outlook was anything but bright. The two men, however, were quite cheerful. And they were proud, too. They were doing the thing in style, with fourteen dogs. They had seen other sleds depart over the Pass for Dawson, or come in from Dawson, but never had they seen a sled with so many as fourteen dogs. In the nature of Arctic travel there was a reason why fourteen dogs should not drag one sled, and that was that one sled could not carry the food for fourteen dogs. But Charles and Hal did not know this. They had worked the trip out with a pencil, so much to a dog, so many dogs, so many days, Q.E.D.[28] Mercedes looked over their shoulders and nodded comprehensively, it was all so very simple.

Late next morning Buck led the long team up the street. There was nothing lively about it, no snap or go in him and his fellows. They were starting dead weary. Four times he had covered the distance between Salt Water and Dawson, and the knowledge that, jaded and tired, he was facing the same trail once more, made him bitter. His heart was not in the work, nor was the heart of any dog. The Outsides were timid and frightened, the Insides without confidence in their masters.

Buck felt vaguely that there was no depending upon these two men and the woman. They did not know how to do anything, and as the days went by it became apparent that they could not learn. They were slack in all things, without order or discipline. It took them half the night to pitch a slovenly camp, and half the morning to break that camp and get the sled loaded in fashion

---

28) Q.E.D.: 증명 끝

so slovenly that for the rest of the day they were occupied in stopping and rearranging the load. Some days they did not make ten miles. On other days they were unable to get started at all. And on no day did they succeed in making more than half the distance used by the men as a basis in their dog-food computation.

It was inevitable that they should go short on dog-food. But they hastened it by overfeeding, bringing the day nearer when underfeeding would commence. The Outside dogs, whose digestions had not been trained by chronic famine to make the most of little, had voracious appetites[29]. And when, in addition to this, the worn-out huskies pulled weakly, Hal decided that the orthodox ration[30] was too small. He doubled it. And to cap it all[31], when Mercedes, with tears in her pretty eyes and a quaver in her throat, could not cajole[32] him into giving the dogs still more, she stole from the fish-sacks and fed them slyly. But it was not food that Buck and the huskies needed, but rest. And though they were making poor time, the heavy load they dragged sapped their strength severely.

Then came the underfeeding. Hal awoke one day to the fact that his dog-food was half gone and the distance only quarter covered; further, that for love or money[33] no additional dog-food was to be obtained. So he cut down even the orthodox ration and tried to increase the day's travel. His sister and brother-in-

---

29) voracious appetites: 왕성한 식욕

30) orthodox ration: 옳다고 인정된 할당량

31) to cap it all: 결국에 가서는, 그 결과, 마침내

32) cajole: 감언이설로 속이다, 감언으로 꾀다, 아첨하다

33) for love or money: 수단 방법을 가리지 않고, 무슨 수를 쓰더라도, 아무리 하여도

law seconded him; but they were frustrated by their heavy outfit and their own incompetence. It was a simple matter to give the dogs less food; but it was impossible to make the dogs travel faster, while their own inability to get under way earlier in the morning prevented them from travelling longer hours. Not only did they not know how to work dogs, but they did not know how to work themselves.

The first to go was Dub. Poor blundering thief that he was, always getting caught and punished, he had none the less been a faithful worker. His wrenched shoulder-blade[34], untreated and unrested, went from bad to worse, till finally Hal shot him with the big Colt's revolver. It is a saying of the country that an Outside dog starves to death on the ration of the husky[35], so the six Outside dogs under Buck could do no less than die on half the ration of the husky. The Newfoundland went first, followed by the three short-haired pointers, the two mongrels hanging more grittily on to life, but going in the end[36].

By this time all the amenities[37] and gentlenesses of the Southland had fallen away from the three people. Shorn of its glamour and romance, Arctic travel became to them a reality too harsh for their manhood and womanhood. Mercedes ceased weeping over the dogs, being too occupied with weeping over herself and with quarrelling with her husband and brother. To quarrel was the one thing they were never too weary to do.

34) wrenched shoulder-blade: 뒤틀린 어깨뼈(견갑골)

35) on half the ration of the husky: 허스키 개가 먹는 반 정도의 배급식량으로

36) the two mongrel15s hanging more grittily on to life, but going in the end: 투지있게 살려고 집착했던 두마리 잡종개들이 마침내 죽었다.

37) amenities: 기분 좋은 응대[태도], 예의 바른 행동[말], 예의

Their irritability[38] arose out of their misery, increased with it, doubled upon it, outdistanced[39] it. The wonderful patience of the trail which comes to men who toil hard and suffer sore, and remain sweet of speech and kindly, did not come to these two men and the woman. They had no inkling[40] of such a patience. They were stiff and in pain; their muscles ached, their bones ached, their very hearts ached; and because of this they became sharp of speech, and hard words were first on their lips in the morning and last at night.

Charles and Hal wrangled whenever Mercedes gave them a chance. It was the cherished belief of each that he did more than his share of the work, and neither forbore to speak this belief at every opportunity. Sometimes Mercedes sided with her husband, sometimes with her brother. The result was a beautiful and unending family quarrel. Starting from a dispute as to which should chop a few sticks for the fire (a dispute which concerned only Charles and Hal), presently would be lugged in the rest of the family, fathers, mothers, uncles, cousins, people thousands of miles away, and some of them dead. That Hal's views on art, or the sort of society plays his mother's brother wrote, should have anything to do with the chopping of a few sticks of firewood, passes comprehension; nevertheless the quarrel was as likely to tend in that direction as in the direction of Charles's political prejudices. And that Charles's sister's tale-bearing tongue should be relevant to the building of a Yukon fire, was apparent only to Mercedes, who disburdened herself of copious opinions upon

---

38) irritability: 성미가 급함, 민감, [생리] 자극 감(반)응성, 과민성

39) outdistanced: 훨씬 앞서다, 《경주 · 경마에서》을 능가하다

40) inkling: 암시, 어렴풋이 눈치 챔, 약간의 지식

that topic, and incidentally upon a few other traits unpleasantly peculiar to her husband's family. In the meantime the fire remained unbuilt, the camp half pitched, and the dogs unfed.

Mercedes nursed a special grievance—the grievance of sex. She was pretty and soft, and had been chivalrously treated all her days. But the present treatment by her husband and brother was everything save chivalrous. It was her custom to be helpless. They complained. Upon which impeachment of what to her was her most essential sex-prerogative[41], she made their lives unendurable. She no longer considered the dogs, and because she was sore and tired, she persisted in riding on the sled. She was pretty and soft, but she weighed one hundred and twenty pounds—a lusty last straw to the load dragged by the weak and starving animals. She rode for days, till they fell in the traces and the sled stood still. Charles and Hal begged her to get off and walk, pleaded with her, entreated, the while she wept and importuned[42] Heaven with a recital of their brutality.

On one occasion they took her off the sled by main strength. They never did it again. She let her legs go limp like a spoiled child, and sat down on the trail. They went on their way, but she did not move. After they had travelled three miles they unloaded the sled, came back for her, and by main strength put her on the sled again.

In the excess of their own misery they were callous[43] to the suffering of their animals. Hal's theory, which he practised on others, was that one must get hardened. He had started out

---

41) sex-prerogative: 성의 특권

42) importuned: 에게 끈덕지게(성가시게) 조르다, 청하다, 괴롭히다

43) callous: 냉담한, 무감각한, 무신경한

preaching it to his sister and brother-in-law. Failing there, he hammered it into the dogs with a club. At the Five Fingers the dog-food gave out, and a toothless old squaw[44] offered to trade them a few pounds of frozen horse-hide[45] for the Colt's revolver that kept the big hunting-knife company at Hal's hip. A poor substitute for food was this hide, just as it had been stripped from the starved horses of the cattlemen six months back. In its frozen state it was more like strips of galvanized[46] iron, and when a dog wrestled it into his stomach it thawed into thin and innutritious leathery strings and into a mass of short hair, irritating and indigestible.

And through it all Buck staggered along at the head of the team as in a nightmare. He pulled when he could; when he could no longer pull, he fell down and remained down till blows from whip or club drove him to his feet again. All the stiffness and gloss had gone out of his beautiful furry coat. The hair hung down, limp and draggled, or matted with dried blood where Hal's club had bruised him. His muscles had wasted away to knotty strings, and the flesh pads had disappeared, so that each rib and every bone in his frame were outlined cleanly through the loose hide that was wrinkled in folds of emptiness. It was heartbreaking, only Buck's heart was unbreakable. The man in the red sweater had proved that.

As it was with Buck, so was it with his mates. They were perambulating skeletons[47]. There were seven all together,

---

44) squaw: 북아메리카 원주민의 여자, 《미국속어 · 우스개》 아내, 여자

45) frozen horse-hide: 얼어붙은 말 의 생가죽

46) galvanized: 아연 도금을 하다

47) perambulating skeletons: 걸어다니는 해골(피로와 굶주림으로 피골이 상접한 썰

including him. In their very great misery they had become insensible to the bite of the lash or the bruise of the club. The pain of the beating was dull and distant, just as the things their eyes saw and their ears heard seemed dull and distant. They were not half living, or quarter living. They were simply so many bags of bones in which sparks of life fluttered faintly. When a halt was made, they dropped down in the traces like dead dogs, and the spark dimmed and paled and seemed to go out. And when the club or whip fell upon them, the spark fluttered feebly up, and they tottered to their feet and staggered on.

There came a day when Billee, the good-natured, fell and could not rise. Hal had traded off his revolver, so he took the axe and knocked Billee on the head as he lay in the traces, then cut the carcass out of the harness and dragged it to one side. Buck saw, and his mates saw, and they knew that this thing was very close to them. On the next day Koona went, and but five of them remained: Joe, too far gone to be malignant[48]; Pike, crippled and limping, only half conscious and not conscious enough longer to malinger; Sol-leks, the one-eyed, still faithful to the toil of trace and trail, and mournful in that he had so little strength with which to pull; Teek, who had not travelled so far that winter and who was now beaten more than the others because he was fresher; and Buck, still at the head of the team, but no longer enforcing discipline or striving to enforce it, blind with weakness half the time and keeping the trail by the loom of it and by the dim feel of his feet.

It was beautiful spring weather, but neither dogs nor humans

매개들)

48) too far gone to be malignant: 악성보다는 훨씬 더 심각한

were aware of it. Each day the sun rose earlier and set later. It was dawn by three in the morning, and twilight lingered till nine at night. The whole long day was a blaze of sunshine. The ghostly winter silence had given way to the great spring murmur of awakening life. This murmur arose from all the land, fraught with[49] the joy of living. It came from the things that lived and moved again, things which had been as dead and which had not moved during the long months of frost. The sap was rising in the pines. The willows and aspens[50] were bursting out in young buds. Shrubs and vines were putting on fresh garbs of green. Crickets[51] sang in the nights, and in the days all manner of creeping, crawling things rustled forth into the sun. Partridges[52] and woodpeckers were booming and knocking in the forest. Squirrels were chattering, birds singing, and overhead honked the wild-fowl driving up from the south in cunning wedges that split the air.

From every hill slope came the trickle of running water, the music of unseen fountains. All things were thawing, bending, snapping. The Yukon was straining to break loose the ice that bound it down. It ate away from beneath; the sun ate from above. Air-holes[53] formed, fissures sprang and spread apart, while thin sections of ice fell through bodily into the river. And amid all this bursting, rending, throbbing of awakening life, under the blazing sun and through the soft-sighing breezes, like wayfarers[54]

49) fraught with: ~이 투성이인, ~이 충만한

50) aspens: 사시나무포플러

51) Crickets: 귀뚜라미

52) Partridges: 반시(半翅), 자고(鷓鴣)류 《유럽 · 아시아산 엽조(獵鳥)》 목도리뇌조, (북아메리카산) 메추라기의 일종

53) air hole: 기공, 공기 구멍, 수면에 언 얼음의 일부가 녹아 생긴 구멍

54) wayfarer: 도보 여행자, 일시적 투숙객, 나그네

to death, staggered the two men, the woman, and the huskies.

With the dogs falling, Mercedes weeping and riding, Hal swearing innocuously, and Charles's eyes wistfully watering, they staggered into John Thornton's camp at the mouth of White River. When they halted, the dogs dropped down as though they had all been struck dead. Mercedes dried her eyes and looked at John Thornton. Charles sat down on a log to rest. He sat down very slowly and painstakingly[55] what of his great stiffness. Hal did the talking. John Thornton was whittling the last touches on an axe-handle he had made from a stick of birch. He whittled and listened, gave monosyllabic replies, and, when it was asked, terse advice. He knew the breed, and he gave his advice in the certainty that it would not be followed.

"They told us up above that the bottom was dropping out of the trail and that the best thing for us to do was to lay over," Hal said in response to Thornton's warning to take no more chances on the rotten ice. "They told us we couldn't make White River, and here we are." This last with a sneering ring of triumph in it.

"And they told you true," John Thornton answered. "The bottom's likely to drop out at any moment[56]. Only fools, with the blind luck of fools, could have made it. I tell you straight, I wouldn't risk my carcass[57] on that ice for all the gold in Alaska."

"That's because you're not a fool, I suppose," said Hal. "All the same, we'll go on to Dawson." He uncoiled his whip. "Get up there, Buck! Hi! Get up there! Mush on!"

---

55) painstakingly: 수고를 아끼지 않고

56) The bottom's likely to drop out at any moment.: (얼음)의 바닥이 언제라도 꺼질 것 같다.

57) carcass: 몸, 인체

Thornton went on whittling[58]. It was idle, he knew, to get between a fool and his folly; while two or three fools more or less would not alter the scheme of things.

But the team did not get up at the command. It had long since passed into the stage where blows were required to rouse it. The whip flashed out, here and there, on its merciless errands. John Thornton compressed his lips. Sol-leks was the first to crawl to his feet. Teek followed. Joe came next, yelping with pain. Pike made painful efforts. Twice he fell over, when half up, and on the third attempt managed to rise. Buck made no effort. He lay quietly where he had fallen. The lash bit into him again and again, but he neither whined nor struggled. Several times Thornton started, as though to speak, but changed his mind. A moisture came into his eyes, and, as the whipping continued, he arose and walked irresolutely up and down.

This was the first time Buck had failed, in itself a sufficient reason to drive Hal into a rage. He exchanged the whip for the customary club. Buck refused to move under the rain of heavier blows which now fell upon him. Like his mates, he was barely able to get up, but, unlike them, he had made up his mind not to get up. He had a vague feeling of impending doom. This had been strong upon him when he pulled in to the bank, and it had not departed from him. What of the thin and rotten ice he had felt under his feet all day, it seemed that he sensed disaster close at hand, out there ahead on the ice where his master was trying to drive him. He refused to stir. So greatly had he suffered, and so far gone was he, that the blows did not hurt much. And as they continued to fall upon him, the spark of life within flickered and

---

58) whittling: 조금씩 깎다, [나무껍질 등을] 깎아내다

went down. It was nearly out. He felt strangely numb. As though from a great distance, he was aware that he was being beaten. The last sensations of pain left him. He no longer felt anything, though very faintly he could hear the impact of the club upon his body. But it was no longer his body, it seemed so far away.

And then, suddenly, without warning, uttering a cry that was inarticulate[59] and more like the cry of an animal, John Thornton sprang upon the man who wielded the club[60]. Hal was hurled backward, as though struck by a falling tree. Mercedes screamed. Charles looked on wistfully[61], wiped his watery eyes, but did not get up because of his stiffness.

John Thornton stood over Buck, struggling to control himself, too convulsed with rage to speak.

"If you strike that dog again, I'll kill you," he at last managed to say in a choking voice.

"It's my dog," Hal replied, wiping the blood from his mouth as he came back. "Get out of my way, or I'll fix you[62]. I'm going to Dawson."

Thornton stood between him and Buck, and evinced no intention of getting out of the way. Hal drew his long hunting-knife. Mercedes screamed, cried, laughed, and manifested the chaotic abandonment of hysteria. Thornton rapped Hal's knuckles with the axe-handle, knocking the knife to the ground. He rapped his knuckles again as he tried to pick it up. Then he stooped, picked it

---

59) inarticulate: (사람이) 똑똑히 말을 못하는, 발음이 분명치 않은

60) wielded the club: 곤봉을 휘두르다

61) wistfully: 바라는 듯이, 깊이 생각에 잠기어, 슬픈 듯이

62) Get out of my way, or I'll fix you.: 내일을 방해하지 마라, 그렇지 않으면 혼내주겠다

up himself, and with two strokes cut Buck's traces[63].

Hal had no fight left in him. Besides, his hands were full with his sister, or his arms, rather; while Buck was too near dead to be of further use in hauling the sled. A few minutes later they pulled out from the bank and down the river. Buck heard them go and raised his head to see, Pike was leading, Sol-leks was at the wheel, and between were Joe and Teek. They were limping and staggering. Mercedes was riding the loaded sled. Hal guided at the gee-pole[64], and Charles stumbled along in the rear.

As Buck watched them, Thornton knelt beside him and with rough, kindly hands searched for broken bones. By the time his search had disclosed nothing more than many bruises and a state of terrible starvation, the sled was a quarter of a mile away. Dog and man watched it crawling along over the ice. Suddenly, they saw its back end drop down, as into a rut[65], and the gee-pole, with Hal clinging to it, jerk into the air. Mercedes's scream came to their ears. They saw Charles turn and make one step to run back, and then a whole section of ice give way and dogs and humans disappear. A yawning hole[66] was all that was to be seen. The bottom had dropped out of the trail[67].

John Thornton and Buck looked at each other.

"You poor devil," said John Thornton, and Buck licked his hand.

---

63) traces: 끈, 줄

64) gee-pole: 개썰매의 끌채

65) as into a rut: 틀에 박히는 것처럼

66) yawning hole: 크게 벌어져 있는 구멍

67) The bottom had dropped out of the trail. : 그 썰매길의 얼음바닥이 꺼져버렸다

Chapter VI
For the Love of a Man

When John Thornton froze his feet in the previous December his partners had made him comfortable and left him to get well, going on themselves up the river to get out a raft of saw-logs for Dawson. He was still limping slightly at the time he rescued Buck, but with the continued warm weather even the slight limp left him. And here, lying by the river bank through the long spring days, watching the running water, listening lazily to the songs of birds and the hum of nature, Buck slowly won back his strength.

A rest comes very good after one has travelled three thousand miles, and it must be confessed that Buck waxed lazy as his wounds healed, his muscles swelled out, and the flesh came back to cover his bones. For that matter, they were all loafing,—Buck, John Thornton, and Skeet and Nig,—waiting for the raft to come that was to carry them down to Dawson. Skeet was a little Irish setter[1] who early made friends with Buck, who, in a dying condition, was unable to resent her first advances. She had the doctor trait which some dogs possess; and as a mother cat washes her kittens, so she washed and cleansed Buck's wounds. Regularly, each morning after he had finished his breakfast, she performed her self-appointed[2] task, till he came to look for her

1) setter: 세터(개), 스파이, 밀고자, 배구의 세터

2) self-appointed: 독단적인, 자기 멋대로 정한, 자천의

ministrations[3] as much as he did for Thornton's. Nig, equally friendly, though less demonstrative, was a huge black dog, half bloodhound and half deerhound, with eyes that laughed and a boundless good nature.

To Buck's surprise these dogs manifested no jealousy toward him. They seemed to share the kindliness and largeness of John Thornton. As Buck grew stronger they enticed him into all sorts of ridiculous games, in which Thornton himself could not forbear to join; and in this fashion Buck romped through his convalescence and into a new existence. Love, genuine passionate love, was his for the first time. This he had never experienced at Judge Miller's down in the sun-kissed Santa Clara Valley. With the Judge's sons, hunting and tramping, it had been a working partnership; with the Judge's grandsons, a sort of pompous guardianship; and with the Judge himself, a stately and dignified friendship. But love that was feverish and burning, that was adoration, that was madness, it had taken John Thornton to arouse.

This man had saved his life, which was something; but, further, he was the ideal master. Other men saw to the welfare of their dogs from a sense of duty and business expediency; he saw to the welfare of his as if they were his own children, because he could not help it. And he saw further. He never forgot a kindly greeting or a cheering word, and to sit down for a long talk with them ("gas"[4] he called it) was as much his delight as theirs. He had a way of taking Buck's head roughly between his hands, and resting his own head upon Buck's, of shaking

---

3) ministration: 돌보기, 봉사, 원조, 예배, 목사의 직무

4) gas: 개들과의 대화

him back and forth, the while calling him ill names that to Buck were love names. Buck knew no greater joy than that rough embrace and the sound of murmured oaths, and at each jerk back and forth it seemed that his heart would be shaken out of his body so great was its ecstasy. And when, released, he sprang to his feet, his mouth laughing, his eyes eloquent, his throat vibrant with unuttered sound, and in that fashion remained without movement, John Thornton would reverently exclaim, "God! you can all but speak![5]"

Buck had a trick of love expression that was akin to hurt. He would often seize Thornton's hand in his mouth and close so fiercely that the flesh bore the impress of his teeth for some time afterward. And as Buck understood the oaths to be love words, so the man understood this feigned bite for a caress.

For the most part, however, Buck's love was expressed in adoration. While he went wild with happiness when Thornton touched him or spoke to him, he did not seek these tokens. Unlike Skeet, who was wont to shove her nose under Thornton's hand and nudge and nudge[6] till petted, or Nig, who would stalk up[7] and rest his great head on Thornton's knee, Buck was content to adore at a distance. He would lie by the hour, eager, alert, at Thornton's feet, looking up into his face, dwelling upon it, studying it, following with keenest interest each fleeting expression, every movement or change of feature. Or, as chance might have it, he would lie farther away, to the side or rear, watching the outlines of the man and the occasional movements

---

5) God! you can all but speak! : 야! 너는 말하는 것 빼고 모든 것을 할 수 있구나!

6) nudge and nudge: 가볍게 계속 밀다, 주의를 끌기 위해 살짝 찌르다

7) stalk up: (사냥감 등에) 몰래 다가가다, 살그머니 접근하다, 몰래 추적하다

of his body. And often, such was the communion in which they lived, the strength of Buck's gaze would draw John Thornton's head around, and he would return the gaze, without speech, his heart shining out of his eyes as Buck's heart shone out.

For a long time after his rescue, Buck did not like Thornton to get out of his sight. From the moment he left the tent to when he entered it again, Buck would follow at his heels. His transient masters since he had come into the Northland had bred in him a fear that no master could be permanent. He was afraid that Thornton would pass out of his life as Perrault and Francois and the Scotch half-breed had passed out. Even in the night, in his dreams, he was haunted by this fear. At such times he would shake off sleep and creep through the chill to the flap of the tent, where he would stand and listen to the sound of his master' s breathing.

But in spite of this great love he bore John Thornton, which seemed to bespeak[8] the soft civilizing influence, the strain of the primitive, which the Northland had aroused in him, remained alive and active. Faithfulness and devotion, things born of fire and roof, were his; yet he retained his wildness and wiliness. He was a thing of the wild, come in from the wild to sit by John Thornton's fire, rather than a dog of the soft Southland stamped with the marks of generations of civilization. Because of his very great love, he could not steal from this man, but from any other man, in any other camp, he did not hesitate an instant; while the cunning with which he stole enabled him to escape detection.

His face and body were scored by the teeth of many dogs, and he fought as fiercely as ever and more shrewdly. Skeet

---

8) bespeak : ~을 나타내다, ~의 증거가 되다; ~을 예시하다

and Nig were too good-natured for quarrelling,—besides, they belonged to John Thornton; but the strange dog, no matter what the breed or valor, swiftly acknowledged Buck's supremacy or found himself struggling for life with a terrible antagonist. And Buck was merciless. He had learned well the law of club and fang, and he never forewent an advantage[9] or drew back from a foe he had started on the way to Death. He had lessoned from Spitz, and from the chief fighting dogs of the police and mail, and knew there was no middle course. He must master or be mastered; while to show mercy was a weakness. Mercy did not exist in the primordial life[10]. It was misunderstood for fear[11], and such misunderstandings made for death. Kill or be killed, eat or be eaten, was the law; and this mandate, down out of the depths of Time, he obeyed.

He was older than the days he had seen and the breaths he had drawn. He linked the past with the present, and the eternity behind him throbbed through him in a mighty rhythm to which he swayed as the tides and seasons swayed. He sat by John Thornton's fire, a broad-breasted dog, white-fanged and long-furred; but behind him were the shades of all manner of dogs, half-wolves and wild wolves, urgent and prompting, tasting the savor of the meat he ate, thirsting for the water he drank, scenting the wind with him, listening with him and telling him the sounds made by the wild life in the forest, dictating his moods, directing his actions, lying down to sleep with him when he lay down, and dreaming with him and beyond him and

---

9) forewent an advantage: 우세, 우위,이점을 버리지 않았다

10) primordial life: 원시의 삶, 최초의 삶

11) It was misunderstood for fear,: 그것은 두려움으로 오해를 받았다

becoming themselves the stuff of his dreams.

So peremptorily[12] did these shades beckon him, that each day mankind and the claims of mankind slipped farther from him. Deep in the forest a call was sounding, and as often as he heard this call, mysteriously thrilling and luring, he felt compelled to turn his back upon the fire and the beaten earth around it, and to plunge into the forest, and on and on, he knew not where or why; nor did he wonder where or why, the call sounding imperiously[13], deep in the forest. But as often as he gained the soft unbroken earth and the green shade, the love for John Thornton drew him back to the fire again.

Thornton alone held him. The rest of mankind was as nothing. Chance travellers might praise or pet him; but he was cold under it all, and from a too demonstrative man[14] he would get up and walk away. When Thornton's partners, Hans and Pete, arrived on the long-expected raft, Buck refused to notice them till he learned they were close to Thornton; after that he tolerated them in a passive sort of way, accepting favors from them as though he favored them by accepting. They were of the same large type as Thornton, living close to the earth, thinking simply and seeing clearly; and ere they swung the raft into the big eddy by the saw-mill[15] at Dawson, they understood Buck and his ways, and did not insist upon an intimacy such as obtained with Skeet and Nig.

For Thornton, however, his love seemed to grow and grow.

---

12) peremptorily: 강하게

13) imperiously: 고압적으로, 도도하게

14) too demonstrative man: 지나치게 감정이 넘치는 사람

15) saw-mill: 제재소

He, alone among men, could put a pack upon Buck's back in the summer travelling. Nothing was too great for Buck to do, when Thornton commanded. One day (they had grub-staked[16] themselves from the proceeds of the raft and left Dawson for the head-waters [17]of the Tanana) the men and dogs were sitting on the crest of a cliff which fell away, straight down, to naked bed-rock three hundred feet below. John Thornton was sitting near the edge, Buck at his shoulder. A thoughtless whim seized Thornton, and he drew the attention of Hans and Pete to the experiment he had in mind. "Jump, Buck!" he commanded, sweeping his arm out and over the chasm. The next instant he was grappling with Buck on the extreme edge, while Hans and Pete were dragging them back into safety.

"It's uncanny," Pete said, after it was over and they had caught their speech.

Thornton shook his head. "No, it is splendid, and it is terrible, too. Do you know, it sometimes makes me afraid."

"I'm not hankering to[18] be the man that lays hands on you while he's around," Pete announced conclusively, nodding his head toward Buck.

"Py Jingo![19]" was Hans's contribution[20]. "Not mineself either."

It was at Circle City, ere the year was out, that Pete's apprehensions were realized. "Black" Burton, a man evil-tempered and malicious, had been picking a quarrel with a tenderfoot[21] at the

---

16) grub-staked: 탐광자에게의 공여품을 제공하다. 물질원조를 하다.

17) head-waters: 상류, 원류, 급수원

18) hankering to: ~되기(하기)를 갈망하다

19) Py Jingo: By Jingo, 맹세코!, 틀림없이!

20) contribution: 발언

21) tenderfoot: 미경험자, 풋내기, (미국 서부의 목장·광산의) 신참자

bar, when Thornton stepped good-naturedly between. Buck, as was his custom, was lying in a corner, head on paws, watching his master's every action. Burton struck out, without warning, straight from the shoulder. Thornton was sent spinning, and saved himself from falling only by clutching the rail of the bar.

Those who were looking on heard what was neither bark nor yelp, but a something which is best described as a roar, and they saw Buck's body rise up in the air as he left the floor for Burton's throat. The man saved his life by instinctively throwing out his arm, but was hurled backward to the floor with Buck on top of him. Buck loosed his teeth from the flesh of the arm and drove in again for the throat. This time the man succeeded only in partly blocking, and his throat was torn open. Then the crowd was upon Buck, and he was driven off; but while a surgeon checked the bleeding, he prowled[22] up and down, growling furiously, attempting to rush in, and being forced back by an array of hostile clubs. A "miners' meeting," called on the spot, decided that the dog had sufficient provocation[23], and Buck was discharged. But his reputation was made, and from that day his name spread through every camp in Alaska.

Later on, in the fall of the year, he saved John Thornton's life in quite another fashion. The three partners were lining a long and narrow poling-boat down a bad stretch of rapids on the Forty-Mile Creek. Hans and Pete moved along the bank, snubbing with a thin Manila rope from tree to tree, while Thornton remained in the boat, helping its descent by means of a pole, and shouting directions to the shore. Buck, on the bank, worried and

---

22) prowled: 돌아다니다, 배회하다(wander)[about, around]

23) sufficient provocation: 충분한 자극, 분개, 도발

anxious, kept abreast of the boat, his eyes never off his master.

At a particularly bad spot, where a ledge of barely submerged rocks jutted out into the river, Hans cast off the rope, and, while Thornton poled the boat out into the stream, ran down the bank with the end in his hand to snub the boat when it had cleared the ledge. This it did, and was flying down-stream in a current as swift as a mill-race[24], when Hans checked it with the rope and checked too suddenly. The boat flirted over and snubbed in to the bank bottom up, while Thornton, flung sheer out of it, was carried down-stream toward the worst part of the rapids, a stretch of wild water in which no swimmer could live.

Buck had sprung in on the instant; and at the end of three hundred yards, amid a mad swirl of water, he overhauled Thornton. When he felt him grasp his tail, Buck headed for the bank, swimming with all his splendid strength. But the progress shoreward was slow; the progress down-stream amazingly rapid. From below came the fatal roaring where the wild current went wilder and was rent in shreds and spray by the rocks which thrust through like the teeth of an enormous comb. The suck of the water as it took the beginning of the last steep pitch was frightful, and Thornton knew that the shore was impossible. He scraped furiously over a rock, bruised across a second, and struck a third with crushing force. He clutched its slippery top with both hands, releasing Buck, and above the roar of the churning water shouted: "Go, Buck! Go!"

Buck could not hold his own, and swept on down-stream, struggling desperately, but unable to win back. When he heard Thornton's command repeated, he partly reared out of the

24) mill-race: 물레방아용 도랑, 물방아를 돌리는 물줄기

water, throwing his head high, as though for a last look, then turned obediently toward the bank. He swam powerfully and was dragged ashore by Pete and Hans at the very point where swimming ceased to be possible and destruction began.

They knew that the time a man could cling to a slippery rock in the face of that driving current was a matter of minutes, and they ran as fast as they could up the bank to a point far above where Thornton was hanging on. They attached the line with which they had been snubbing the boat to Buck's neck and shoulders, being careful that it should neither strangle[25] him nor impede his swimming, and launched him into the stream. He struck out boldly, but not straight enough into the stream. He discovered the mistake too late, when Thornton was abreast of him and a bare half-dozen strokes away while he was being carried helplessly past.

Hans promptly snubbed with the rope, as though Buck were a boat. The rope thus tightening on him in the sweep of the current, he was jerked under the surface, and under the surface he remained till his body struck against the bank and he was hauled out[26]. He was half drowned, and Hans and Pete threw themselves upon him, pounding the breath into him and the water out of him. He staggered to his feet and fell down. The faint sound of Thornton's voice came to them, and though they could not make out the words of it, they knew that he was in his extremity. His master's voice acted on Buck like an electric shock, He sprang to his feet and ran up the bank ahead of the men to the point of his previous departure.

---

25) strangle: ~을 목 졸라 죽이다, 교살하다, ~을 질식(사)시키다

26) he was hauled out. : 그는 끌려나왔다

Again the rope was attached and he was launched, and again he struck out, but this time straight into the stream. He had miscalculated once, but he would not be guilty of it a second time. Hans paid out the rope, permitting no slack, while Pete kept it clear of coils. Buck held on till he was on a line straight above Thornton; then he turned, and with the speed of an express train headed down upon him. Thornton saw him coming, and, as Buck struck him like a battering ram, with the whole force of the current behind him, he reached up and closed with both arms around the shaggy[27] neck. Hans snubbed the rope around the tree, and Buck and Thornton were jerked under the water. Strangling[28], suffocating, sometimes one uppermost and sometimes the other, dragging over the jagged bottom, smashing against rocks and snags[29], they veered in to the bank[30].

Thornton came to, belly downward and being violently propelled back and forth across a drift log by Hans and Pete. His first glance was for Buck, over whose limp and apparently lifeless body Nig was setting up a howl, while Skeet was licking the wet face and closed eyes. Thornton was himself bruised and battered, and he went carefully over Buck's body, when he had been brought around, finding three broken ribs.

"That settles it," he announced. "We camp right here." And camp they did, till Buck's ribs knitted and he was able to travel.

---

27) shaggy: 털투성이의(hairy), 뒤얽힌, [초목이] 무성한(bushy), 작은 나무투성이의 (scrubby)

28) Strangling: 목이 졸리면서, strangle ~을 목 졸라 죽이다, 교살하다; ~을 질식(사) 시키다.

29) snags: (배의 운행을 방해하는) 유목(流木), 돌기물, (비격식) 뜻하지 않은 장애

30) they veered in to the bank.: 그들은 강둑으로 방향을 바꾸었다.

That winter, at Dawson, Buck performed another exploit, not so heroic, perhaps, but one that put his name many notches[31] higher on the totem-pole[32] of Alaskan fame. This exploit was particularly gratifying to the three men; for they stood in need of the outfit which it furnished, and were enabled to make a long-desired trip into the virgin East, where miners had not yet appeared. It was brought about by a conversation in the Eldorado Saloon, in which men waxed boastful of their favorite dogs. Buck, because of his record, was the target for these men, and Thornton was driven stoutly to defend him. At the end of half an hour one man stated that his dog could start a sled with five hundred pounds and walk off with it; a second bragged six hundred for his dog; and a third, seven hundred.

"Pooh! pooh!" said John Thornton; "Buck can start a thousand pounds."

"And break it out? and walk off with it for a hundred yards?" demanded Matthewson, a Bonanza King, he of the seven hundred vaunt.

"And break it out, and walk off with it for a hundred yards," John Thornton said coolly.

"Well," Matthewson said, slowly and deliberately, so that all could hear, "I've got a thousand dollars that says he can't. And there it is." So saying, he slammed a sack of gold dust of the size of a bologna sausage down upon the bar.

Nobody spoke. Thornton's bluff[33], if bluff it was, had been

---

31) notches: 단계, 등급, 표시, V자형 새김, 벤 자리

32) totem-pole: 토템 폴: 북미 북서부 인디언이 토템상(像)을 그리거나 새겨서 집 앞 등에 세우는 표주(標柱)

33) bluff: 허세, 허풍떨다, 절벽, 엄포놓기, 벼랑

called. He could feel a flush of warm blood creeping up his face. His tongue had tricked him. He did not know whether Buck could start a thousand pounds. Half a ton! The enormousness of it appalled him. He had great faith in Buck's strength and had often thought him capable of starting such a load; but never, as now, had he faced the possibility of it, the eyes of a dozen men fixed upon him, silent and waiting. Further, he had no thousand dollars; nor had Hans or Pete.

"I've got a sled standing outside now, with twenty fiftypound sacks of flour on it," Matthewson went on with brutal directness; "so don't let that hinder you."

Thornton did not reply. He did not know what to say. He glanced from face to face in the absent way of a man who has lost the power of thought and is seeking somewhere to find the thing that will start it going again. The face of Jim O'Brien, a Mastodon King and old-time comrade, caught his eyes. It was as a cue to him, seeming to rouse him to do what he would never have dreamed of doing.

"Can you lend me a thousand?" he asked, almost in a whisper.

"Sure," answered O'Brien, thumping down a plethoric sack[34] by the side of Matthewson's. "Though it's little faith I'm having, John, that the beast can do the trick."

The Eldorado emptied its occupants into the street to see the test. The tables were deserted, and the dealers and gamekeepers came forth to see the outcome of the wager and to lay odds. Several hundred men, furred and mittened, banked around the sled within easy distance. Matthewson's sled, loaded with a thousand pounds of flour, had been standing for a couple of

34) a plethoric sack: 불룩한(과다한) 자루

hours, and in the intense cold (it was sixty below zero) the runners had frozen fast to the hard-packed snow. Men offered odds of two to one that Buck could not budge the sled. A quibble[35] arose concerning the phrase "break out.[36]" O'Brien contended it was Thornton's privilege to knock the runners loose, leaving Buck to "break it out" from a dead standstill. Matthewson insisted that the phrase included breaking the runners from the frozen grip of the snow. A majority of the men who had witnessed the making of the bet decided in his favor, whereat the odds went up to three to one against Buck.

There were no takers[37]. Not a man believed him capable of the feat. Thornton had been hurried into the wager[38], heavy with doubt; and now that he looked at the sled itself, the concrete fact, with the regular team of ten dogs curled up in the snow before it, the more impossible the task appeared. Matthewson waxed jubilant.

"Three to one!" he proclaimed. "I'll lay you another thousand at that figure, Thornton. What d'ye say?"

Thornton's doubt was strong in his face, but his fighting spirit was aroused—the fighting spirit that soars above odds, fails to recognize the impossible, and is deaf to all save the clamor for battle. He called Hans and Pete to him. Their sacks were slim, and with his own the three partners could rake together only two hundred dollars. In the ebb of their fortunes, this sum was their

---

35) quibble: 논란, 트집

36) break out: 부수어 떼어내다, 준비하 다(Buck이 썰매를 끌 수 있도록 바닥에 얼어붙은 썰매의 활주부분을 떼어놓는 것에 대해 논란 여부)

37) There were no takers. : 지원자(응모자)가 없었다.

38) the wager: 내기, 내기의 대상

total capital; yet they laid it unhesitatingly against Matthewson's six hundred.

The team of ten dogs was unhitched[39], and Buck, with his own harness, was put into the sled. He had caught the contagion of the excitement, and he felt that in some way he must do a great thing for John Thornton. Murmurs of admiration at his splendid appearance went up. He was in perfect condition, without an ounce of superfluous flesh, and the one hundred and fifty pounds that he weighed were so many pounds of grit[40] and virility[41]. His furry coat shone with the sheen of silk. Down the neck and across the shoulders, his mane, in repose as it was, half bristled and seemed to lift with every movement, as though excess of vigor made each particular hair alive and active. The great breast and heavy fore legs were no more than in proportion with the rest of the body, where the muscles showed in tight rolls underneath the skin. Men felt these muscles and proclaimed them hard as iron, and the odds went down to two to one.

"Gad, sir! Gad, sir!" stuttered[42] a member of the latest dynasty, a king of the Skookum Benches. "I offer you eight hundred for him, sir, before the test, sir; eight hundred just as he stands."

Thornton shook his head and stepped to Buck's side.

"You must stand off from him," Matthewson protested. "Free play and plenty of room."

The crowd fell silent; only could be heard the voices of the gamblers vainly offering two to one. Everybody acknowledged

---

39) unhitched: 놓아 주다, 떼어내다, 풀어놓다

40) grit: 기개, 기골, 불굴의 정신, 용기, 담력, 배짱

41) virility: 남성임, 남자다움; 힘참, 억셈, 박력, 남성의 장년기[한창때]

42) stuttered: (말을) 더듬다, 더듬거리며 말하다, 더듬는 듯한 소리를 내다.

Buck a magnificent animal, but twenty fifty-pound sacks of flour bulked too large in their eyes for them to loosen their pouch-strings.

Thornton knelt down by Buck's side. He took his head in his two hands and rested cheek on cheek. He did not playfully shake him, as was his wont, or murmur soft love curses; but he whispered in his ear. "As you love me, Buck. As you love me," was what he whispered. Buck whined with suppressed eagerness.

The crowd was watching curiously. The affair was growing mysterious. It seemed like a conjuration[43]. As Thornton got to his feet, Buck seized his mittened hand between his jaws, pressing in with his teeth and releasing slowly, half-reluctantly[44]. It was the answer, in terms, not of speech, but of love. Thornton stepped well back.

"Now, Buck," he said.

Buck tightened the traces, then slacked them for a matter of several inches. It was the way he had learned.

"Gee!" Thornton's voice rang out, sharp in the tense silence.

Buck swung to the right, ending the movement in a plunge that took up the slack and with a sudden jerk arrested his one hundred and fifty pounds. The load quivered, and from under the runners arose a crisp crackling[45].

"Haw!" Thornton commanded.

Buck duplicated the manoeuvre, this time to the left. The crackling turned into a snapping, the sled pivoting and the

---

43) conjuration: 주문, 마법, 요술

44) half-reluctantly: 반쯤 마지못해, 반쯤 억지로

45) a crisp crackling: 파삭하며 탁탁거리는 소리

runners slipping and grating[46] several inches to the side. The sled was broken out. Men were holding their breaths, intensely unconscious of the fact.

"Now, MUSH!"

Thornton's command cracked out like a pistol-shot. Buck threw himself forward, tightening the traces with a jarring lunge[47]. His whole body was gathered compactly together in the tremendous effort, the muscles writhing and knotting like live things under the silky fur. His great chest was low to the ground, his head forward and down, while his feet were flying like mad, the claws scarring the hard-packed snow in parallel grooves[48]. The sled swayed and trembled, half-started forward. One of his feet slipped, and one man groaned aloud. Then the sled lurched[49] ahead in what appeared a rapid succession of jerks, though it never really came to a dead stop again...half an inch...an inch... two inches... The jerks perceptibly diminished; as the sled gained momentum, he caught them up, till it was moving steadily along.

Men gasped and began to breathe again, unaware that for a moment they had ceased to breathe. Thornton was running behind, encouraging Buck with short, cheery words. The distance had been measured off, and as he neared the pile of firewood which marked the end of the hundred yards, a cheer began to grow and grow, which burst into a roar as he passed the firewood and halted at command. Every man was tearing

46) grating: grate. (시끄럽게) 갈리다, 불쾌한 소리를 내다, 삐걱거리게 하다, (강판으로) 갈다, 맞스치다

47) jarring lunge: 삐걱거리며 돌진하기

48) groove: 흠, 강선, 홈, 가늘고 길게 팬 곳

49) lurched: 비틀거리다, 흔들흔들하다

himself loose, even Matthewson. Hats and mittens were flying in the air. Men were shaking hands, it did not matter with whom, and bubbling over in a general incoherent babel[50].

But Thornton fell on his knees beside Buck. Head was against head, and he was shaking him back and forth. Those who hurried up heard him cursing Buck, and he cursed him long and fervently, and softly and lovingly.

"Gad, sir! Gad, sir!" spluttered the Skookum Bench king. "I' ll give you a thousand for him, sir, a thousand, sir—twelve hundred, sir."

Thornton rose to his feet. His eyes were wet. The tears were streaming frankly down his cheeks. "Sir," he said to the Skookum Bench king, "no, sir. You can go to hell, sir. It's the best I can do for you, sir."

Buck seized Thornton's hand in his teeth. Thornton shook him back and forth. As though animated by a common impulse, the onlookers drew back to a respectful distance; nor were they again indiscreet enough to interrupt.

50) babel: 대혼란, 왁자지껄한 말소리, 소란(한 땅), 떠들썩한(혼란한)장소

Chapter VII
The Sounding of the Call

When Buck earned sixteen hundred dollars in five minutes for John Thornton, he made it possible for his master to pay off certain debts and to journey with his partners into the East after a fabled lost mine, the history of which was as old as the history of the country. Many men had sought it; few had found it; and more than a few there were who had never returned from the quest. This lost mine was steeped in tragedy and shrouded in mystery. No one knew of the first man. The oldest tradition stopped before it got back to him. From the beginning there had been an ancient and ramshackle[1] cabin. Dying men had sworn to it, and to the mine the site of which it marked, clinching their testimony with nuggets[2] that were unlike any known grade of gold in the Northland.

But no living man had looted this treasure house, and the dead were dead; wherefore John Thornton and Pete and Hans, with Buck and half a dozen other dogs, faced into the East on an unknown trail to achieve where men and dogs as good as themselves had failed. They sledded seventy miles up the Yukon, swung to the left into the Stewart River, passed the Mayo and the McQuestion, and held on until the Stewart itself became a

---

1) ramshackle: (당장이라도) 넘어질 듯한《집 따위》, 흔들〔덜컥〕거리는《차 따위》 줏대없는, 절조가 없는

2) nuggets: (광상(鑛床)에 박힌) 금괴(金塊), (천연의) 귀금속 덩어리, 뭉치, (pl.) 귀중한 것, 돈

streamlet[3], threading[4] the upstanding peaks which marked the backbone of the continent.

John Thornton asked little of man or nature. He was unafraid of the wild. With a handful of salt and a rifle he could plunge into the wilderness and fare wherever he pleased and as long as he pleased. Being in no haste, Indian fashion, he hunted his dinner in the course of the day's travel; and if he failed to find it, like the Indian, he kept on travelling, secure in the knowledge that sooner or later he would come to it. So, on this great journey into the East, straight meat was the bill of fare, ammunition and tools principally made up the load on the sled, and the time-card was drawn upon the limitless future.

To Buck it was boundless delight, this hunting, fishing, and indefinite wandering through strange places. For weeks at a time they would hold on steadily, day after day; and for weeks upon end they would camp, here and there, the dogs loafing and the men burning holes through frozen muck and gravel and washing countless pans of dirt by the heat of the fire. Sometimes they went hungry, sometimes they feasted riotously, all according to the abundance of game and the fortune of hunting. Summer arrived, and dogs and men packed on their backs, rafted across blue mountain lakes, and descended or ascended unknown rivers in slender boats whipsawed from the standing forest.

The months came and went, and back and forth they twisted through the uncharted vastness, where no men were and yet where men had been if the Lost Cabin were true. They went across divides in summer blizzards, shivered under the midnight

3) streamlet: (작은) 시내, 실개천

4) threading: 전체에 스며[꿰뚫고] 흐르다, 뚫고 나가다, 누비듯이 나아가다

sun on naked mountains between the timber line and the eternal snows, dropped into summer valleys amid swarming gnats[5] and flies, and in the shadows of glaciers picked strawberries and flowers as ripe and fair as any the Southland could boast. In the fall of the year they penetrated a weird lake country, sad and silent, where wildfowl had been, but where then there was no life nor sign of life—only the blowing of chill winds, the forming of ice in sheltered places, and the melancholy rippling of waves on lonely beaches.

And through another winter they wandered on the obliterated[6] trails of men who had gone before. Once, they came upon a path blazed through the forest, an ancient path, and the Lost Cabin seemed very near. But the path began nowhere and ended nowhere, and it remained mystery, as the man who made it and the reason he made it remained mystery. Another time they chanced upon the time-graven wreckage[7] of a hunting lodge, and amid the shreds of rotted blankets John Thornton found a long-barrelled flint-lock[8]. He knew it for a Hudson Bay Company gun of the young days in the Northwest, when such a gun was worth its height in beaver skins packed flat, And that was all—no hint as to the man who in an early day had reared the lodge and left the gun among the blankets.

Spring came on once more, and at the end of all their wandering they found, not the Lost Cabin, but a shallow placer in a broad valley where the gold showed like yellow butter

---

5) gnats: 각다귀, 모기

6) obliterate: 지우다, 말살하다, 망각하다

7) the time-graven wreckage: 그 시간으로 새겨진 난파선 같은

8) a long-barrelled flint-lock: 긴 통의 부싯돌 조절장치

across the bottom of the washing-pan. They sought no farther. Each day they worked earned them thousands of dollars in clean dust and nuggets[9], and they worked every day. The gold was sacked in moose-hide bags, fifty pounds to the bag, and piled like so much firewood outside the spruce-bough lodge. Like giants they toiled, days flashing on the heels of days like dreams as they heaped the treasure up.

There was nothing for the dogs to do, save the hauling in of meat now and again that Thornton killed, and Buck spent long hours musing by the fire. The vision of the short-legged hairy man came to him more frequently[10], now that there was little work to be done; and often, blinking by the fire, Buck wandered with him in that other world which he remembered.

The salient thing[11] of this other world seemed fear. When he watched the hairy man sleeping by the fire, head between his knees and hands clasped above, Buck saw that he slept restlessly, with many starts and awakenings, at which times he would peer fearfully into the darkness and fling more wood upon the fire. Did they walk by the beach of a sea, where the hairy man gathered shellfish and ate them as he gathered, it was with eyes that roved everywhere for hidden danger and with legs prepared to run like the wind at its first appearance. Through the forest they crept noiselessly, Buck at the hairy man's heels; and they were alert and vigilant, the pair of them, ears twitching and

---

9) nugget: (귀금속 등의) 덩어리, (특히) 천연의 금괴

10) The vision of the short-legged hairy man came to him more frequently.: 다리가 짧고 털투성이 인간의 환영이 그에게 더 자주 나타났다. (Buck은 원시인간의 환영을 보게되며 이것은 인간이 문명화 되기 이전의 야생적인 생명체였음을 보여주려는 작가의 의도라고 볼 수 있다.)

11) salient thing: 두드러진 것, 눈에 띄는 것

moving and nostrils quivering, for the man heard and smelled as keenly as Buck. The hairy man could spring up into the trees and travel ahead as fast as on the ground, swinging by the arms from limb to limb, sometimes a dozen feet apart, letting go and catching, never falling, never missing his grip. In fact, he seemed as much at home among the trees as on the ground; and Buck had memories of nights of vigil spent beneath trees wherein the hairy man roosted, holding on tightly as he slept.

And closely akin to the visions of the hairy man was the call still sounding in the depths of the forest[12]. It filled him with a great unrest and strange desires. It caused him to feel a vague, sweet gladness, and he was aware of wild yearnings and stirrings for he knew not what. Sometimes he pursued the call into the forest, looking for it as though it were a tangible thing, barking softly or defiantly, as the mood might dictate. He would thrust his nose into the cool wood moss, or into the black soil where long grasses grew, and snort with joy at the fat earth smells; or he would crouch for hours, as if in concealment, behind fungus-covered trunks of fallen trees, wide-eyed and wide-eared to all that moved and sounded about him. It might be, lying thus, that he hoped to surprise this call he could not understand. But he did not know why he did these various things. He was impelled to do them, and did not reason about them at all.

Irresistible impulses seized him. He would be lying in camp, dozing lazily in the heat of the day, when suddenly his head would lift and his ears cock up, intent and listening, and he would spring to his feet and dash away, and on and on, for

12) the call still sounding in the depths of the forest.: 그 외침소리는 숲의 심연에서 계속 들려왔다. (Buck은 본능적으로 문명 이전의 야성의 부름을 느끼게 된다.)

hours, through the forest aisles and across the open spaces where the niggerheads[13] bunched. He loved to run down dry watercourses, and to creep and spy upon the bird life in the woods. For a day at a time he would lie in the underbrush where he could watch the partridges drumming and strutting[14] up and down. But especially he loved to run in the dim twilight of the summer midnights, listening to the subdued and sleepy murmurs of the forest, reading signs and sounds as man may read a book, and seeking for the mysterious something that called—called, waking or sleeping, at all times, for him to come.

One night he sprang from sleep with a start, eager-eyed, nostrils quivering and scenting, his mane bristling in recurrent waves. From the forest came the call (or one note of it, for the call was many noted), distinct and definite as never before,—a long-drawn howl, like, yet unlike, any noise made by husky dog. And he knew it, in the old familiar way, as a sound heard before. He sprang through the sleeping camp and in swift silence dashed through the woods. As he drew closer to the cry he went more slowly, with caution in every movement, till he came to an open place among the trees, and looking out saw, erect on haunches, with nose pointed to the sky, a long, lean, timber wolf[15].

He had made no noise, yet it ceased from its howling and tried to sense his presence. Buck stalked into the open, half crouching, body gathered compactly together, tail straight and stiff, feet falling with unwonted care. Every movement

---

13) niggerheads: 니거헤드탄(炭)《석탄층 중에서 나는 둥근 탄 덩어리》, 산호초가 파괴되어 생기는 검은 덩어리

14) strutting: 뽐내며 걷다

15) timber wolf: 늑대의 일종, 얼룩이리

advertised commingled[16] threatening and overture of friendliness. It was the menacing truce that marks the meeting of wild beasts that prey. But the wolf fled at sight of him. He followed, with wild leapings, in a frenzy to overtake[17]. He ran him into a blind channel, in the bed of the creek where a timber jam barred the way. The wolf whirled about, pivoting on his hind legs[18] after the fashion of Joe and of all cornered husky dogs, snarling and bristling, clipping his teeth together in a continuous and rapid succession of snaps.

Buck did not attack, but circled him about and hedged him in with friendly advances. The wolf was suspicious and afraid; for Buck made three of him in weight, while his head barely reached Buck's shoulder. Watching his chance, he darted away, and the chase was resumed. Time and again he was cornered, and the thing repeated, though he was in poor condition, or Buck could not so easily have overtaken him. He would run till Buck's head was even with his flank, when he would whirl around at bay, only to dash away again at the first opportunity.

But in the end Buck's pertinacity[19] was rewarded; for the wolf, finding that no harm was intended, finally sniffed noses with him. Then they became friendly, and played about in the nervous, half-coy way with which fierce beasts belie their fierceness. After some time of this the wolf started off at an easy lope in a manner that plainly showed he was going somewhere. He made it clear to Buck that he was to come, and they ran side

16) commingled: ~을 혼합하다, 뒤섞이다, 합치다

17) in a frenzy to overtake : 따라잡으려고 미친듯이

18) pivoting on his hind legs: 뒷다리를 회전축으로 회전하다

19) pertinacity: 끈덕짐, 끈질김, 불굴

by side through the sombre twilight, straight up the creek bed, into the gorge from which it issued, and across the bleak divide where it took its rise.

On the opposite slope of the watershed they came down into a level country where were great stretches of forest and many streams, and through these great stretches they ran steadily, hour after hour, the sun rising higher and the day growing warmer. Buck was wildly glad. He knew he was at last answering the call, running by the side of his wood brother toward the place from where the call surely came. Old memories were coming upon him fast, and he was stirring to them as of old he stirred to the realities of which they were the shadows. He had done this thing before, somewhere in that other and dimly remembered world, and he was doing it again, now, running free in the open, the unpacked earth underfoot, the wide sky overhead.

They stopped by a running stream to drink, and, stopping, Buck remembered John Thornton. He sat down. The wolf started on toward the place from where the call surely came, then returned to him, sniffing noses and making actions as though to encourage him. But Buck turned about and started slowly on the back track. For the better part of an hour the wild brother ran by his side, whining softly. Then he sat down, pointed his nose upward, and howled. It was a mournful howl, and as Buck held steadily on his way he heard it grow faint and fainter until it was lost in the distance.

John Thornton was eating dinner when Buck dashed into camp and sprang upon him in a frenzy of affection, overturning him, scrambling upon him, licking his face, biting his hand—"playing the general tom-fool," as John Thornton characterized it, the while he shook Buck back and forth and cursed him lovingly.

For two days and nights Buck never left camp, never let Thornton out of his sight. He followed him about at his work, watched him while he ate, saw him into his blankets at night and out of them in the morning. But after two days the call in the forest began to sound more imperiously than ever. Buck's restlessness came back on him, and he was haunted by recollections of the wild brother, and of the smiling land beyond the divide and the run side by side through the wide forest stretches. Once again he took to wandering in the woods, but the wild brother came no more; and though he listened through long vigils, the mournful howl was never raised.

He began to sleep out at night, staying away from camp for days at a time; and once he crossed the divide at the head of the creek and went down into the land of timber and streams. There he wandered for a week, seeking vainly for fresh sign of the wild brother, killing his meat as he travelled and travelling with the long, easy lope that seems never to tire. He fished for salmon in a broad stream that emptied somewhere into the sea, and by this stream he killed a large black bear, blinded by the mosquitoes while likewise fishing, and raging[20] through the forest helpless and terrible. Even so, it was a hard fight, and it aroused the last latent remnants of Buck's ferocity[21]. And two days later, when he returned to his kill and found a dozen wolverenes[22] quarrelling over the spoil, he scattered them like chaff[23]; and those that fled

---

20) ranging: range, 돌아다니다, 싸다니다, 헤매다

21) the last latent remnants of Buck's ferocity: Buck의 마지막 잠재되어 남아있는 흉포스러움

22) wolverenes: (북미산) 오소리들

23) like chaff: 쓰레기처럼, 잡동사니처럼

left two behind who would quarrel no more.

The blood-longing became stronger than ever before. He was a killer, a thing that preyed, living on the things that lived, unaided, alone, by virtue of his own strength and prowess[24], surviving triumphantly in a hostile environment where only the strong survived. Because of all this he became possessed of a great pride in himself, which communicated itself like a contagion to his physical being. It advertised itself in all his movements, was apparent in the play of every muscle, spoke plainly as speech in the way he carried himself, and made his glorious furry coat if anything more glorious. But for the stray brown on his muzzle and above his eyes[25], and for the splash of white hair that ran midmost down his chest, he might well have been mistaken for a gigantic wolf, larger than the largest of the breed. From his St. Bernard father he had inherited size and weight, but it was his shepherd mother who had given shape to that size and weight. His muzzle was the long wolf muzzle, save that it was larger than the muzzle of any wolf; and his head, somewhat broader, was the wolf head on a massive scale.

His cunning was wolf cunning, and wild cunning; his intelligence, shepherd intelligence and St. Bernard intelligence; and all this, plus an experience gained in the fiercest of schools, made him as formidable a creature as any that roamed the wild. A carnivorous[26] animal living on a straight meat diet, he was in

24) prowess : 용기, 역량, 용감한 행위

25) But for the stray brown on his muzzle and above his eyes,: 그의 주둥이와 눈 위쪽에 우연히 흩어져 있는 갈색이 없었더라면

26) carnivorous: 육식성의, 식충류의, (익살) [사람이] 육식의

full flower, at the high tide of his life, overspilling[27] with vigor and virility. When Thornton passed a caressing hand along his back, a snapping and crackling followed the hand, each hair discharging its pent magnetism at the contact[28]. Every part, brain and body, nerve tissue and fibre, was keyed to the most exquisite pitch; and between all the parts there was a perfect equilibrium or adjustment[29]. To sights and sounds and events which required action, he responded with lightning-like rapidity. Quickly as a husky dog could leap to defend from attack or to attack, he could leap twice as quickly. He saw the movement, or heard sound, and responded in less time than another dog required to compass the mere seeing or hearing. He perceived and determined and responded in the same instant. In point of fact the three actions of perceiving, determining, and responding were sequential[30]; but so infinitesimal[31] were the intervals of time between them that they appeared simultaneous. His muscles were surcharged with vitality, and snapped into play sharply, like steel springs. Life streamed through him in splendid flood, glad and rampant, until it seemed that it would burst him asunder in sheer ecstasy and pour forth generously over the world.

"Never was there such a dog," said John Thornton one day, as the partners watched Buck marching out of camp.

"When he was made, the mould was broke," said Pete.

---

27) overspilling: 넘쳐흐르다

28) discharging its pent magnetism at the contact: 각가의 털들이 그 접촉에 감춰진 자성(매력)을 발산하며

29) equilibrium or adjustment: 균형과 조화

30) sequential: 순차적인, 연속적인

31) infinitesimal: 미소한, 극미의, 극소한, 극미량의

"Py jingo! I t'ink so mineself," Hans affirmed.

They saw him marching out of camp, but they did not see the instant and terrible transformation which took place as soon as he was within the secrecy of the forest. He no longer marched. At once he became a thing of the wild, stealing along softly, cat-footed, a passing shadow that appeared and disappeared among the shadows. He knew how to take advantage of every cover, to crawl on his belly like a snake, and like a snake to leap and strike. He could take a ptarmigan[32] from its nest, kill a rabbit as it slept, and snap in mid air the little chipmunks[33] fleeing a second too late for the trees. Fish, in open pools, were not too quick for him; nor were beaver, mending their dams, too wary. He killed to eat, not from wantonness[34]; but he preferred to eat what he killed himself. So a lurking humor ran through his deeds, and it was his delight to steal upon the squirrels, and, when he all but had them, to let them go, chattering in mortal fear to the treetops.

As the fall of the year came on, the moose appeared in greater abundance, moving slowly down to meet the winter in the lower and less rigorous valleys. Buck had already dragged down a stray part-grown calf; but he wished strongly for larger and more formidable quarry[35], and he came upon it one day on the divide at the head of the creek. A band of twenty moose had crossed over from the land of streams and timber, and chief among them

---

32) ptarmigan: [조류] 뇌조, 들꿩, 멧닭

33) chipmunk: 다람쥐: 아시아 · 북미산

34) wantonness: 문란함, 즐거움, 장난난, 방종

35) quarry: 채석장, 원천의 의미가 아니라 사냥 동물[새], (개·매·사냥꾼 등이 찾는) 사냥감(game)

was a great bull. He was in a savage temper, and, standing over six feet from the ground, was as formidable an antagonist as even Buck could desire. Back and forth the bull tossed his great palmated antlers[36], branching to fourteen points and embracing seven feet within the tips. His small eyes burned with a vicious and bitter light, while he roared with fury at sight of Buck.

From the bull's side, just forward of the flank, protruded a feathered arrow-end, which accounted for his savageness. Guided by that instinct which came from the old hunting days of the primordial world, Buck proceeded to cut the bull out from the herd. It was no slight task. He would bark and dance about in front of the bull, just out of reach of the great antlers and of the terrible splay hoofs[37] which could have stamped his life out with a single blow. Unable to turn his back on the fanged danger and go on, the bull would be driven into paroxysms[38] of rage. At such moments he charged Buck, who retreated craftily, luring him on by a simulated inability to escape. But when he was thus separated from his fellows, two or three of the younger bulls would charge back upon Buck and enable the wounded bull to rejoin the herd.

There is a patience of the wild—dogged, tireless, persistent as life itself—that holds motionless for endless hours the spider in its web, the snake in its coils, the panther in its ambuscade[39]; this patience belongs peculiarly to life when it hunts its living food; and it belonged to Buck as he clung to the flank of the

---

36) palmated antlers: 손바닥 모양의 가지진 뿔, 또는 그 뿔의 가지

37) splay hoofs: 바깥으로 벌어진 발굽들

38) paroxysms: (감정·행동 등의) 격발, 발작적 활동

39) panther in its ambuscade: 매복하여 숨어있는 퓨마, (아메리카 산) 표범

herd, retarding its march, irritating the young bulls, worrying the cows with their half-grown calves, and driving the wounded bull mad with helpless rage. For half a day this continued. Buck multiplied himself, attacking from all sides, enveloping the herd in a whirlwind of menace, cutting out his victim as fast as it could rejoin its mates, wearing out the patience of creatures preyed upon, which is a lesser patience than that of creatures preying.

As the day wore along and the sun dropped to its bed in the northwest (the darkness had come back and the fall nights were six hours long), the young bulls retraced their steps more and more reluctantly to the aid of their beset leader. The down-coming winter was harrying them on to the lower levels, and it seemed they could never shake off this tireless creature that held them back. Besides, it was not the life of the herd, or of the young bulls, that was threatened. The life of only one member was demanded, which was a remoter interest than their lives, and in the end they were content to pay the toll.

As twilight fell the old bull stood with lowered head, watching his mates—the cows he had known, the calves he had fathered, the bulls he had mastered—as they shambled[40] on at a rapid pace through the fading light. He could not follow, for before his nose leaped the merciless fanged terror that would not let him go. Three hundredweight more than half a ton he weighed; he had lived a long, strong life, full of fight and struggle, and at the end he faced death at the teeth of a creature whose head did not reach beyond his great knuckled knees.

From then on, night and day, Buck never left his prey, never

---

40) shambled: 휘청휘청[발을 질질 끌며] 걷다

gave it a moment's rest, never permitted it to browse the leaves of trees or the shoots of young birch and willow. Nor did he give the wounded bull opportunity to slake his burning thirst in the slender trickling streams they crossed. Often, in desperation, he burst into long stretches of flight. At such times Buck did not attempt to stay him, but loped easily at his heels, satisfied with the way the game was played, lying down when the moose stood still, attacking him fiercely when he strove to eat or drink.

The great head drooped more and more under its tree of horns, and the shambling trot grew weak and weaker. He took to standing for long periods, with nose to the ground and dejected ears dropped limply[41]; and Buck found more time in which to get water for himself and in which to rest. At such moments, panting with red lolling tongue and with eyes fixed upon the big bull, it appeared to Buck that a change was coming over the face of things. He could feel a new stir in the land. As the moose were coming into the land, other kinds of life were coming in. Forest and stream and air seemed palpitant[42] with their presence. The news of it was borne in upon him, not by sight, or sound, or smell, but by some other and subtler sense. He heard nothing, saw nothing, yet knew that the land was somehow different; that through it strange things were afoot[43] and ranging; and he resolved to investigate after he had finished the business in hand.

At last, at the end of the fourth day, he pulled the great moose down. For a day and a night he remained by the kill, eating and sleeping, turn and turn about. Then, rested, refreshed and strong,

---

41) dejected ears dropped limply: 낙심한 귀들이 힘없이 떨어졌다

42) palpitant : 두근거리는, 떨리는, 맥박이 뛰는

43) afoot: 진행 중에, 일어나, 움직여

he turned his face toward camp and John Thornton. He broke into the long easy lope, and went on, hour after hour, never at loss for the tangled way, heading straight home through strange country with a certitude of direction that put man and his magnetic needle to shame.[44]

As he held on he became more and more conscious of the new stir in the land. There was life abroad in it different from the life which had been there throughout the summer. No longer was this fact borne in upon him in some subtle, mysterious way. The birds talked of it, the squirrels chattered about it, the very breeze whispered of it. Several times he stopped and drew in the fresh morning air in great sniffs, reading a message which made him leap on with greater speed. He was oppressed with a sense of calamity happening, if it were not calamity already happened; and as he crossed the last watershed and dropped down into the valley toward camp, he proceeded with greater caution.

Three miles away he came upon a fresh trail that sent his neck hair rippling and bristling, It led straight toward camp and John Thornton. Buck hurried on, swiftly and stealthily, every nerve straining and tense, alert to the multitudinous[45] details which told a story—all but the end. His nose gave him a varying description of the passage of the life on the heels of which he was travelling. He remarked the pregnant silence of the forest. The bird life had flitted. The squirrels were in hiding. One only he saw,—a sleek gray fellow, flattened against a gray dead limb

---

44) with a certitude of direction that put man and his magnetic needle to shame: 사람과 그의 (나침판의) 자침을 무기력하게 하는 확실한 방향감각을 가지고

45) multitudinous: 다수의, 떼를 이루는, 가지가지의; 여러 부분(모양, 항목)으로 된; 광대한, 거대한

so that he seemed a part of it, a woody excrescence[46] upon the wood itself.

As Buck slid along with the obscureness of a gliding shadow, his nose was jerked suddenly to the side as though a positive force had gripped and pulled it. He followed the new scent into a thicket[47] and found Nig. He was lying on his side, dead where he had dragged himself, an arrow protruding, head and feathers, from either side of his body.

A hundred yards farther on, Buck came upon one of the sled-dogs Thornton had bought in Dawson. This dog was thrashing about in a death-struggle, directly on the trail, and Buck passed around him without stopping. From the camp came the faint sound of many voices, rising and falling in a sing-song chant. Bellying forward to the edge of the clearing, he found Hans, lying on his face, feathered with arrows like a porcupine. At the same instant Buck peered out where the spruce-bough lodge had been and saw what made his hair leap straight up on his neck and shoulders. A gust of overpowering rage swept over him. He did not know that he growled, but he growled aloud with a terrible ferocity. For the last time in his life he allowed passion to usurp cunning and reason, and it was because of his great love for John Thornton that he lost his head.

The Yeehats[48] were dancing about the wreckage of the spruce-bough lodge when they heard a fearful roaring and saw rushing

---

46) a woody excrescence: 나무 같은 이상 생성물, 이상 성장, 방해물

47) thicket: 덤불, 관목의 숲, 잡목림

48) Yeehats: John Thornton과 그의 광산채 굴 친구들을 살해한 인디언 부족, 그들은 Buck에게 다수가 살해되고 살아남은 자들은 Buck을 두려워하여 "Ghost Dog" 또는 "Evil Spirit"이라고 부른다.

upon them an animal the like of which they had never seen before. It was Buck, a live hurricane of fury, hurling himself upon them in a frenzy to destroy. He sprang at the foremost man (it was the chief of the Yeehats), ripping the throat wide open till the rent jugular[49] spouted a fountain of blood. He did not pause to worry the victim, but ripped in passing, with the next bound tearing wide the throat of a second man. There was no withstanding him. He plunged about in their very midst, tearing, rending, destroying, in constant and terrific motion which defied the arrows they discharged at him. In fact, so inconceivably rapid were his movements, and so closely were the Indians tangled together, that they shot one another with the arrows; and one young hunter, hurling a spear at Buck in mid air, drove it through the chest of another hunter with such force that the point broke through the skin of the back and stood out beyond. Then a panic seized the Yeehats, and they fled in terror to the woods, proclaiming[50] as they fled the advent of the Evil Spirit.

And truly Buck was the Fiend incarnate, raging at their heels and dragging them down like deer as they raced through the trees. It was a fateful day for the Yeehats. They scattered far and wide over the country, and it was not till a week later that the last of the survivors gathered together in a lower valley and counted their losses. As for Buck, wearying of the pursuit, he returned to the desolated camp. He found Pete where he had been killed in his blankets in the first moment of surprise. Thornton's desperate struggle was fresh-written on the earth, and Buck scented every detail of it down to the edge of a deep pool.

---

49) rent jugular: 찢어진 경정맥

50) proclaiming: 공포하다, 성명하다

By the edge, head and fore feet in the water, lay Skeet, faithful to the last. The pool itself, muddy and discolored from the sluice[51] boxes, effectually hid what it contained, and it contained John Thornton; for Buck followed his trace into the water, from which no trace led away.

All day Buck brooded by the pool or roamed restlessly about the camp. Death, as a cessation of movement, as a passing out and away from the lives of the living, he knew, and he knew John Thornton was dead. It left a great void in him, somewhat akin to hunger, but a void which ached and ached, and which food could not fill, At times, when he paused to contemplate the carcasses of the Yeehats, he forgot the pain of it; and at such times he was aware of a great pride in himself,—a pride greater than any he had yet experienced. He had killed man, the noblest game of all, and he had killed in the face of the law of club and fang. He sniffed the bodies curiously. They had died so easily. It was harder to kill a husky dog than them. They were no match at all, were it not for their arrows and spears and clubs. Thenceforward[52] he would be unafraid of them except when they bore in their hands their arrows, spears, and clubs.

Night came on, and a full moon rose high over the trees into the sky, lighting the land till it lay bathed in ghostly day. And with the coming of the night, brooding and mourning by the pool, Buck became alive to a stirring of the new life in the forest other than that which the Yeehats had made, He stood up, listening and scenting. From far away drifted a faint, sharp yelp, followed by a chorus of similar sharp yelps. As the moments

51) sluice: [채광] (사금 채취장의) 인공 수로(sluiceway)

52) Thenceforward: 거기서부터, 그때부터, 그때 이래

passed the yelps grew closer and louder. Again Buck knew them as things heard in that other world which persisted in his memory. He walked to the centre of the open space and listened. It was the call, the many-noted call[53], sounding more luringly and compellingly than ever before. And as never before, he was ready to obey. John Thornton was dead. The last tie was broken. Man and the claims of man no longer bound him.

Hunting their living meat, as the Yeehats were hunting it, on the flanks of the migrating moose, the wolf pack had at last crossed over from the land of streams and timber and invaded Buck's valley. Into the clearing where the moonlight streamed, they poured in a silvery flood; and in the centre of the clearing stood Buck, motionless as a statue, waiting their coming. They were awed, so still and large he stood, and a moment's pause fell, till the boldest one leaped straight for him. Like a flash Buck struck, breaking the neck. Then he stood, without movement, as before, the stricken wolf rolling in agony behind him. Three others tried it in sharp succession; and one after the other they drew back, streaming blood from slashed throats or shoulders.

This was sufficient to fling the whole pack forward, pell-mell[54], crowded together, blocked and confused by its eagerness to pull down the prey. Buck's marvellous quickness and agility stood him in good stead. Pivoting on his hind legs, and snapping and gashing[55], he was everywhere at once, presenting a front which was apparently unbroken so swiftly did he whirl and

53) the many-noted call: 여러 번 감지되어 확실한 부름의 소리 (야생으로부터의 부름에 Buck은 본능적으로 굴복하게 됨)

54) pell-mell: 황급히, 허둥지둥, 무모하게, 난잡하게

55) snapping and gashing: 달려들어 덥썩 물거나 깊은 상처를 입히면서

guard from side to side. But to prevent them from getting behind him, he was forced back, down past the pool and into the creek bed, till he brought up against a high gravel bank. He worked along to a right angle in the bank which the men had made in the course of mining, and in this angle he came to bay, protected on three sides and with nothing to do but face the front[56].

And so well did he face it, that at the end of half an hour the wolves drew back discomfited. The tongues of all were out and lolling, the white fangs showing cruelly white in the moonlight. Some were lying down with heads raised and ears pricked forward; others stood on their feet, watching him; and still others were lapping water from the pool. One wolf, long and lean and gray, advanced cautiously, in a friendly manner, and Buck recognized the wild brother with whom he had run for a night and a day. He was whining softly, and, as Buck whined, they touched noses.

Then an old wolf, gaunt and battle-scarred, came forward. Buck writhed his lips into the preliminary of a snarl[57], but sniffed noses with him, Whereupon the old wolf sat down, pointed nose at the moon, and broke out thc long wolf howl. The others sat down and howled. And now the call came to Buck in unmistakable accents. He, too, sat down and howled. This over, he came out of his angle and the pack crowded around him, sniffing in half-friendly, half-savage manner. The leaders lifted the yelp of the pack and sprang away into the woods. The wolves swung in behind, yelping in chorus. And

56) with nothing to do but face the front: 그는 단지 정면만 방어하면 되었다

57) Buck writhed his lips into the preliminary of a snarl: Buck은 으르렁 거리기 전의 예비동작으로 그의 입술을 뒤틀게 했다

Buck ran with them, side by side with the wild brother, yelping as he ran.

And here may well end the story of Buck. The years were not many when the Yeehats noted a change in the breed of timber wolves; for some were seen with splashes of brown on head and muzzle, and with a rift of white centring down the chest. But more remarkable than this, the Yeehats tell of a Ghost Dog that runs at the head of the pack. They are afraid of this Ghost Dog, for it has cunning greater than they, stealing from their camps in fierce winters, robbing their traps, slaying their dogs, and defying their bravest hunters.

Nay, the tale grows worse. Hunters there are who fail to return to the camp, and hunters there have been whom their tribesmen found with throats slashed cruelly open and with wolf prints about them in the snow greater than the prints of any wolf. Each fall, when the Yeehats follow the movement of the moose, there is a certain valley which they never enter. And women there are who become sad when the word goes over the fire of how the Evil Spirit came to select that valley for an abiding-place.

In the summers there is one visitor, however, to that valley, of which the Yeehats do not know. It is a great, gloriously coated wolf, like, and yet unlike, all other wolves. He crosses alone from the smiling timber land and comes down into an open space among the trees. Here a yellow stream flows from rotted moose-hide sacks and sinks into the ground, with long grasses growing through it and vegetable mould overrunning it and hiding its yellow from the sun; and here he muses for a time, howling once, long and mournfully, ere he departs.

But he is not always alone. When the long winter nights come on and the wolves follow their meat into the lower valleys, he may be seen running at the head of the pack through the pale moonlight or glimmering borealis, leaping gigantic above his fellows, his great throat a-bellow as he sings a song of the younger world, which is the song of the pack.

OTHER STORIES

THE WHITE SILENCE

(1899)

Jack London

"Carmen[1] won't last more than a couple of days." Mason spat out a chunk of ice and surveyed the poor animal ruefully, then put her foot in his mouth and proceeded to bite out the ice which clustered cruelly between the toes.

"I never saw a dog with a highfalutin[2]' name that ever was worth a rap[3]," he said, as he concluded his task and shoved her aside. "They just fade away and die under the responsibility. Did ye ever see one go wrong with a sensible name like Cassiar, Siwash, or Husky? No, sir! Take a look at Shookum here, he's – "

Snap! The lean brute flashed up, the white teeth just missing Mason's throat.

"Ye will, will ye?" A shrewd clout behind the ear with the butt of the dog-whip stretched the animal in the snow, quivering softly, a yellow slaver[4] dripping from its fangs.

---

1) Carmen: 썰매개의 이름. 어원적 의미는 God's vineyard, 또는 [F. karmɛn] 카르멘: Mérimée의 동명 소설(1845) 및 이에 따른 Bizet의 오페라(1875)의 정열적인 여주인공의 이름. Mason은 썰매개의 이름으로는 너무 고상하다고 생각한다.

2) highfalutin: 과장한, 거만한, 거드름 피우는, 고상한 척하는

3) worth a rap: 거의 가치가 없는

4) slaver: 군침

"As I was saying, just look at Shookum, here -- he's got the spirit. Bet ye he eats Carmen before the week's out."

"I'll bank another proposition against that," replied Malemute Kid, reversing the frozen bread placed before the fire to thaw. "We' ll eat Shookum before the trip is over. What d' ye say, Ruth?"

The Indian woman settled the coffee with a piece of ice, glanced from Malemute Kid to her husband, then at the dogs, but vouchsafed[5] no reply. It was such a palpable truism that none was necessary. Two hundred miles of unbroken trail in prospect, with a scant six days' grub for themselves and none for the dogs, could admit no other alternative. The two men and the woman grouped about the fire and began their meager meal. The dogs lay in their harnesses, for it was a mid-day halt, and watched each mouthful enviously.

"No more lunches after to-day," said Malemute Kid. "And we' ve got to keep a close eye on the dogs, -- they're getting vicious. They'd just as soon pull a fellow down as not, if they get a chance[6]."

"And I was president of an Epworth once, and taught in the Sunday school." Having irrelevantly delivered himself of this, Mason fell into a dreamy contemplation of his steaming moccasins, but was aroused by Ruth filling his cup. "Thank

---

5) vouchsafed: 주다, 허용하다, ~을 특별한 호의로써 허락하다

6) They'd just as soon pull a fellow down as not, if they get a chance.: 그들은 기회가 있다면 동료를 쓰러뜨리고 싶어한다(would~as soon~as not: 어느 쪽이냐 하면 ~하고 싶다)

God, we've got slathers of[7] tea! I've seen it growing, down in Tennessee. What wouldn't I give for a hot corn pone[8] just now! Never mind, Ruth; you won't starve much longer, nor wear moccasins either."

The woman threw off her gloom at this, and in her eyes welled up a great love for her white lord, -- the first white man she had ever seen, -- the first man whom she had known to treat a woman as something better than a mere animal or beast of burden.

"Yes, Ruth," continued her husband, having recourse[9] to the macaronic jargon[10] in which it was alone possible for them to understand each other, "wait till we clean up and pull for the Outside. We'll take the White Man's canoe and go to the Salt Water. Yes, bad water, rough water, -- great mountains dance up and down all the time. And so big, so far, so far away, -- you travel ten sleep, twenty sleep, forty sleep" (he graphically enumerated[11] the days on his fingers,) "all the time water, bad water. Then you come to great village, plenty people, just the same mosquitoes next summer. Wigwams oh, so high, -- ten, twenty pines. Hi-yu skookum!"

He paused impotently, cast an appealing glance at Malemute

---

7) slathers of: lots of, 많이, 듬뿍, 다수수

8) corn pone: 옥수수 빵

9) recourse: 의지, 의존

10) macaronic jargon: 혼합방언

11) enumerated: ~을 하나하나 열거하다, 차례로 들다, ~을 하나하나 세다

Kid, then laboriously placed the twenty pines, end on end, by sign language. Malemute Kid smiled with cheery cynicism; but Ruth's eyes were wide with wonder, and with pleasure; for she half believed he was joking, and such condescension[12] pleased her poor woman's heart.

"And then you step into a -- a box, and pouf! up you go." He tossed his empty cup in the air by way of illustration, and as he deftly caught it, cried: "And biff! down you come. Oh, great medicine-men! You go Fort Yukon, I go Arctic City, -- twenty-five sleep, -- big string, all the time, -- I catch him string, -- I say, 'Hello, Ruth! How are ye?' -- and you say, 'Is that my good husband?' -- and I say, 'Yes,' -- and you say, 'No can bake good bread, no more soda,' -- then I say, 'Look in cache[13], under flour; good-by.' You look and catch plenty soda. All the time you Fort Yukon, me Arctic City. Hi-yu medicine-man![14]"

Ruth smiled so ingenuously[15] at the fairy story, that both men burst into laughter. A row among the dogs cut short the wonders of the Outside, and by the time the snarling combatants were separated, she had lashed the sleds and all was ready for the trail.

"Mush! Baldy! Hi! Mush on!" Mason worked his whip smartly, and as the dogs whined low in the traces, broke out

---

12) condescension: (손아랫사람에 대한) 겸손, 공손, 정중, 생색 내는 듯한 태도

13) cache: 은닉처, 저장하다, 저장소

14) medicine-man: 북미 인디언의 병을 고치는 마술사, (특히 1900년 이전의) 약 행상인

15) ingenuously: 솔직하게, 순진하게

the sled with the gee-pole. Ruth followed with the second team, leaving Malemute Kid, who had helped her start, to bring up the rear. Strong man, noble brute that he was, capable of felling an ox at a blow, he could not bear to beat the poor animals, but humored them as a dog-driver rarely does, -- nay, almost wept with them in their misery.

"Come, mush on there, you poor sore-footed brutes," he murmured, after several ineffectual attempts to start the load. But his patience was at last rewarded, and though whimpering with pain, they hastened to join their fellows.

No more conversation; the toil of the trail will not permit such extravagance. And of all deadening[16] labors, that of the Northland trail is the worst. Happy is the man who can weather a day's travel at the price of silence, and that on a beaten track.

And of all heart-breaking labors, that of breaking trail is the worst. At every step the great webbed shoe sinks till the snow is level with the knee. Then up, straight up, the deviation[17] of a fraction of an inch being a certain precursor[18] of disaster, the snowshoe must be lifted till the surface is cleared; then forward, down, and the other foot is raised perpendicularly[19] for the matter of half a yard. He who tries this for the first time, if haply he avoids bringing his shoes in dangerous propinquity and

16) deadening: 치명적인, 말라죽게 하는

17) deviation: 편차, 일탈, 이탈

18) precursor: 선구자, 선배, 전조

19) perpendicularly: 수직으로, 직각으로

measures not his length on the treacherous footing, will give up exhausted at the end of a hundred yards; he who can keep out of the way of the dogs for a whole day may well crawl into his sleeping-bag with a clear conscience, and a pride which passeth all understanding; and he who travels twenty sleeps on the Long Trail is a man whom the gods may envy.

The afternoon wore on, and with the awe, born of the White Silence, the voiceless travelers bent to their work. Nature has many tricks wherewith she convinces man of his finity[20], -- the ceaseless flow of the tides, the fury of the storm, the shock of the earthquake, the long roll of heaven's artillery, -- but the most tremendous, the most stupefying of all, is the passive phase of the White Silence. All movement ceases, the sky clears, the heavens are as brass; the slightest whisper seems sacrilege, and man becomes timid, affrighted at the sound of his own voice. Sole speck of life journeying across the ghostly wastes of a dead world, he trembles at his audacity, realizes that his is a maggot's life, nothing more. Strange thoughts arise unsummoned, and the mystery of all things strives for utterance. And the fear of death, of God, of the universe, comes over him, -- the hope of the Resurrection and the Life, the yearning for immortality, the vain striving of the imprisoned essence, -- it is then, if ever, man walks alone with God.

So wore the day away[21]. The river took a great bend, and Mason headed his team for the cut-off across the narrow neck

20) finity: 유한함, 한계, 제한

21) So wore the day away.: 그날도 그렇게 그럭저럭 지나갔다.

of land. But the dogs balked at the high bank. Again and again, though Ruth and Malemute Kid were shoving on the sled, they slipped back. Then came the concerted effort. The miserable creatures, weak from hunger, exerted their last strength. Up -- up -- the sled poised on the top of the bank; but the leader swung the string of dogs behind him to the right, fouling Mason's snowshoes. The result was grievous[22]. Mason was whipped off his feet; one of the dogs fell in the traces; and the sled toppled back, dragging everything to the bottom again.

Slash! the whip fell among the dogs savagely, especially upon the one which had fallen.

"Don't, Mason," entreated Malemute Kid; "the poor devil's on its last legs. Wait and we'll put my team on.[23]"

Mason deliberately withheld the whip till the last word had fallen, then out flashed the long lash, completely curling about the offending creature's body. Carmen, -- for it was Carmen, -- cowered in the snow, cried piteously, then rolled over on her side.

It was a tragic moment, a pitiful incident of the trail, -- a dying dog, two comrades in anger. Ruth glanced solicitously[24] from man to man. But Malemute Kid restrained himself, though there was a world of reproach in his eyes, and bending over

22) The result was grievous.: 그 결과는 참혹했다

23) we'll put my team on. : 우리가 나의 팀을 움직이게 할 것이다

24) solicitous: 열심인, 간절히 ~하려 하는, 갈망하는

the dog, cut the traces. No word was spoken. The teams were double-spanned and the difficulty overcome; the sleds were under way again, the dying dog dragging herself along in the rear. As long as an animal can travel, it is not shot, and this last chance is accorded it, -- the crawling into camp, if it can, in the hope of a moose being killed.

Already penitent for his angry action, but too stubborn to make amends, Mason toiled on at the head of the cavalcade[25], little dreaming that danger hovered in the air. The timber clustered thick in the sheltered bottom, and through this they threaded their way. Fifty feet or more from the trail towered a lofty pine. For generations it had stood there, and for generations destiny had had this one end in view, -- perhaps the same had been decreed of Mason.

He stooped to fasten the loosened thong of his moccasin. The sleds came to a halt and the dogs lay down in the snow without a whimper. The stillness was weird; not a breath rustled the frost-encrusted forest; the cold and silence of outer space had chilled the heart and smote the trembling lips of nature. A sigh pulsed through the air, -- they did not seem to actually hear it, but rather felt it, like the premonition of movement in a motionless void. Then the great tree, burdened with its weight of years and snow, played its last part in the tragedy of life. He heard the warning crash and attempted to spring up, but almost erect, caught the blow squarely on the shoulder.

---

25) cavalcade: 기마대, 마차대, 기마〔마차〕 행렬〔행진, (화려한) 행렬, 퍼레이드, 사건의 진전, (별의) 운행

The sudden danger, the quick death, -- how often had Malemute Kid faced it! The pine needles were still quivering as he gave his commands and sprang into action. Nor did the Indian girl faint or raise her voice in idle wailing, as would many of her white sisters. At his order, she threw her weight on the end of a quickly extemporized handspike[26], easing the pressure and listening to her husband's groans, while Malemute Kid attacked the tree with his ax. The steel rang merrily as it bit into the frozen trunk, each stroke being accompanied by a forced, audible respiration, the "Huh!" "Huh!" of the woodsman.

At last the Kid laid the pitiable thing that was once a man in the snow. But worse than his comrade's pain, was the dumb anguish in the woman's face, the blended look of hopeful, hopeless query. Little was said; those of the Northland are early taught the futility of words and the inestimable[27] value of deeds. With the temperature at sixty-five below zero, a man cannot lie many minutes in the snow and live. So the sled-lashings were cut, and the sufferer, rolled in furs, laid on a couch of boughs. Before him roared a fire, built of the very wood which wrought the mishap. Behind and partially over him was stretched the primitive fly, -- a piece of canvas, which caught the radiating heat and threw it back and down upon him, -- a trick which men may know who study physics at the fount.

---

26) extemporized handspike: 급조한 지레

27) inestimable: 평가(계산)할 수 없는, 헤아릴 수 없는, 헤아릴 수 없을 만큼 큰, 더없이 귀중한

And men who have shared their bed with death know when the call is sounded. Mason was terribly crushed. The most cursory[28] examination revealed it. His right arm, leg, and back, were broken; his limbs were paralyzed from the hips; and the likelihood of internal injuries was large. An occasional moan was his only sign of life.

No hope; nothing to be done. The pitiless night crept slowly by, -- Ruth's portion, the despairing stoicism[29] of her race, and Malemute Kid adding new lines to his face of bronze. In fact, Mason suffered least of all, for he spent his time in Eastern Tennessee, in the Great Smoky Mountains, living over the scenes of his childhood. And most pathetic was the melody of his long-forgotten Southern vernacular, as he raved of swimming-holes and coon-hunts and watermelon raids. It was as Greek to Ruth, but the Kid understood and felt, -- felt as only one can feel who has been shut out for years from all that civilization means.

Morning brought consciousness to the stricken man, and Malemute Kid bent closer to catch his whispers.

"You remember when we foregathered[30] on the Tanana, four years come next ice-run? I didn't care so much for her then. It was more like she was pretty, and there was a smack of excitement[31] about it, I think. But d' ye know, I've come to

---

28) cursory: 몹시 서두른, 조잡한, 엉성한

29) despairing stoicism: 자포자기의 금욕주의

30) foregathered: 우연히 만났다

31) a smack of excitement: 약간의 흥분

think a heap of her. She's been a good wife to me, always at my shoulder in the pinch. And when it comes to trading, you know there isn't her equal. D' ye recollect the time she shot the Moosehorn Rapids to pull you and me off that rock, the bullets whipping the water like hailstones[32]? -- and the time of the famine at Nuklukyeto? -- or when she raced the ice-run to bring the news? Yes, she's been a good wife to me, better 'n that other one. Didn't know I'd been there? Never told you, eh? Well, I tried it once, down in the States. That's why I'm here. Been raised together, too. I came away to give her a chance for divorce. She got it.

"But that's got nothing to do with Ruth. I had thought of cleaning up and pulling for the Outside next year, -- her and I, -- but it's too late. Don't send her back to her people, Kid. It's beastly hard for a woman to go back. Think of it! -- nearly four years on our bacon and beans and flour and dried fruit, and then to go back to her fish and cariboo. It's not good for her to have tried our ways, to come to know they're better 'n her people's, and then return to them. Take care of her, Kid, -- why don't you, -- but no, you always fought shy of them, -- and you never told me why you came to this country. Be kind to her, and send her back to the States as soon as you can. But fix it so as she can come back, -- liable to get homesick, you know.

"And the youngster -- it's drawn us closer, Kid. I only hope it is a boy. Think of it! -- flesh of my flesh, Kid. He mustn't stop in this country. And if it's a girl, why she can't. Sell my furs; they'll

32) hailstones: 싸락눈, 우박

fetch at least five thousand, and I've got as much more with the company. And handle my interests with yours. I think that bench claim will show up. See that he gets a good schooling; and Kid, above all, don't let him come back. This country was not made for white men.

"I'm a gone man[33], Kid. Three or four sleeps at the best[34]. You've got to go on. You must go on! Remember, it's my wife, it's my boy, -- O God! I hope it's a boy! You can't stay by me, -- and I charge you, a dying man, that you pull on."

"Give me three days," pleaded Malemute Kid. "You may change for the better;[35] something may turn up."

"No."

"Just three days."

"You must pull on."[36]

"Two days."

"It's my wife and my boy, Kid. You would not ask it."

"One day."

---

33) I'm a gone man.: 나는 가망없어.

34) at the best: 기껏해야

35) You may change for the better: 자네는 몸이 호전될지도 몰라

36) "You must pull on." : 방아쇠를 당겨.

"No, no! I charge --"

"Only one day. We can shave it through on the grub[37], and I might knock over a moose."

"No, -- all right; one day, but not a minute more. And Kid, don't -- don't leave me to face it alone. Do as you would ask of me. Just a shot, one pull on the trigger. You understand. Think of it! Think of it! Flesh of my flesh, and I'll never live to see him!

"Send Ruth here. I want to say good-by and tell her that she must think of the boy and not wait till I'm dead. She might refuse to go with you if I didn't. Good-by, old man; good-by.

"Kid! I say -- a -- sink a hole above the pup, next to the slide. I panned out forty cents on my shovel there.

"And Kid!" he stooped lower to catch the last faint words, the dying man's surrender of his pride. "I'm sorry -- for -- you know -- Carmen."

Leaving the girl crying softly over her man, Malemute Kid slipped into his parka and snowshoes, tucked his rifle under his arm, and crept away into the forest. He was no tyro in the stern sorrows of the Northland, but never had he faced so stiff a problem as this. In the abstract, it was a plain, mathematical

---

37) We can shave it through on the grub: 우리는 그 식량으로 간신히 버틸 수 있어. shave through(아슬아슬하게 스치듯이 지나가다), grub(비격식으로 음식을 의미함)

proposition, -- three possible lives as against one doomed one. But now he hesitated. For five years, shoulder to shoulder, on the rivers and trails, in the camps and mines, facing death by field and flood and famine, had they knitted the bonds of their comradeship. So close was the tie, that he had often been conscious of a vague jealousy of Ruth, from the first time she had come between. And now it must be severed by his own hand.

Though he prayed for a moose, just one moose, all game seemed to have deserted the land, and nightfall found the exhausted man crawling into camp, light-handed, heavy-hearted. An uproar from the dogs and shrill cries from Ruth hastened him.

Bursting into the camp, he saw the girl in the midst of the snarling pack, laying about her with an ax. The dogs had broken the iron rule of their masters and were rushing the grub. He joined the issue with his rifle reversed, and the hoary game of natural selection was played out with all the ruthlessness of its primeval environment. Rifle and ax went up and down, hit or missed with monotonous regularity; lithe bodies flashed, with wild eyes and dripping fangs; and man and beast fought for supremacy to the bitterest conclusion. Then the beaten brutes crept to the edge of the firelight, licking their wounds, voicing their misery to the stars.

The whole stock of dried salmon had been devoured, and perhaps five pounds of flour remained to tide them over two hundred miles of wilderness. Ruth returned to her husband, while Malemute Kid cut up the warm body of one of the dogs, the skull of which had been crushed by the ax. Every portion was carefully put away, save the hide and offal, which were cast to his fellows of the moment before.

Morning brought fresh trouble. The animals were turning on each other. Carmen, who still clung to her slender thread of life, was downed by the pack. The lash fell among them unheeded. They cringed and cried under the blows, but refused to scatter till the last wretched bit had disappeared, -- bones, hide, hair, everything.

Malemute Kid went about his work, listening to Mason, who was back in Tennessee, delivering tangled discourses and wild exhortations[38] to his brethren of other days.

Taking advantage of neighboring pines, he worked rapidly, and Ruth watched him make a cache similar to those sometimes used by hunters to preserve their meat from the wolverines and dogs. One after the other, he bent the tops of two small pines toward each other and nearly to the ground, making them fast with thongs of moose hide. Then he beat the dogs into submission and harnessed them to two of the sleds, loading the same with everything but the furs which enveloped Mason. These he wrapped and lashed tightly about him, fastening either end of the robes to the bent pines. A single stroke of his hunting knife would release them and send the body high in the air.

Ruth had received her husband's last wishes and made no struggle. Poor girl, she had learned the lesson of obedience well. From a child, she had bowed, and seen all women bow to the

38) exhortations: 간곡한 권유, 권고, 충고, 경고, 훈계

lords of creation, and it did not seem in the nature of things for woman to resist. The Kid permitted her one outburst of grief, as she kissed her husband, -- her own people had no such custom, -- then led her to the foremost sled and helped her into her snowshoes. Blindly, instinctively, she took the gee-pole and whip, and "mushed" the dogs out on the trail. Then he returned to Mason, who had fallen into a coma; and long after she was out of sight, he crouched by the fire, waiting, hoping, praying for his comrade to die.

It is not pleasant to be alone with painful thoughts in the White Silence. The silence of gloom is merciful, shrouding one as with protection and breathing a thousand intangible sympathies; but the bright White Silence, clear and cold, under steely skies, in pitiless.

An hour passed, -- two hours, -- but the man would not die. At high noon, the sun, without raising its rim above the southern horizon, threw a suggestion of fire athwart the heavens, then quickly drew it back. Malemute Kid roused and dragged himself to his comrade's side. He cast one glance about him. The White Silence seemed to sneer[39], and a great fear came upon him. There was a sharp report[40]; Mason swung into his aerial sepulcher[41], and Malemute Kid lashed the dogs into a wild gallop as he fled across the snow.

---

39) The White Silence seemed to sneer.: 하얀 침묵이 조소하는 것처럼 보였다.

40) a sharp report: 날카로운 총성

41) aerial sepulcher: 천상(공중, 대기)의 무덤

THE LAW OF LIFE

Jack London

(First published in McClure's Magazine Vol. 16, March, 1901)

Old Koskoosh listened greedily. Though his sight had long since faded, his hearing was still acute, and the slightest sound penetrated to the glimmering intelligence which yet abode behind the withered forehead, but which no longer gazed forth upon the things of the world. Ah! that was Sit-cum-to-ha, shrilly anathematizing[1] the dogs as she cuffed and beat them into the harnesses. Sit-cum-to-ha was his daughter's daughter, but she was too busy to waste a thought upon her broken grandfather, sitting alone there in the snow, forlorn and helpless. Camp must be broken. The long trail waited while the short day refused to linger. Life called her, and the duties of life, not death. And he was very close to death now.

The thought made the old man panicky for the moment, and he stretched forth a palsied hand which wandered tremblingly over the small heap of dry wood beside him. Reassured that it was indeed there, his hand returned to the shelter of his mangy furs, and he again fell to listening. The sulky crackling[2] of half-frozen hides told him that the chief's moose-skin lodge had been struck, and even then was being rammed and jammed into

1) anathematizing: 공식적으로 저주하다, 파문하다, 저주하여 추방하다

2) crackling: 딱딱거리는 소리

portable compass. The chief was his son, stalwart[3] and strong, head man of the tribesmen, and a mighty hunter. As the women toiled with the camp luggage, his voice rose, chiding[4] them for their slowness. Old Koskoosh strained his ears. It was the last time he would hear that voice. There went Geehow's lodge! And Tusken's! Seven, eight, nine; only the shaman's[5] could be still standing. There! They were at work upon it now. He could hear the shaman grunt as he piled it on the sled. A child whimpered, and a woman soothed it with soft, crooning gutturals[6]. Little Koo-tee, the old man thought, a fretful child, and not overstrong. It would die soon, perhaps, and they would burn a hole through the frozen tundra and pile rocks above to keep the wolverines away. Well, what did it matter? A few years at best, and as many an empty belly as a full one. And in the end, Death waited, ever-hungry and hungriest of them all.

What was that? Oh, the men lashing the sleds and drawing tight the thongs[7]. He listened, who would listen no more. The whip-lashes snarled and bit among the dogs. Hear them whine! How they hated the work and the trail! They were off![8] Sled after sled churned[9] slowly away into the silence. They were gone. They had passed out of his life, and he faced the last

3) stalwart: 튼튼한(strongly-built), 건장한(stout). 용감한

4) chiding: chide, 꾸짖다(scold), 비난하다《for doing》, ~에게 잔소리하다

5) shaman: 샤먼, 방술사(方術師), 마술사, 무당

6) crooning gutturals: 작은 소리로 웅얼거리는 목구멍에서 나오는 소리

7) thong: 끈, 가죽끈, 고무 슬리퍼(flip-flop)

8) They were off!: 그들은 떠났다

9) churned: churn, 거품이 일다, 거품을 일으키며 나아가다

bitter hour alone. No. The snow crunched beneath a moccasin; a man stood beside him; upon his head a hand rested gently. His son was good to do this thing. He remembered other old men whose sons had not waited after the tribe. But his son had. He wandered away into the past, till the young man's voice brought him back.

"Is it well with you?" he asked.

And the old man answered, "It is well."

"There be wood beside you," the younger man continued, "and the fire burns bright. The morning is gray, and the cold has broken. It will snow presently. Even now is it snowing."

"Ay, even now is it snowing."

"The tribesmen hurry. Their bales are heavy, and their bellies flat with lack of feasting. The trail is long and they travel fast. go now. It is well?"

"It is well. I am as a last year's leaf, clinging lightly to the stem. The first breath that blows, and I fall. My voice is become like an old woman's. My eyes no longer show me the way of my feet, and my feet are heavy, and I am tired. It is well."

He bowed his head in content till the last noise of the complaining snow[10] had died away, and he knew his son was

10) complaining snow: 구슬픈 소리를 내며 내리는 눈

beyond recall. Then his hand crept out in haste to the wood. It alone stood between him and the eternity that yawned in upon him. At last the measure of his life was a handful of fagots[11]. One by one they would go to feed the fire, and just so, step by step, death would creep upon him. When the last stick had surrendered up its heat, the frost would begin to gather strength. First his feet would yield, then his hands; and the numbness would travel, slowly, from the extremities to the body. His head would fall forward upon his knees, and he would rest. It was easy. All men must die.

He did not complain. It was the way of life, and it was just. He had been born close to the earth, close to the earth had he lived, and the law thereof was not new to him. It was the law of all flesh. Nature was not kindly to the flesh. She had no concern for that concrete thing called the individual. Her interest lay in the species, the race. This was the deepest abstraction old Koskoosh's barbaric mind was capable of, but he grasped it firmly. He saw it exemplified in all life. The rise of the sap, the bursting greenness of the willow bud, the fall of the yellow leaf -- in this alone was told the whole history. But one task did Nature set the individual. Did he not perform it, he died. Did he perform it, it was all the same, he died. Nature did not care; there were plenty who were obedient, and it was only the obedience in this matter, not the obedient, which lived and lived always. The tribe of Koskoosh was very old. The old men he had known when a boy, had known old men before them. Therefore it was true that the tribe lived, that it stood for the

11) fagot: 장작뭇(단), 섶(나무)단

obedience of all its members, way down into the forgotten past, whose very resting-places were unremembered. They did not count; they were episodes. They had passed away like clouds from a summer sky. He also was an episode, and would pass away. Nature did not care. To life she set one task, gave one law. To perpetuate[12] was the task of life, its law was death. A maiden was a good creature to look upon, full-breasted and strong, with spring to her step and light in her eyes. But her task was yet before her. The light in her eyes brightened, her step quickened, she was now bold with the young men, now timid, and she gave them of her own unrest. And ever she grew fairer and yet fairer to look upon, till some hunter, able no longer to withhold himself, took her to his lodge to cook and toil for him and to become the mother of his children. And with the coming of her offspring her looks left her. Her limbs dragged and shuffled[13], her eyes dimmed and bleared[14], and only the little children found joy against the withered cheek of the old squaw by the fire. Her task was done. But a little while, on the first pinch of famine or the first long trail, and she would be left, even as he had been left, in the snow, with a little pile of wood. Such was the law. He placed a stick carefully upon the fire and resumed his meditations. It was the same everywhere, with all things. The mosquitoes vanished with the first frost. The little tree-squirrel crawled away to die. When age settled upon the rabbit it became slow and heavy, and could no longer outfoot its enemies. Even the big bald-face grew clumsy and blind and

12) perpetuate: 영속시키다, 불멸〔불후(不朽)〕케 하다

13) shuffled: 발을 질질 끌다, 지척거리다, 발을 끌다

14) bleared: 흐릿해지다

quarrelsome, in the end to be dragged down by a handful of yelping huskies. He remembered how he had abandoned his own father on an upper reach of the Klondike one winter, the winter before the missionary came with his talk-books and his box of medicines. Many a time had Koskoosh smacked his lips over the recollection of that box, though now his mouth refused to moisten. The "painkiller[15]" had been especially good. But the missionary was a bother after all, for he brought no meat into the camp, and he ate heartily, and the hunters grumbled. But he chilled his lungs on the divide by the Mayo, and the dogs afterwards nosed the stones away and fought over his bones.

Koskoosh placed another stick on the fire and harked back deeper into the past. There was the time of the Great Famine, when the old men crouched empty-bellied to the fire, and let fall from their lips dim traditions of the ancient day when the Yukon ran wide open for three winters, and then lay frozen for three summers. He had lost his mother in that famine. In the summer the salmon run had failed, and the tribe looked forward to the winter and the coming of the caribou. Then the winter came, but with it there were no caribou[16]. Never had the like been known, not even in the lives of the old men. But the caribou did not come, and it was the seventh year, and the rabbits had not replenished[17], and the dogs were naught but bundles of bones. And through the long darkness the children wailed and died,

---

15) painkiller: 진통제

16) caribou: 순록

17) replenish: 채우다, 다시 채우다, (연료를) 계속 공급하다, 대다, 새로 보충〔보급〕하다 《with》

and the women, and the old men; and not one in ten of the tribe lived to meet the sun when it came back in the spring. That was a famine!

But he had seen times of plenty, too, when the meat spoiled on their hands, and the dogs were fat and worthless with overeating -- times when they let the game go unkilled, and the women were fertile, and the lodges were cluttered with sprawling men-children and women-children[18]. Then it was the men became high-stomached, and revived ancient quarrels, and crossed the divides to the south to kill the Pellys, and to the west that they might sit by the dead fires of the Tananas. He remembered, when a boy, during a time of plenty, when he saw a moose pulled down by the wolves. Zing-ha lay with him in the snow and watched -- Zing-ha, who later became the craftiest of hunters, and who, in the end, fell through an air-hole on the Yukon. They found him, a month afterward, just as he had crawled halfway out and frozen stiff to the ice.

But the moose. Zing-ha and he had gone out that day to play at hunting after the manner of their fathers. On the bed of the creek they struck the fresh track of a moose, and with it the tracks of many wolves. "An old one," Zing-ha, who was quicker at reading the sign, said -- "an old one who cannot keep up with the herd. The wolves have cut him out from his brothers, and they will never leave him." And it was so. It was their way. By

18) the lodges were cluttered with sprawling men-children and women-children.: 오두막들에는 팔다리를 보기 흉하게 벌리고 있는 사내아이들과 여자아이들이 가득했다.

day and by night, never resting, snarling on his heels, snapping at his nose, they would stay by him to the end. How Zing-ha and he felt the blood-lust quicken! The finish would be a sight to see!

Eager-footed, they took the trail, and even he, Koskoosh, slow of sight and an unversed tracker[19], could have followed it blind, it was so wide. Hot were they on the heels of the chase, reading the grim tragedy, fresh-written, at every step. Now they came to where the moose had made a stand. Thrice the length of a grown man's body, in every direction, had the snow been stamped about and uptossed. In the midst were the deep impressions of the splay-hoofed game[20], and all about, everywhere, were the lighter footmarks of the wolves. Some, while their brothers harried the kill[21], had lain to one side and rested. The full-stretched impress of their bodies in the snow was as perfect as though made the moment before. One wolf had been caught in a wild lunge of the maddened victim and trampled to death. A few bones, well picked, bore witness.

Again, they ceased the uplift of their snowshoes at a second stand. Here the great animal had fought desperately. Twice had he been dragged down, as the snow attested, and twice had he shaken his assailants[22] clear and gained footing once more. He had done his task long since, but none the less was life dear to

19) unversed tracker: 숙달되지 못한, 익숙하지 못한 사냥꾼, 추적자

20) splay-hoofed game: 바깥으로 벌어진 말발굽의 사냥감

21) harried the kill: 그 사냥감을 괴롭혔다

22) assailants: 공격자, 가해자, 적

him. Zing-ha said it was a strange thing, a moose once down to get free again; but this one certainly had. The shaman would see signs and wonders in this when they told him.

And yet again, they come to where the moose had made to mount the bank and gain the timber. But his foes had laid on from behind, till he reared and fell back upon them, crushing two deep into the snow. It was plain the kill was at hand, for their brothers had left them untouched. Two more stands were hurried past, brief in time-length and very close together. The trail was red now, and the clean stride of the great beast had grown short and slovenly. Then they heard the first sounds of the battle -- not the full-throated chorus of the chase, but the short, snappy[23] bark which spoke of close quarters and teeth to flesh. Crawling up the wind, Zing-ha bellied it through the snow, and with him crept he, Koskoosh, who was to be chief of the tribesmen in the years to come. Together they shoved aside the under branches of a young spruce and peered forth. It was the end they saw.

The picture, like all of youth's impressions, was still strong with him, and his dim eyes watched the end played out as vividly as in that far-off time. Koskoosh marvelled at this, for in the days which followed, when he was a leader of men and a head of councillors, he had done great deeds and made his name a curse in the mouths of the Pellys, to say naught of the strange white man he had killed, knife to knife, in open fight.

For long he pondered on the days of his youth, till the fire

---

23) snappy: 팔팔한, 활기찬, 일을 척척 잘하는

died down and the frost bit deeper. He replenished[24] it with two sticks this time, and gauged his grip on life by what remained. If Sit-cum-to-ha had only remembered her grandfather, and gathered a larger armful, his hours would have been longer. It would have been easy. But she was ever a careless child, and honored not her ancestors from the time the Beaver, son of the son of Zing-ha, first cast eyes upon her. Well, what mattered it? Had he not done likewise in his own quick youth? For a while he listened to the silence. Perhaps the heart of his son might soften, and he would come back with the dogs to take his old father on with the tribe to where the caribou ran thick and the fat hung heavy upon them.

He strained his ears[25], his restless brain for the moment stilled. Not a stir, nothing[26]. He alone took breath in the midst of the great silence. It was very lonely. Hark! What was that? A chill passed over his body. The familiar, long-drawn howl broke the void, and it was close at hand. Then on his darkened eyes was projected the vision of the moose -- the old bull moose -- the torn flanks and bloody sides, the riddled mane, and the great branching horns, down low and tossing to the last. He saw the flashing forms of gray, the gleaming eyes, the lolling[27] tongues, the slavered fangs. And he saw the inexorable[28] circle close in till it became a dark point in the midst of the stamped snow.

---

24) replenished: 다시 채우다, 보충하다

25) He strained his ears: 그는 귀를 집중해서 들었다

26) Not a stir, nothing.: 조금의 움직임도 전혀 없었다

27) lolling: 늘어뜨린

28) inexorable: 무정한, 냉혹한, 굽힐 수 없는, 움직일 수 없는

A cold muzzle thrust against his cheek, and at its touch his soul leaped back to the present. His hand shot into the fire and dragged out a burning faggot. Overcome for the nonce[29] by his hereditary fear of man, the brute retreated, raising a prolonged call to his brothers; and greedily they answered, till a ring of crouching, jaw-slobbered[30] gray was stretched round about. The old man listened to the drawing in of this circle. He waved his brand wildly, and sniffs turned to snarls; but the panting brutes refused to scatter. Now one wormed his chest forward, dragging his haunches[31] after, now a second, now a third; but never a one drew back. Why should he cling to life? he asked, and dropped the blazing stick into the snow. It sizzled and went out. The circle grunted[32] uneasily, but held its own. Again he saw the last stand of the old bull moose, and Koskoosh dropped his head wearily upon his knees. What did it matter after all? Was it not the law of life?

29) for the nonce: 당분간은, 당장은

30) jaw-slobbered: 턱에 군침이 흐르는

31) haunches: (보통 pl.) 허리, 궁둥이, (양고기 따위의) 허리 부분

32) grunt: 으르렁 거리다

Bâtard

(1902, Jack London)

Batard[1] was a devil. This was recognized throughout the Northland. "Hell's Spawn" he was called by many men, but his master, Black Leclere, chose for him the shameful name "Batard." Now Black Leclere was also a devil, and the twain were well matched. There is a saying that when two devils come together, hell is to pay[2]. This is to be expected, and this certainly was to be expected when Batard and Black Leclere came together. The first time they met, Batard was a part-grown puppy, lean and hungry, with bitter eyes; and they met with snap and snarl, and wicked looks, for Leclere's upper lip had a wolfish way of lifting and showing the white, cruel teeth. And it lifted then, and his eyes glinted viciously, as he reached for Batard and dragged him out from the squirming litter. It was certain that they divined each other, for on the instant Batard had buried his puppy fangs in Leclere's hand, and Leclere, thumb and finger, was coolly choking his young life out of him.

"Sacredam[3]," the Frenchman said softly, flirting the quick blood from his bitten hand and gazing down on the little puppy

---

1) Batard: 서자, (동식물의) 잡종(hybrid), 가짜, 서출인, 가짜인(원래는 트기 또는 사생아를 의미하는 프랑스어 Bâtard임.)

2) hell is to pay: 후환이 있을 것이다

3) Sacredam: (F) Sacrebleu=Goddamn

choking and gasping in the snow.

Leclere turned to John Hamlin, storekeeper of the Sixty Mile Post. "Dat fo' w'at Ah lak heem. 'Ow moch, eh, you, M'sieu'? 'Ow moch? Ah buy heem, now; Ah buy heem queek."

And because he hated him with an exceeding bitter hate, Leclere bought Batard and gave him his shameful name. And for five years the twain adventured across the Northland, from St. Michael' s and the Yukon delta to the head-reaches of the Pelly and even so far as the Peace River, Athabasca, and the Great Slave. And they acquired a reputation for uncompromising wickedness, the like of which never before attached itself to man and dog.

Batard did not know his father--hence his name--but, as John Hamlin knew, his father was a great grey timber wolf. But the mother of Batard, as he dimly remembered her, was snarling, bickering, obscene, husky, full-fronted and heavy-chested, with a malign eye, a cat-like grip on life, and a genius for trickery and evil. There was neither faith nor trust in her. Her treachery alone could be relied upon, and her wild-wood amours attested her general depravity. Much of evil and much of strength were there in these, Batard's progenitors, and, bone and flesh of their bone and flesh, he had inherited it all. And then came Black Leclere, to lay his heavy hand on the bit of pulsating puppy life, to press and prod and mould till it became a big bristling beast, acute in knavery, overspilling with hate, sinister, malignant, diabolical. With a proper master Batard might have made an ordinary, fairly efficient sled-dog. He never got the chance: Leclere but confirmed him in his congenital iniquity[4].

---

4) congenital iniquity: 타고난 사악함

The history of Batard and Leclere is a history of war--of five cruel, relentless years, of which their first meeting is fit summary. To begin with, it was Leclere's fault, for he hated with understanding and intelligence, while the long-legged, ungainly puppy hated only blindly, instinctively, without reason or method. At first there were no refinements of cruelty (these were to come later), but simple beatings and crude brutalities. In one of these Batard had an ear injured. He never regained control of the riven muscles, and ever after the ear drooped limply down to keep keen the memory of his tormentor. And he never forgot.

His puppyhood was a period of foolish rebellion. He was always worsted, but he fought back because it was his nature to fight back. And he was unconquerable. Yelping shrilly from the pain of lash and club, he none the less contrived always to throw in the defiant snarl, the bitter vindictive menace of his soul which fetched without fail more blows and beatings. But his was his mother's tenacious grip on life. Nothing could kill him. He flourished under misfortune, grew fat with famine, and out of his terrible struggle for life developed a preternatural intelligence. His were the stealth and cunning of the husky, his mother, and the fierceness and valour of the wolf, his father.

Possibly it was because of his father that he never wailed. His puppy yelps passed with his lanky legs[5], so that he became grim and taciturn[6], quick to strike, slow to warn. He answered curse with snarl, and blow with snap, grinning the while his

---

5) lanky legs: 빼빼 마른(피골이 상접한) 다리들

6) grim and taciturn: 험상궂고 음침하게 무뚝뚝한

implacable hatred; but never again, under the extremest agony, did Leclere bring from him the cry of fear nor of pain. This unconquerableness but fanned Leclere's wrath and stirred him to greater deviltries.

Did Leclere give Batard half a fish and to his mates whole ones, Batard went forth to rob other dogs of their fish. Also he robbed caches and expressed himself in a thousand rogueries, till he became a terror to all dogs and masters of dogs. Did Leclere beat Batard and fondle Babette--Babette who was not half the worker he was--why, Batard threw her down in the snow and broke her hind leg in his heavy jaws, so that Leclere was forced to shoot her. Likewise, in bloody battles, Batard mastered all his team-mates, set them the law of trail and forage, and made them live to the law he set.

In five years he heard but one kind word, received but one soft stroke of a hand, and then he did not know what manner of things they were. He leaped like the untamed thing he was, and his jaws were together in a flash. It was the missionary at Sunrise, a newcomer in the country, who spoke the kind word and gave the soft stroke of the hand. And for six months after, he wrote no letters home to the States, and the surgeon at McQuestion travelled two hundred miles on the ice to save him from blood-poisoning.

Men and dogs looked askance at[7] Batard when he drifted into their camps and posts. The men greeted him with feet

---

7) looked askance at: ~을 옆눈으로 보다

threateningly lifted for the kick, the dogs with bristling manes and bared fangs. Once a man did kick Batard, and Batard, with quick wolf snap, closed his jaws like a steel trap on the man's calf and crunched down to the bone. Whereat the man was determined to have his life, only Black Leclere, with ominous eyes and naked hunting-knife, stepped in between. The killing of Batard--ah, SACREDAM, THAT was a pleasure Leclere reserved for himself. Some day it would happen, or else--bah! who was to know? Anyway, the problem would be solved.

For they had become problems to each other. The very breath each drew was a challenge and a menace to the other. Their hate bound them together as love could never bind. Leclere was bent on the coming of the day when Batard should wilt in spirit and cringe and whimper at his feet. And Batard--Leclere knew what was in Batard's mind, and more than once had read it in Batard's eyes. And so clearly had he read, that when Batard was at his back, he made it a point to glance often over his shoulder.

Men marvelled[8] when Leclere refused large money for the dog. "Some day you'll kill him and be out his price," said John Hamlin once, when Batard lay panting in the snow where Leclere had kicked him, and no one knew whether his ribs were broken, and no one dared look to see.

"Dat," said Leclere, dryly, "dat is my biz'ness, M'sieu'."

And the men marvelled that Batard did not run away. They did not understand. But Leclere understood. He was a man who

8) marvelled: 놀랐다

lived much in the open, beyond the sound of human tongue, and he had learned the voices of wind and storm, the sigh of night, the whisper of dawn, the clash of day. In a dim way he could hear the green things growing, the running of the sap, the bursting of the bud. And he knew the subtle speech of the things that moved, of the rabbit in the snare, the moody raven beating the air with hollow wing, the baldface shuffling under the moon, the wolf like a grey shadow gliding betwixt the twilight and the dark. And to him Batard spoke clear and direct. Full well he understood why Batard did not run away, and he looked more often over his shoulder.

When in anger, Batard was not nice to look upon, and more than once had he leapt for Leclere's throat, to be stretched quivering and senseless in the snow, by the butt of the ever ready dogwhip. And so Batard learned to bide his time. When he reached his full strength and prime of youth, he thought the time had come. He was broad-chested, powerfully muscled, of far more than ordinary size, and his neck from head to shoulders was a mass of bristling hair-- to all appearances a full-blooded wolf. Leclere was lying asleep in his furs when Batard deemed the time to be ripe. He crept upon him stealthily, head low to earth and lone ear laid back, with a feline softness of tread. Batard breathed gently, very gently, and not till he was close at hand did he raise his head. He paused for a moment and looked at the bronzed bull throat, naked and knotty, and swelling to a deep steady pulse. The slaver dripped down his fangs and slid off his tongue at the sight, and in that moment he remembered his drooping ear, his uncounted blows and prodigious wrongs, and without a sound sprang on the sleeping man.

Leclere awoke to the pang of the fangs in his throat, and, perfect animal that he was, he awoke clear-headed and with full comprehension. He closed on Batard's windpipe with both his hands, and rolled out of his furs to get his weight uppermost. But the thousands of Batard's ancestors had clung at the throats of unnumbered moose and caribou and dragged them down, and the wisdom of those ancestors was his. When Leclere's weight came on top of him, he drove his hind legs upwards and in, and clawed down chest and abdomen[9], ripping and tearing through skin and muscle. And when he felt the man's body wince above him and lift, he worried and shook at the man's throat. His team-mates closed around in a snarling circle, and Batard, with failing breath and fading sense, knew that their jaws were hungry for him. But that did not matter- -it was the man, the man above him, and he ripped and clawed, and shook and worried, to the last ounce of his strength. But Leclere choked him with both his hands, till Batard's chest heaved and writhed for the air denied, and his eyes glazed and set, and his jaws slowly loosened, and his tongue protruded black and swollen.

"Eh? Bon, you devil!" Leclere gurgled mouth and throat clogged with his own blood, as he shoved the dizzy dog from him.

And then Leclere cursed the other dogs off as they fell upon Batard. They drew back into a wider circle, squatting alertly on their haunches and licking their chops, the hair on every neck bristling and erect.

---

9) abdomen: 복부, 배

Batard recovered quickly, and at sound of Leclere's voice, tottered to his feet and swayed weakly back and forth.

"A-h-ah! You beeg devil!" Leclere spluttered. "Ah fix you; Ah fix you plentee, by GAR!"

Batard, the air biting into his exhausted lungs like wine, flashed full into the man's face, his jaws missing and coming together with a metallic clip. They rolled over and over on the snow, Leclere striking madly with his fists. Then they separated, face to face, and circled back and forth before each other. Leclere could have drawn his knife. His rifle was at his feet. But the beast in him was up and raging. He would do the thing with his hands--and his teeth. Batard sprang in, but Leclere knocked him over with a blow of the fist, fell upon him, and buried his teeth to the bone in the dog's shoulder.

It was a primordial setting and a primordial scene, such as might have been in the savage youth of the world. An open space in a dark forest, a ring of grinning wolf-dogs, and in the centre two beasts, locked in combat, snapping and snarling raging madly about panting, sobbing, cursing, straining, wild with passion, in a fury of murder, ripping and tearing and clawing in elemental brutishness.

But Leclere caught Batard behind the ear with a blow from his fist, knocking him over, and, for the instant, stunning him. Then Leclere leaped upon him with his feet, and sprang up and down, striving to grind him into the earth. Both Batard's hind legs were broken ere Leclere ceased that he might catch breath.

"A-a-ah! A-a-ah!" he screamed, incapable of speech, shaking his fist, through sheer impotence of throat and larynx.

But Batard was indomitable. He lay there in a helpless welter, his lip feebly lifting and writhing to the snarl he had not the strength to utter. Leclere kicked him, and the tired jaws closed on the ankle, but could not break the skin.

Then Leclere picked up the whip and proceeded almost to cut him to pieces, at each stroke of the lash crying: "Dis taim Ah break you! Eh? By GAR! Ah break you!"

In the end, exhausted, fainting from loss of blood, he crumpled up and fell by his victim, and when the wolf-dogs closed in to take their vengeance, with his last consciousness dragged his body on top of Batard to shield him from their fangs.

This occurred not far from Sunrise, and the missionary, opening the door to Leclere a few hours later, was surprised to note the absence of Batard from the team. Nor did his surprise lessen when Leclere threw back the robes from the sled, gathered Batard into his arms and staggered across the threshold. It happened that the surgeon of McQuestion, who was something of a gadabout, was up on a gossip, and between them they proceeded to repair Leclere,

"Merci, non," said he. "Do you fix firs' de dog. To die? NON. Eet is not good. Becos' heem Ah mus' yet break. Dat fo' w'at he mus' not die."

The surgeon called it a marvel, the missionary a miracle, that Leclere pulled through at all; and so weakened was he, that in the spring the fever got him, and he went on his back again. Batard had been in even worse plight, but his grip on life prevailed, and the bones of his hind legs knit, and his organs righted themselves, during the several weeks he lay strapped to the floor. And by the time Leclere, finally convalescent, sallow and shaky, took the sun by the cabin door, Batard had reasserted his supremacy among his kind, and brought not only his own team-mates but the missionary's dogs into subjection.

He moved never a muscle, nor twitched a hair, when, for the first time, Leclere tottered out on the missionary's arm, and sank down slowly and with infinite caution on the three-legged stool.

"BON!" he said. "BON! De good sun!" And he stretched out his wasted hands and washed them in the warmth.

Then his gaze fell on the dog, and the old light blazed back in his eyes. He touched the missionary lightly on the arm. "Mon pere, dat is one beeg devil, dat Batard. You will bring me one pistol, so, dat Ah drink de sun in peace."

And thenceforth for many days he sat in the sun before the cabin door. He never dozed, and the pistol lay always across his knees. Batard had a way, the first thing each day, of looking for the weapon in its wonted place. At sight of it he would lift his lip faintly in token that he understood, and Leclere would lift his own lip in an answering grin. One day the missionary took note of the trick.

"Bless me!" he said. "I really believe the brute comprehends."

Leclere laughed softly. "Look you, mon pere. Dat w'at Ah now spik, to dat does he lissen."

As if in confirmation, Batard just perceptibly wriggled[10] his lone ear up to catch the sound.

"Ah say 'keel'."

Batard growled deep down in his throat, the hair bristled along his neck, and every muscle went tense and expectant.

"Ah lift de gun, so, like dat." And suiting action to word, he sighted the pistol at Batard. Batard, with a single leap, sideways, landed around the corner of the cabin out of sight.

"Bless me!" he repeated at intervals. Leclere grinned proudly.

"But why does he not run away?"

The Frenchman's shoulders went up in the racial shrug that means all things from total ignorance to infinite understanding.

"Then why do you not kill him?"

Again the shoulders went up.

"Mon pere," he said after a pause, "de taim is not yet. He is one beeg devil. Some taim Ah break heem, so an' so, all to leetle

10) wriggled: 꿈틀거리다, 굼실거리다, 몸부림치다, 안절부절못하다

bits. Hey? some taim. BON!"

A day came when Leclere gathered his dogs together and floated down in a bateau to Forty Mile, and on to the Porcupine, where he took a commission from the P. C. Company, and went exploring for the better part of a year. After that he poled up the Koyokuk to deserted Arctic City, and later came drifting back, from camp to camp, along the Yukon. And during the long months Batard was well lessoned. He learned many tortures, and, notably, the torture of hunger, the torture of thirst, the torture of fire, and, worst of all, the torture of music.

Like the rest of his kind, he did not enjoy music. It gave him exquisite anguish[11], racking him nerve by nerve, and ripping apart every fibre of his being. It made him howl, long and wolf-life, as when the wolves bay the stars on frosty nights. He could not help howling. It was his one weakness in the contest with Leclere, and it was his shame. Leclere, on the other hand, passionately loved music--as passionately as he loved strong drink. And when his soul clamoured for expression, it usually uttered itself in one or the other of the two ways, and more usually in both ways. And when he had drunk, his brain a-lilt with unsung song and the devil in him aroused and rampant, his soul found its supreme utterance in torturing Batard.

"Now we will haf a leetle museek," he would say. "Eh? W'at you t'ink, Batard?"

It was only an old and battered harmonica, tenderly treasured and patiently repaired; but it was the best that money could buy,

---

11) exquisite anguish: 예리한 고통

and out of its silver reeds he drew weird vagrant airs that men had never heard before. Then Batard, dumb of throat, with teeth tight clenched, would back away, inch by inch, to the farthest cabin corner. And Leclere, playing, playing, a stout club tucked under his arm, followed the animal up, inch by inch, step by step, till there was no further retreat.

At first Batard would crowd himself into the smallest possible space, grovelling[12] close to the floor; but as the music came nearer and nearer, he was forced to uprear, his back jammed into the logs, his fore legs fanning the air as though to beat off the rippling waves of sound. He still kept his teeth together, but severe muscular contractions attacked his body, strange twitchings and jerkings, till he was all a-quiver and writhing in silent torment. As he lost control, his jaws spasmodically wrenched apart, and deep throaty vibrations issued forth, too low in the register of sound for human ear to catch. And then, nostrils distended, eyes dilated, hair bristling in helpless rage, arose the long wolf howl. It came with a slurring rush upwards, swelling to a great heart- breaking burst of sound, and dying away in sadly cadenced woe--then the next rush upward, octave upon octave; the bursting heart; and the infinite sorrow and misery, fainting, fading, falling, and dying slowly away.

It was fit for hell. And Leclere, with fiendish ken, seemed to divine each particular nerve and heartstring, and with long wails and tremblings and sobbing minors to make it yield up its last shred of grief. It was frightful, and for twenty-four hours after,

---

12) grovel: [동물이] 기다, 기며 나아가다, [사람이] 엎드리다, 부복하다, 엎드려 기다

Batard was nervous and unstrung, starting at common sounds, tripping over his own shadow, but, withal, vicious and masterful with his team-mates. Nor did he show signs of a breaking spirit. Rather did he grow more grim and taciturn[13], biding his time with an inscrutable patience that began to puzzle and weigh upon Leclere. The dog would lie in the firelight, motionless, for hours, gazing straight before him at Leclere, and hating him with his bitter eyes.

Often the man felt that he had bucked against the very essence of life--the unconquerable essence that swept the hawk down out of the sky like a feathered thunderbolt[14], that drove the great grey goose across the zones, that hurled the spawning salmon through two thousand miles of boiling Yukon flood. At such times he felt impelled to--express his own unconquerable essence; and with strong drink, wild music, and Batard, he indulged in vast orgies, wherein he pitted his puny strength in the face of things, and challenged all that was, and had been, and was yet to be.

"Dere is somet'ing dere," he affirmed, when the rhythmed vagaries of his mind touched the secret chords of Batard's being and brought forth the long lugubrious howl[15]. "Ah pool eet out wid bot' my han's, so, an' so. Ha! ha! Eet is fonee! Eet is ver' fonee! De priest chant, de womans pray, de mans swear, de

---

13) taciturn: 말이 없는 (성격의), 무언의, 입이 무거운, 말수가 적은(silent), 음침하고 무뚝뚝한

14) like a feathered thunderbolt: 날개달린 벼락처럼

15) lugubrious howl : 가련한 울음소리

leetle bird go peep-peep, Batard, heem go yow-yow--an' eet is all de ver' same t'ing. Ha! ha!"

Father Gautier, a worthy priest, one reproved him with instances of concrete perdition. He never reproved him again.

"Eet may be so, mon pere," he made answer. "An' Ah t'ink Ah go troo hell a-snappin', lak de hemlock troo de fire. Eh, mon pere?"

But all bad things come to an end as well as good, and so with Black Leclere. On the summer low water, in a poling boat, he left McDougall for Sunrise. He left McDougall in company with Timothy Brown, and arrived at Sunrise by himself. Further, it was known that they had quarrelled just previous to pulling out; for the Lizzie, a wheezy[16] ten-ton stern-wheeler, twenty-four hours behind, beat Leclere in by three days. And when he did get in, it was with a clean-drilled bullet-hole through his shoulder muscle, and a tale of ambush and murder.

A strike had been made at Sunrise, and things had changed considerably. With the infusion of several hundred gold-seekers, a deal of whisky, and half-a-dozen equipped gamblers, the missionary had seen the page of his years of labour with the Indians wiped clean. When the squaws became preoccupied with cooking beans and keeping the fire going for the wifeless miners, and the bucks with swapping their warm furs for black bottles and broken time-pieces, he took to his bed, said "Bless

16) wheezy: 숨가쁜, 씨근거리는, 헐떡거리는

me" several times, and departed to his final accounting in a rough-hewn[17], oblong box. Whereupon the gamblers moved their roulette and faro tables into the mission house, and the click of chips and clink of glasses went up from dawn till dark and to dawn again.

Now Timothy Brown was well beloved among these adventurers of the North. The one thing against him was his quick temper and ready fist--a little thing, for which his kind heart and forgiving hand more than atoned. On the other hand, there was nothing to atone for Black Leclere. He was "black," as more than one remembered deed bore witness, while he was as well hated as the other was beloved. So the men of Sunrise put an antiseptic dressing on his shoulder and haled him before Judge Lynch.

It was a simple affair. He had quarrelled with Timothy Brown at McDougall. With Timothy Brown he had left McDougall. Without Timothy Brown he had arrived at Sunrise. Considered in the light of his evilness, the unanimous conclusion[18] was that he had killed Timothy Brown. On the other hand, Leclere acknowledged their facts, but challenged their conclusion, and gave his own explanation. Twenty miles out of Sunrise he and Timothy Brown were poling the boat along the rocky shore. From that shore two rifle- shots rang out. Timothy Brown pitched out of the boat and went down bubbling red, and that was the last of Timothy Brown. He, Leclere, pitched into the

17) rough-hewn: 대충 깎은, 두손매무리한, 투박한

18) unanimous conclusion: 만장일치의 결론

bottom of the boat with a stinging shoulder. He lay very quiet, peeping at the shore. After a time two Indians stuck up their heads and came out to the water's edge, carrying between them a birch-bark canoe. As they launched it, Leclere let fly. He potted one, who went over the side after the manner of Timothy Brown. The other dropped into the bottom of the canoe, and then canoe and poling boat went down the stream in a drifting battle. After that they hung up on a split current, and the canoe passed on one side of an island, the poling boat on the other. That was the last of the canoe, and he came on into Sunrise. Yes, from the way the Indian in the canoe jumped, he was sure he had potted him. That was all. This explanation was not deemed adequate. They gave him ten hours' grace while the Lizzie steamed down to investigate. Ten hours later she came wheezing back to Sunrise. There had been nothing to investigate. No evidence had been found to back up his statements. They told him to make his will, for he possessed a fifty-thousand dollar Sunrise claim, and they were a law-abiding as well as a law-giving breed.

Leclere shrugged his shoulders. "Bot one t'ing," he said; "a leetle, w'at you call, favour--a leetle favour, dat is eet. I gif my feefty t'ousan' dollair to de church. I gif my husky dog, Batard, to de devil. De leetle favour? Firs' you hang heem, an' den you hang me. Eet is good, eh?"

Good it was, they agreed, that Hell's Spawn should break trail for his master across the last divide, and the court was adjourned down to the river bank, where a big spruce tree stood by itself. Slackwater Charley put a hangman's knot in the end of a hauling- line, and the noose was slipped over Leclere's head and pulled tight around his neck. His hands were tied behind his back, and he was assisted to the top of a cracker box. Then the running end of the line was passed over an over-hanging branch, drawn taut, and made fast. To kick the box out from under would leave him dancing on the air.

"Now for the dog," said Webster Shaw, sometime mining engineer. "You'll have to rope him, Slackwater."

Leclere grinned. Slackwater took a chew of tobacco, rove a running noose[19], and proceeded leisurely to coil a few turns in his hand. He paused once or twice to brush particularly offensive mosquitoes from off his face. Everybody was brushing mosquitoes, except Leclerc, about whose head a small cloud was visible. Even Batard, lying full-stretched on the ground with his fore paws rubbed the pests away from eyes and mouth.

But while Slackwater waited for Batard to lift his head, a faint call came from the quiet air, and a man was seen waving his arms and running across the flat from Sunrise. It was the store-keeper.

"C-call 'er off, boys," he panted, as he came in among them.

"Little Sandy and Bernadotte's jes' got in," he explained with returning breath. "Landed down below an' come up by the short cut. Got the Beaver with 'm. Picked 'm up in his canoe, stuck in a back channel, with a couple of bullet-holes in 'm. Other buck

19) running noose: 당기면 죄어지게 만든 올가미

was Klok Kutz, the one that knocked spots out of his squaw and dusted."

"Eh? W'at Ah say? Eh?" Leclere cried exultantly. "Dat de one fo' sure! Ah know. Ah spik true."

"The thing to do is to teach these damned Siwashes a little manners," spoke Webster Shaw. "They're getting fat and sassy, and we'll have to bring them down a peg. Round in all the bucks and string up the Beaver for an object lesson. That's the programme. Come on and let's see what he's got to say for himself."

"Heh, M'sieu!" Leclere called, as the crowd began to melt away through the twilight in the direction of Sunrise. "Ah lak ver' moch to see de fon."

"Oh, we'll turn you loose when we come back," Webster Shaw shouted over his shoulder. "In the meantime meditate on your sins and the ways of Providence. It will do you good, so be grateful."

As is the way with men who are accustomed to great hazards, whose nerves are healthy and trained in patience, so it was with Leclere who settled himself to the long wait--which is to say that he reconciled his mind to it. There was no settling of the body, for the taut rope forced him to stand rigidly erect. The least relaxation of the leg muscles pressed the rough-fibred noose into his neck, while the upright position caused him much pain in his wounded shoulder. He projected his under lip and expelled his breath upwards along his face to blow the mosquitoes away from his eyes. But the situation had its compensation. To be snatched from the maw of death was well worth a little bodily suffering, only it was unfortunate that he should miss the hanging of the Beaver.

And so he mused, till his eyes chanced to fall upon Batard, head between fore paws and stretched on the ground asleep. And their Leclere ceased to muse. He studied the animal closely, striving to sense if the sleep were real or feigned. Batard's sides were heaving regularly, but Leclere felt that the breath came and went a shade too quickly; also he felt that there was a vigilance or alertness to every hair that belied unshackling sleep[20]. He would have given his Sunrise claim to be assured that the dog was not awake, and once, when one of his joints cracked, he looked quickly and guiltily at Batard to see if he roused. He did not rouse then but a few minutes later he got up slowly and lazily, stretched, and looked carefully about him.

"Sacredam," said Leclere under his breath.

Assured that no one was in sight or hearing, Batard sat down, curled his upper lip almost into a smile, looked up at Leclere, and licked his chops.

"Ah see my feenish," the man said, and laughed sardonically[21] aloud.

---

20) unshackling sleep: 자유로운 수면

21) sardonically: 냉소적으로, 빈정대듯이

Batard came nearer, the useless ear wabbling, the good ear cocked forward with devilish comprehension. He thrust his head on one side quizzically[22], and advanced with mincing[23], playful steps. He rubbed his body gently against the box till it shook and shook again. Leclere teetered[24] carefully to maintain his equilibrium.

"Batard," he said calmly, "look out. Ah keel you."

Batard snarled at the word and shook the box with greater force. Then he upreared, and with his fore paws threw his weight against it higher up. Leclere kicked out with one foot, but the rope bit into his neck and checked so abruptly as nearly to overbalance him.

"Hi, ya! Chook![25] Mush-on!" he screamed.

Batard retreated, for twenty feet or so, with a fiendish levity[26] in his bearing that Leclere could not mistake. He remembered the dog often breaking the scum of ice on the water hole by lifting up and throwing his weight upon it; and remembering, he understood what he now had in mind. Batard faced about and paused. He showed his white teeth in a grin, which Leclere answered; and then hurled his body through the air, in full

---

22) quizzically: 묻는 듯이

23) mincing: 뽐내는, 으스대는, 점잔빼는

24) teeter: 시소놀이를 하다, 위아래로 움직이다, ~을 동요시키다

25) Chook!: 늙은 암탉, 욕설

26) a fiendish levity: 교묘한, 악마같은 변덕, 경솔

charge, straight for the box.

Fifteen minutes later, Slackwater Charley and Webster Shaw returning, caught a glimpse of a ghostly pendulum swinging back and forth in the dim light. As they hurriedly drew in closer, they made out the man's inert body, and a live thing that clung to it, and shook and worried, and gave to it the swaying motion.

"Hi, ya! Chook! you Spawn of Hell![27]" yelled Webster Shaw.

But Batard glared at him, and snarled threateningly, without loosing his jaws.

Slackwater Charley got out his revolver, but his hand was shaking, as with a chill, and he fumbled.

"Here you take it," he said, passing the weapon over.

Webster Shaw laughed shortly, drew a sight between the gleaming eyes, and pressed the trigger. Batard's body twitched with the shock, threshed the ground spasmodically[28] for a moment, and went suddenly limp. But his teeth still held fast locked.

---

27) Spawn of Hell: 지옥의 새끼들, 욕설

28) spasmodically: 발작적으로

LOVE OF LIFE

Jack London

(First printed in McClure's Magazine, Vol. 26, Dec., 1905)

"This out of all will remain --
They have lived and have tossed:
So much of the game will be gain,
Though the gold of the dice has been lost."

They limped painfully down the bank, and once the foremost of the two men staggered among the rough-strewn[1] rocks. They were tired and weak, and their faces had the drawn expression of patience which comes of hardship long endured. They were heavily burdened with blanket packs which were strapped to their shoulders. Head-straps, passing across the forehead, helped support these packs. Each man carried a rifle. They walked in a stooped posture, the shoulders well forward, the head still farther forward, the eyes bent upon the ground.

"I wish we had just about two of them cartridges that's layin' in that cache of ourn," said the second man.

His voice was utterly and drearily expressionless. He spoke without enthusiasm; and the first man, limping into the milky stream that foamed over the rocks, vouchsafed no reply.

---

1) rough-strewn; 거칠게 흩어져 있는

The other man followed at his heels. They did not remove their foot-gear[2], though the water was icy cold -- so cold that their ankles ached and their feet went numb. In places the water dashed against their knees, and both men staggered for footing.

The man who followed slipped on a smooth boulder, nearly fell, but recovered himself with a violent effort, at the same time uttering a sharp exclamation of pain. He seemed faint and dizzy and put out his free hand while he reeled, as though seeking support against the air. When he had steadied himself he stepped forward, but reeled again and nearly fell. Then he stood still and looked at the other man, who had never turned his head.

The man stood still for fully a minute, as though debating with himself. Then he called out:

"I say, Bill, I've sprained my ankle."

Bill staggered on through the milky water. He did not look around. The man watched him go, and though his face was expressionless as ever, his eyes were like the eyes of a wounded deer.

The other man limped up the farther bank and continued straight on without looking back. The man in the stream watched him. His lips trembled a little, so that the rough thatch of brown hair which covered them was visibly agitated. His tongue even strayed out to moisten them.

---

2) foot-gear: (집합적) 신는 것, 신발·덧신·양말 등

"Bill!" he cried out. It was the pleading cry of a strong man in distress, but Bill's head did not turn. The man watched him go, limping grotesquely and lurching forward with stammering gait up the slow slope toward the soft sky-line of the low-lying hill. He watched him go till he passed over the crest and disappeared. Then he turned his gaze and slowly took in the circle of the world that remained to him now that Bill was gone.

Near the horizon the sun was smouldering[3] dimly, almost obscured by formless mists and vapors, which gave an impression of mass and density without outline or tangibility. The man pulled out his watch, the while resting his weight on one leg. It was four o'clock, and as the season was near the last of July or first of August, -- he did not know the precise date within a week or two, -- he knew that the sun roughly marked the northwest. He looked to the south and knew that somewhere beyond those bleak hills lay the Great Bear Lake; also, he knew that in that direction the Arctic Circle cut its forbidding way across the Canadian Barrens. This stream in which he stood was a feeder to the Coppermine River, which in turn flowed north and emptied into Coronation Gulf and the Arctic Ocean. He had never been there, but he had seen it, once, on a Hudson Bay Company chart.

Again his gaze completed the circle of the world about him. It was not a heartening spectacle. Everywhere was soft sky-line. The hills were all low-lying. There were no trees, no shrubs, no grasses -- naught but a tremendous and terrible desolation that

---

3) smouldering: 이글거리 는, 타오르는

sent fear swiftly dawning into his eyes.

"Bill!" he whispered, once and twice; "Bill!"

He cowered in the midst of the milky water, as though the vastness were pressing in upon him with overwhelming force, brutally crushing him with its complacent awfulness. He began to shake as with an ague-fit, till the gun fell from his hand with a splash. This served to rouse him. He fought with his fear and pulled himself together, groping in the water and recovering the weapon. He hitched his pack farther over on his left shoulder, so as to take a portion of its weight from off the injured ankle. Then he proceeded, slowly and carefully, wincing with pain, to the bank.

He did not stop. With a desperation that was madness, unmindful of the pain, he hurried up the slope to the crest of the hill over which his comrade had disappeared -- more grotesque and comical by far than that limping, jerking comrade. But at the crest he saw a shallow valley, empty of life. He fought with his fear again, overcame it, hitched the pack still farther over on his left shoulder, and lurched on down the slope.

The bottom of the valley was soggy with water, which the thick moss held, spongelike, close to the surface. This water squirted out from under his feet at every step, and each time he lifted a foot the action culminated in a sucking sound as the wet moss reluctantly released its grip. He picked his way from muskeg[4] to

4) muskeg: 북미 북부의(마른 나뭇잎이 쌓인) 소택 지대

muskeg, and followed the other man's footsteps along and across the rocky ledges which thrust like islets through the sea of moss.

Though alone, he was not lost. Farther on he knew he would come to where dead spruce and fir, very small and weazened, bordered the shore of a little lake, the titchin-nichilie, in the tongue of the country, the "land of little sticks." And into that lake flowed a small stream, the water of which was not milky. There was rush-grass on that stream -- this he remembered well -- but no timber, and he would follow it till its first trickle ceased at a divide. He would cross this divide to the first trickle of another stream, flowing to the west, which he would follow until it emptied into the river Dease, and here he would find a cache under an upturned canoe and piled over with many rocks. And in this cache would be ammunition for his empty gun, fish-hooks and lines, a small net -- all the utilities for the killing and snaring of food. Also, he would find flour, -- not much, -- a piece of bacon, and some beans.

Bill would be waiting for him there, and they would paddle away south down the Dease to the Great Bear Lake. And south across the lake they would go, ever south, till they gained the Mackenzie. And south, still south, they would go, while the winter raced vainly after them, and the ice formed in the eddies, and the days grew chill and crisp, south to some warm Hudson Bay Company post, where timber grew tall and generous and there was grub without end.

These were the thoughts of the man as he strove onward. But hard as he strove with his body, he strove equally hard with his mind, trying to think that Bill had not deserted him, that Bill would surely wait for him at the cache. He was compelled to think this thought, or else there would not be any use to strive, and he would have lain down and died. And as the dim ball of the sun sank slowly into the northwest he covered every inch -- and many times -- of his and Bill's flight south before the downcoming winter. And he conned the grub of the cache and the grub of the Hudson Bay Company post over and over again. He had not eaten for two days; for a far longer time he had not had all he wanted to eat. Often he stooped and picked pale muskeg berries, put them into his mouth, and chewed and swallowed them. A muskeg berry is a bit of seed enclosed in a bit of water. In the mouth the water melts away and the seed chews sharp and bitter. The man knew there was no nourishment in the berries, but he chewed them patiently with a hope greater than knowledge and defying experience.

At nine o'clock he stubbed his toe on a rocky ledge, and from sheer weariness and weakness staggered and fell. He lay for some time, without movement, on his side. Then he slipped out of the pack-straps and clumsily dragged himself into a sitting posture. It was not yet dark, and in the lingering twilight he groped about among the rocks for shreds of dry moss. When he had gathered a heap he built a fire, -- a smouldering, smudgy[5] fire, -- and put a tin pot of water on to boil.

He unwrapped his pack and the first thing he did was to count his matches. There were sixty-seven. He counted them

5) smudgy: 얼룩투성이의, 선명치 않은, 더러워진

three times to make sure. He divided them into several portions, wrapping them in oil paper, disposing of one bunch in his empty tobacco pouch, of another bunch in the inside band of his battered hat, of a third bunch under his shirt on the chest. This accomplished, a panic came upon him, and he unwrapped them all and counted them again. There were still sixty-seven.

He dried his wet foot-gear by the fire. The moccasins were in soggy shreds. The blanket socks were worn through in places, and his feet were raw and bleeding. His ankle was throbbing, and he gave it an examination. It had swollen to the size of his knee. He tore a long strip from one of his two blankets and bound the ankle tightly. He tore other strips and bound them about his feet to serve for both moccasins and socks. Then he drank the pot of water, steaming hot, wound his watch, and crawled between his blankets.

He slept like a dead man. The brief darkness around midnight came and went. The sun arose in the northeast -- at least the day dawned in that quarter, for the sun was hidden by gray clouds.

At six o'clock he awoke, quietly lying on his back. He gazed straight up into the gray sky and knew that he was hungry. As he rolled over on his elbow he was startled by a loud snort, and saw a bull caribou regarding him with alert curiosity. The animal was not more than fifty feet away, and instantly into the man's mind leaped the vision and the savor of a caribou steak sizzling and frying over a fire. Mechanically he reached for the empty gun, drew a bead, and pulled the trigger. The bull snorted and leaped away, his hoofs rattling and clattering as he fled across the ledges.

The man cursed and flung the empty gun from him. He groaned aloud as he started to drag himself to his feet. It was a slow and arduous[6] task. His joints were like rusty hinges. They worked harshly in their sockets, with much friction, and each bending or unbending was accomplished only through a sheer exertion of will. When he finally gained his feet, another minute or so was consumed in straightening up, so that he could stand erect as a man should stand.

He crawled up a small knoll and surveyed the prospect. There were no trees, no bushes, nothing but a gray sea of moss scarcely diversified by gray rocks, gray lakelets, and gray streamlets. The sky was gray. There was no sun nor hint of sun. He had no idea of north, and he had forgotten the way he had come to this spot the night before. But he was not lost. He knew that. Soon he would come to the land of the little sticks. He felt that it lay off to the left somewhere, not far -- possibly just over the next low hill.

He went back to put his pack into shape for travelling. He assured himself of the existence of his three separate parcels of matches, though he did not stop to count them. But he did linger, debating, over a squat moose-hide sack. It was not large. He could hide it under his two hands. He knew that it weighed fifteen pounds, -- as much as all the rest of the pack, -- and it worried him. He finally set it to one side and proceeded to roll

6) arduous: [일·훈련 등이] 몹시 힘드는, 견디기 어려운, 벅찬

the pack. He paused to gaze at the squat moose-hide sack. He picked it up hastily with a defiant glance about him, as though the desolation were trying to rob him of it; and when he rose to his feet to stagger on into the day, it was included in the pack on his back.

He bore away to the left, stopping now and again to eat muskeg berries. His ankle had stiffened, his limp was more pronounced, but the pain of it was as nothing compared with the pain of his stomach. The hunger pangs were sharp. They gnawed and gnawed[7] until he could not keep his mind steady on the course he must pursue to gain the land of little sticks. The muskeg berries did not allay this gnawing, while they made his tongue and the roof of his mouth sore with their irritating bite.

He came upon a valley where rock ptarmigan rose on whirring wings from the ledges and muskegs. Ker -- ker -- ker was the cry they made. He threw stones at them, but could not hit them. He placed his pack on the ground and stalked them as a cat stalks a sparrow. The sharp rocks cut through his pants' legs till his knees left a trail of blood; but the hurt was lost in the hurt of his hunger. He squirmed over the wet moss, saturating[8] his clothes and chilling his body; but he was not aware of it, so great was his fever for food. And always the ptarmigan rose, whirring, before him, till their ker -- ker -- ker became a mock to him, and he cursed them and cried aloud at them with their own cry.

Once he crawled upon one that must have been asleep. He did

---

7) gnawed and gnawed: 계속 괴롭히다

8) saturate: 흠뻑 적시다, 담그다, 젖어 버리게 하다

not see it till it shot up in his face from its rocky nook. He made a clutch as startled as was the rise of the ptarmigan, and there remained in his hand three tail-feathers. As he watched its flight he hated it, as though it had done him some terrible wrong. Then he returned and shouldered his pack.

As the day wore along he came into valleys or swales where game was more plentiful. A band of caribou passed by, twenty and odd animals, tantalizingly[9] within rifle range. He felt a wild desire to run after them, a certitude that he could run them down. A black fox came toward him, carrying a ptarmigan in his mouth. The man shouted. It was a fearful cry, but the fox, leaping away in fright, did not drop the ptarmigan.

Late in the afternoon he followed a stream, milky with lime, which ran through sparse patches of rush-grass. Grasping these rushes firmly near the root, he pulled up what resembled a young onion-sprout no larger than a shingle-nail. It was tender, and his teeth sank into it with a crunch that promised deliciously of food. But its fibers were tough. It was composed of stringy filaments saturated with water, like the berries, and devoid of nourishment. He threw off his pack and went into the rush-grass on hands and knees, crunching and munching, like some bovine creature.

He was very weary and often wished to rest -- to lie down and sleep; but he was continually driven on -- not so much by his desire to gain the land of little sticks as by his hunger. He

9) tantalizingly: 보이기만 하여도 감질나게, 애태우게, 흥미를 돋게 하여

searched little ponds for frogs and dug up the earth with his nails for worms, though he knew in spite that neither frogs nor worms existed so far north.

He looked into every pool of water vainly, until, as the long twilight came on, he discovered a solitary fish, the size of a minnow, in such a pool. He plunged his arm in up to the shoulder, but it eluded him. He reached for it with both hands and stirred up the milky mud at the bottom. In his excitement he fell in, wetting himself to the waist. Then the water was too muddy to admit of his seeing the fish, and he was compelled to wait until the sediment had settled.

The pursuit was renewed, till the water was again muddied. But he could not wait. He unstrapped the tin bucket and began to bale the pool. He baled wildly at first, splashing himself and flinging the water so short a distance that it ran back into the pool. He worked more carefully, striving to be cool, though his heart was pounding against his chest and his hands were trembling. At the end of half an hour the pool was nearly dry. Not a cupful of water remained. And there was no fish. He found a hidden crevice among the stones through which it had escaped to the adjoining and larger pool -- a pool which he could not empty in a night and a day. Had he known of the crevice, he could have closed it with a rock at the beginning and the fish would have been his.

Thus he thought, and crumpled up and sank down upon the wet earth. At first he cried softly to himself, then he cried loudly to the pitiless desolation that ringed him around; and for a long time after he was shaken by great dry sobs.

He built a fire and warmed himself by drinking quarts of hot water, and made camp on a rocky ledge in the same fashion he had the night before. The last thing he did was to see that his matches were dry and to wind his watch. The blankets were wet and clammy[10]. His ankle pulsed with pain. But he knew only that he was hungry, and through his restless sleep he dreamed of feasts and banquets and of food served and spread in all imaginable ways.

He awoke chilled and sick. There was no sun. The gray of earth and sky had become deeper, more profound. A raw wind was blowing, and the first flurries of snow were whitening the hilltops. The air about him thickened and grew white while he made a fire and boiled more water. It was wet snow, half rain, and the flakes were large and soggy. At first they melted as soon as they came in contact with the earth, but ever more fell, covering the ground, putting out the fire, spoiling his supply of moss-fuel.

This was a signal for him to strap on his pack and stumble onward, he knew not where. He was not concerned with the land of little sticks, nor with Bill and the cache under the upturned canoe by the river Dease. He was mastered by the verb "to eat." He was hunger-mad. He took no heed of the course he pursued, so long as that course led him through the swale bottoms. He felt his way through the wet snow to the watery

---

10) clammy: 진득거리고 차가운, 차갑고 습한

muskeg berries, and went by feel as he pulled up the rush-grass by the roots. But it was tasteless stuff and did not satisfy. He found a weed that tasted sour and he ate all he could find of it, which was not much, for it was a creeping growth, easily hidden under the several inches of snow.

He had no fire that night, nor hot water, and crawled under his blanket to sleep the broken hunger-sleep. The snow turned into a cold rain. He awakened many times to feel it falling on his upturned face. Day came -- a gray day and no sun. It had ceased raining. The keenness of his hunger had departed. Sensibility, as far as concerned the yearning for food, had been exhausted. There was a dull, heavy ache in his stomach, but it did not bother him so much. He was more rational, and once more he was chiefly interested in the land of little sticks and the cache by the river Dease.

He ripped the remnant of one of his blankets into strips and bound his bleeding feet. Also, he recinched the injured ankle and prepared himself for a day of travel. When he came to his pack, he paused long over the squat moose-hide sack, but in the end it went with him.

The snow had melted under the rain, and only the hilltops showed white. The sun came out, and he succeeded in locating the points of the compass, though he knew now that he was lost. Perhaps, in his previous days' wanderings, he had edged away too far to the left. He now bore off to the right to counteract the possible deviation from his true course.

Though the hunger pangs were no longer so exquisite, he

realized that he was weak. He was compelled to pause for frequent rests, when he attacked the muskeg berries and rush-grass patches. His tongue felt dry and large, as though covered with a fine hairy growth, and it tasted bitter in his mouth. His heart gave him a great deal of trouble. When he had travelled a few minutes it would begin a remorseless thump, thump, thump, and then leap up and away in a painful flutter of beats that choked him and made him go faint and dizzy.

In the middle of the day he found two minnows in a large pool. It was impossible to bale it, but he was calmer now and managed to catch them in his tin bucket. They were no longer than his little finger, but he was not particularly hungry. The dull ache in his stomach had been growing duller and fainter. It seemed almost that his stomach was dozing. He ate the fish raw, masticating[11] with painstaking care, for the eating was an act of pure reason. While he had no desire to eat, he knew that he must eat to live.

In the evening he caught three more minnows, eating two and saving the third for breakfast. The sun had dried stray shreds of moss, and he was able to warm himself with hot water. He had not covered more than ten miles that day; and the next day, travelling whenever his heart permitted him, he covered no more than five miles. But his stomach did not give him the slightest uneasiness. It had gone to sleep. He was in a strange country, too, and the caribou were growing more plentiful, also the wolves. Often their yelps drifted across the desolation, and once

11) masticate: (~을) 씹다, (고무 등을) 곤죽으로 하다, 저작하다

he saw three of them slinking away before his path.

Another night; and in the morning, being more rational, he untied the leather string that fastened the squat moose-hide sack. From its open mouth poured a yellow stream of coarse gold-dust and nuggets. He roughly divided the gold in halves, caching one half on a prominent ledge, wrapped in a piece of blanket, and returning the other half to the sack. He also began to use strips of the one remaining blanket for his feet. He still clung to his gun, for there were cartridges in that cache by the river Dease. This was a day of fog, and this day hunger awoke in him again. He was very weak and was afflicted with a giddiness which at times blinded him. It was no uncommon thing now for him to stumble and fall; and stumbling once, he fell squarely into a ptarmigan nest. There were four newly hatched chicks, a day old -- little specks of pulsating life no more than a mouthful; and he ate them ravenously, thrusting them alive into his mouth and crunching them like egg-shells between his teeth. The mother ptarmigan beat about him with great outcry. He used his gun as a club with which to knock her over, but she dodged out of reach. He threw stones at her and with one chance shot broke a wing. Then she fluttered away, running, trailing the broken wing, with him in pursuit.

The little chicks had no more than whetted his appetite. He hopped and bobbed clumsily along on his injured ankle, throwing stones and screaming hoarsely at times; at other times hopping and bobbing silently along, picking himself up grimly and patiently when he fell, or rubbing his eyes with his hand when the giddiness threatened to overpower him.

The chase led him across swampy ground in the bottom of the valley, and he came upon footprints in the soggy moss. They were not his own -- he could see that. They must be Bill's. But he could not stop, for the mother ptarmigan was running on. He would catch her first, then he would return and investigate.

He exhausted the mother ptarmigan; but he exhausted himself. She lay panting on her side. He lay panting on his side, a dozen feet away, unable to crawl to her. And as he recovered she recovered, fluttering out of reach as his hungry hand went out to her. The chase was resumed. Night settled down and she escaped. He stumbled from weakness and pitched head foremost on his face, cutting his cheek, his pack upon his back. He did not move for a long while; then he rolled over on his side, wound his watch, and lay there until morning.

Another day of fog. Half of his last blanket had gone into foot-wrappings. He failed to pick up Bill's trail. It did not matter. His hunger was driving him too compellingly -- only -- only he wondered if Bill, too, were lost. By midday the irk of his pack became too oppressive. Again he divided the gold, this time merely spilling half of it on the ground. In the afternoon he threw the rest of it away, there remaining to him only the half-blanket, the tin bucket, and the rifle.

An hallucination began to trouble him. He felt confident that one cartridge remained to him. It was in the chamber of the rifle and he had overlooked it. On the other hand, he knew all the time that the chamber was empty. But the hallucination persisted. He fought it off for hours, then threw his rifle open and was confronted with emptiness. The disappointment was as bitter as though he had really expected to find the cartridge.

He plodded on for half an hour, when the hallucination arose again. Again he fought it, and still it persisted, till for very relief he opened his rifle to unconvince himself. At times his mind wandered farther afield, and he plodded on, a mere automaton, strange conceits and whimsicalities[12] gnawing at his brain like worms. But these excursions out of the real were of brief duration, for ever the pangs of the hunger-bite called him back. He was jerked back abruptly once from such an excursion by a sight that caused him nearly to faint. He reeled and swayed, doddering like a drunken man to keep from falling. Before him stood a horse. A horse! He could not believe his eyes. A thick mist was in them, intershot with sparkling points of light. He rubbed his eyes savagely to clear his vision, and beheld, not a horse, but a great brown bear. The animal was studying him with bellicose[13] curiosity.

The man had brought his gun halfway to his shoulder before he realized. He lowered it and drew his hunting-knife from its beaded sheath at his hip. Before him was meat and life. He ran his thumb along the edge of his knife. It was sharp. The point was sharp. He would fling himself upon the bear and kill it. But his heart began its warning thump, thump, thump. Then followed the wild upward leap and tattoo of flutters, the pressing

12) whimsicalities: [불가산] 변덕(스러움), 일시적 기분, [가산] (보통 -ies) 별난 생각, 기행(奇行)

13) bellicose: (문어) 호전적인(belligerent), 싸우기 좋아하는

as of an iron band about his forehead, the creeping of the dizziness into his brain.

His desperate courage was evicted by a great surge of fear. In his weakness, what if the animal attacked him? He drew himself up to his most imposing stature, gripping the knife and staring hard at the bear. The bear advanced clumsily a couple of steps, reared up, and gave vent to a tentative growl. If the man ran, he would run after him; but the man did not run. He was animated now with the courage of fear. He, too, growled, savagely, terribly, voicing the fear that is to life germane and that lies twisted about life's deepest roots.

The bear edged away to one side, growling menacingly, himself appalled by this mysterious creature that appeared upright and unafraid. But the man did not move. He stood like a statue till the danger was past, when he yielded to a fit of trembling and sank down into the wet moss.

He pulled himself together and went on, afraid now in a new way. It was not the fear that he should die passively from lack of food, but that he should be destroyed violently before starvation had exhausted the last particle of the endeavor in him that made toward surviving. There were the wolves. Back and forth across the desolation drifted their howls, weaving the very air into a fabric of menace that was so tangible that he found himself, arms in the air, pressing it back from him as it might be the walls of a wind-blown tent.

Now and again the wolves, in packs of two and three, crossed his path. But they sheered clear of him. They were not in sufficient numbers, and besides they were hunting the caribou, which did not battle, while this strange creature that walked erect might scratch and bite.

In the late afternoon he came upon scattered bones where the wolves had made a kill. The d bris had been a caribou calf an hour before, squawking and running and very much alive. He contemplated the bones, clean-picked and polished, pink with the cell-life in them which had not yet died. Could it possibly be that he might be that ere the day was done! Such was life, eh? A vain and fleeting thing. It was only life that pained. There was no hurt in death. To die was to sleep. It meant cessation, rest. Then why was he not content to die?

But he did not moralize long. He was squatting in the moss, a bone in his mouth, sucking at the shreds of life that still dyed it faintly pink. The sweet meaty taste, thin and elusive almost as a memory, maddened him. He closed his jaws on the bones and crunched. Sometimes it was the bone that broke, sometimes his teeth. Then he crushed the bones between rocks, pounded them to a pulp, and swallowed them. He pounded his fingers, too, in his haste, and yet found a moment in which to feel surprise at the fact that his fingers did not hurt much when caught under the descending rock.

Came frightful days of snow and rain. He did not know when he made camp, when he broke camp. He travelled in the night as much as in the day. He rested wherever he fell, crawled on whenever the dying life in him flickered up and burned less dimly. He, as a man, no longer strove. It was the life in him, unwilling to die, that drove him on. He did not suffer. His nerves had become blunted, numb, while his mind was filled with weird visions and delicious dreams.

But ever he sucked and chewed on the crushed bones of the caribou calf, the least remnants of which he had gathered up and carried with him. He crossed no more hills or divides, but automatically followed a large stream which flowed through a wide and shallow valley. He did not see this stream nor this valley. He saw nothing save visions. Soul and body walked or crawled side by side, yet apart, so slender was the thread that bound them.

He awoke in his right mind, lying on his back on a rocky ledge. The sun was shining bright and warm. Afar off he heard the squawking of caribou calves. He was aware of vague memories of rain and wind and snow, but whether he had been beaten by the storm for two days or two weeks he did not know.

For some time he lay without movement, the genial sunshine pouring upon him and saturating his miserable body with its warmth. A fine day, he thought. Perhaps he could manage to locate himself. By a painful effort he rolled over on his side. Below him flowed a wide and sluggish river. Its unfamiliarity puzzled him. Slowly he followed it with his eyes, winding in wide sweeps among the bleak, bare hills, bleaker and barer and lower-lying than any hills he had yet encountered. Slowly, deliberately, without excitement or more than the most casual interest, he followed the course of the strange stream toward the sky-line and saw it emptying into a bright and shining sea. He was still unexcited. Most unusual, he thought, a vision or a mirage -- more likely a vision, a trick of his disordered mind. He was confirmed in this by sight of a ship lying at anchor in the midst of the shining sea. He closed his eyes for a while, then opened them. Strange how the vision persisted! Yet not strange. He knew there were no seas or ships in the heart of the barren lands, just as he had known there was no cartridge in the empty rifle.

He heard a snuffle behind him -- a half-choking gasp or cough. Very slowly, because of his exceeding weakness and stiffness, he rolled over on his other side. He could see nothing near at hand, but he waited patiently. Again came the snuffle and cough, and outlined between two jagged rocks not a score of feet away he made out the gray head of a wolf. The sharp ears were not pricked so sharply as he had seen them on other wolves; the eyes were bleared and bloodshot[14], the head seemed to droop limply and forlornly. The animal blinked continually in the sunshine. It seemed sick. As he looked it snuffled[15] and coughed again.

This, at least, was real, he thought, and turned on the other side so that he might see the reality of the world which had been veiled from him before by the vision. But the sea still shone in the distance and the ship was plainly discernible. Was it reality, after all? He closed his eyes for a long while and thought, and then it came to him. He had been making north by east, away from the Dease Divide and into the Coppermine Valley. This wide and sluggish river[16] was the Coppermine. That shining

---

14) bloodshot: [눈이] 충혈된, 핏발이 선

15) snuffle: 코를 킁킁거리다, 코멘소리를 내며 호흡하다, 콧물을 훌쩍이다

16) wide and sluggish river: 넓고 느린 강

sea was the Arctic Ocean. That ship was a whaler, strayed east, far east, from the mouth of the Mackenzie, and it was lying at anchor in Coronation Gulf. He remembered the Hudson Bay Company chart he had seen long ago, and it was all clear and reasonable to him.

He sat up and turned his attention to immediate affairs. He had worn through the blanket-wrappings, and his feet were shapeless lumps of raw meat. His last blanket was gone. Rifle and knife were both missing. He had lost his hat somewhere, with the bunch of matches in the band, but the matches against his chest were safe and dry inside the tobacco pouch[17] and oil paper. He looked at his watch. It marked eleven o'clock and was still running. Evidently he had kept it wound.

He was calm and collected. Though extremely weak, he had no sensation of pain. He was not hungry. The thought of food was not even pleasant to him, and whatever he did was done by his reason alone. He ripped off his pants' legs to the knees and bound them about his feet. Somehow he had succeeded in retaining the tin bucket. He would have some hot water before he began what he foresaw was to be a terrible journey to the ship.

His movements were slow. He shook as with a palsy. When he started to collect dry moss, he found he could not rise to his feet. He tried again and again, then contented himself with crawling about on hands and knees. Once he crawled near to the sick wolf. The animal dragged itself reluctantly out of his way, licking its chops with a tongue which seemed hardly to have the

17) tobacco pouch: 살담배 쌈지, 담배 쌈지

strength to curl. The man noticed that the tongue was not the customary healthy red. It was a yellowish brown and seemed coated with a rough and half-dry mucus[18].

After he had drunk a quart of hot water the man found he was able to stand, and even to walk as well as a dying man might be supposed to walk. Every minute or so he was compelled to rest. His steps were feeble and uncertain, just as the wolf's that trailed him were feeble and uncertain; and that night, when the shining sea was blotted out by blackness, he knew he was nearer to it by no more than four miles.

Throughout the night he heard the cough of the sick wolf, and now and then the squawking of the caribou calves. There was life all around him, but it was strong life, very much alive and well, and he knew the sick wolf clung to the sick man's trail in the hope that the man would die first. In the morning, on opening his eyes, he beheld it regarding him with a wistful and hungry stare. It stood crouched, with tail between its legs, like a miserable and woe-begone dog. It shivered in the chill morning wind, and grinned dispiritedly when the man spoke to it in a voice that achieved no more than a hoarse whisper.

The sun rose brightly, and all morning the man tottered and fell toward the ship on the shining sea. The weather was perfect. It was the brief Indian Summer of the high latitudes. It might last a week. To-morrow or next day it might be gone.

---

18) mucus: [불가산] 점액, (식물의) 진, 콧물, 코딱지

In the afternoon the man came upon a trail. It was of another man, who did not walk, but who dragged himself on all fours. The man thought it might be Bill, but he thought in a dull, uninterested way. He had no curiosity. In fact, sensation and emotion had left him. He was no longer susceptible to pain. Stomach and nerves had gone to sleep. Yet the life that was in him drove him on. He was very weary, but it refused to die. It was because it refused to die that he still ate muskeg berries and minnows[19], drank his hot water, and kept a wary eye on the sick wolf.

He followed the trail of the other man who dragged himself along, and soon came to the end of it -- a few fresh-picked bones where the soggy moss was marked by the foot-pads of many wolves. He saw a squat moose-hide sack, mate to his own, which had been torn by sharp teeth. He picked it up, though its weight was almost too much for his feeble fingers. Bill had carried it to the last. Ha! ha! He would have the laugh on Bill. He would survive and carry it to the ship in the shining sea. His mirth was hoarse and ghastly, like a raven's croak, and the sick wolf joined him, howling lugubriously. The man ceased suddenly. How could he have the laugh on Bill if that were Bill; if those bones, so pinky-white and clean, were Bill?

He turned away. Well, Bill had deserted him; but he would not take the gold, nor would he suck Bill's bones. Bill would have, though, had it been the other way around, he mused as he staggered on. He came to a pool of water. Stooping over in quest of minnows, he jerked his head back as though he had

19) minnow: 작은 물고기, 유럽산 잉엇과의 작은 물고기

been stung. He had caught sight of his reflected face. So horrible was it that sensibility awoke long enough to be shocked. There were three minnows in the pool, which was too large to drain; and after several ineffectual attempts to catch them in the tin bucket he forbore. He was afraid, because of his great weakness, that he might fall in and drown. It was for this reason that he did not trust himself to the river astride one of the many drift-logs which lined its sand-spits[20].

That day he decreased the distance between him and the ship by three miles; the next day by two -- for he was crawling now as Bill had crawled; and the end of the fifth day found the ship still seven miles away and him unable to make even a mile a day. Still the Indian Summer held on, and he continued to crawl and faint, turn and turn about; and ever the sick wolf coughed and wheezed at his heels. His knees had become raw meat like his feet, and though he padded them with the shirt from his back it was a red track he left behind him on the moss and stones. Once, glancing back, he saw the wolf licking hungrily his bleeding trail, and he saw sharply what his own end might be -- unless -- unless he could get the wolf. Then began as grim a tragedy of existence as was ever played -- a sick man that crawled, a sick wolf that limped, two creatures dragging their dying carcasses across the desolation and hunting each other's lives.

Had it been a well wolf, it would not have mattered so much to the man; but the thought of going to feed the maw of that loathsome and all but dead thing was repugnant[21] to him. He

---

20) sand-spits: (좁고 뾰족한) 곳, 모래톱(spit)

21) repugnant: 싫은, 불쾌한, 일치하지 않는

was finicky. His mind had begun to wander again, and to be perplexed by hallucinations[22], while his lucid intervals grew rarer and shorter.

He was awakened once from a faint by a wheeze close in his ear. The wolf leaped lamely back, losing its footing and falling in its weakness. It was ludicrous, but he was not amused. Nor was he even afraid. He was too far gone for that. But his mind was for the moment clear, and he lay and considered. The ship was no more than four miles away. He could see it quite distinctly when he rubbed the mists out of his eyes, and he could see the white sail of a small boat cutting the water of the shining sea. But he could never crawl those four miles. He knew that, and was very calm in the knowledge. He knew that he could not crawl half a mile. And yet he wanted to live. It was unreasonable that he should die after all he had undergone. Fate asked too much of him. And, dying, he declined to die. It was stark madness, perhaps, but in the very grip of Death he defied Death and refused to die.

He closed his eyes and composed himself with infinite precaution. He steeled himself to keep above the suffocating languor that lapped like a rising tide through all the wells of his being. It was very like a sea, this deadly languor, that rose and rose and drowned his consciousness bit by bit. Sometimes he was all but submerged, swimming through oblivion with a faltering stroke; and again, by some strange alchemy of soul, he would find another shred of will and strike out more strongly.

Without movement he lay on his back, and he could hear, slowly

22) hallucination: 환각, 환상, 망상

drawing near and nearer, the wheezing intake and output of the sick wolf's breath. It drew closer, ever closer, through an infinitude of time, and he did not move. It was at his ear. The harsh dry tongue grated like sandpaper against his cheek. His hands shot out – or at least he willed them to shoot out. The fingers were curved like talons, but they closed on empty air. Swiftness and certitude require strength, and the man had not this strength.

The patience of the wolf was terrible. The man's patience was no less terrible. For half a day he lay motionless, fighting off unconsciousness and waiting for the thing that was to feed upon him and upon which he wished to feed. Sometimes the languid sea rose over him and he dreamed long dreams; but ever through it all, waking and dreaming, he waited for the wheezing breath and the harsh caress of the tongue.

He did not hear the breath, and he slipped slowly from some dream to the feel of the tongue along his hand. He waited. The fangs pressed softly; the pressure increased; the wolf was exerting its last strength in an effort to sink teeth in the food for which it had waited so long. But the man had waited long, and the lacerated hand closed on the jaw. Slowly, while the wolf struggled feebly and the hand clutched feebly, the other hand crept across to a grip. Five minutes later the whole weight of the man's body was on top of the wolf. The hands had not sufficient strength to choke the wolf, but the face of the man was pressed close to the throat of the wolf and the mouth of the man was full of hair. At the end of half an hour the man was aware of a warm trickle in his throat. It was not pleasant. It was like molten lead being forced into his stomach, and it was forced by his will alone. Later the man rolled over on his back and slept. * * *

There were some members of a scientific expedition on the whale-ship Bedford. From the deck they remarked a strange object on the shore. It was moving down the beach toward the water. They were unable to classify it, and, being scientific men, they climbed into the whale-boat alongside and went ashore to see. And they saw something that was alive but which could hardly be called a man. It was blind, unconscious. It squirmed along the ground like some monstrous worm. Most of its efforts were ineffectual, but it was persistent, and it writhed and twisted and went ahead perhaps a score of feet an hour. * * *

Three weeks afterward the man lay in a bunk on the whale-ship Bedford, and with tears streaming down his wasted cheeks told who he was and what he had undergone. He also babbled incoherently of his mother, of sunny Southern California, and a home among the orange groves and flowers.

The days were not many after that when he sat at table with the scientific men and ship's officers. He gloated[23] over the spectacle of so much food, watching it anxiously as it went into the mouths of others. With the disappearance of each mouthful an expression of deep regret came into his eyes. He was quite sane, yet he hated those men at meal-time. He was haunted by a fear that the food would not last. He inquired of the cook, the cabin-boy, the captain, concerning the food stores. They reassured him countless times; but he could not believe them,

23) gloated:~을 만족스럽게[기쁘게, 홀린 듯이] 바라보다

and pried cunningly about the lazarette to see with his own eyes.

It was noticed that the man was getting fat. He grew stouter with each day. The scientific men shook their heads and theorized. They limited the man at his meals, but still his girth increased and he swelled prodigiously under his shirt.

The sailors grinned. They knew. And when the scientific men set a watch on the man, they knew too. They saw him slouch for'ard after breakfast, and, like a mendicant, with outstretched palm, accost[24] a sailor. The sailor grinned and passed him a fragment of sea biscuit. He clutched it avariciously, looked at it as a miser looks at gold, and thrust it into his shirt bosom. Similar were the donations from other grinning sailors. The scientific men were discreet. They let him alone. But they privily examined his bunk. It was lined with hardtack[25]; the mattress was stuffed with hardtack; every nook and cranny was filled with hardtack. Yet he was sane. He was taking precautions against another possible famine -- that was all. He would recover from it, the scientific men said; and he did, ere the Bedford's anchor rumbled down[26] in San Francisco Bay.

(Site maintained by Roy Tennant and Clarice Stasz, PhD.)

24) accost: 말을 걸다, 인사하다, 상대방에게 다가가서 말을 걸다

25) hardtack: 건빵, 딱딱한 비스킷, 돈

26) rumbled down: 소리내며 내려갔다

TO BUILD A FIRE

(First published in The Century Magazine, v.76, August, 1908, 525-534)

NOTE: This is the famous, second version of a story first published in a more juvenile treatment for the Youth's Companion on May 29, 1902. To compare the two versions side-by-side, open the earlier version in a new window (you will need to adjust the browser windows to fit them both on your screen). A concordance (a way to find words in context, how often they occur, etc.) is also available.

Day had broken cold and gray, exceedingly cold and gray, when the man turned aside from the main Yukon trail and climbed the high earth-bank, where a dim and little-travelled trail led eastward through the fat spruce timberland. It was a steep bank, and he paused for breath at the top, excusing the act to himself by looking at his watch. It was nine o'clock. There was no sun nor hint of sun, though there was not a cloud in the sky. It was a clear day, and yet there seemed an intangible pall over the face of things, a subtle gloom that made the day dark, and that was due to the absence of sun. This fact did not worry the man. He was used to the lack of sun. It had been days since he had seen the sun, and he knew that a few more days must pass before that cheerful orb, due south, would just peep above the sky-line and dip immediately from view.

The man flung a look back along the way he had come. The Yukon lay a mile wide and hidden under three feet of ice. On top of this ice were as many feet of snow. It was all pure white, rolling in gentle undulations[1] where the ice-jams of the freeze-up had formed. North and south, as far as his eye could see, it was unbroken white, save for a dark hair-line that curved and twisted from around the spruce-covered island to the south, and that curved and twisted away into the north, where it disappeared behind another spruce-covered island. This dark hair-line was the trail -- the main trail -- that led south five hundred miles to the Chilcoot Pass, Dyea, and salt water; and that led north seventy miles to Dawson, and still on to the north a thousand miles to Nulato, and finally to St. Michael on Bering Sea, a thousand miles and half a thousand more.

But all this -- the mysterious, far-reaching hair-line trail, the absence of sun from the sky, the tremendous cold, and the strangeness and weirdness of it all -- made no impression on the man. It was not because he was long used to it. He was a newcomer in the land, a chechaquo[2], and this was his first winter. The trouble with him was that he was without imagination. He was quick and alert in the things of life, but only in the things, and not in the significances. Fifty degrees below zero meant eighty-odd degrees of frost. Such fact impressed him as being cold and uncomfortable, and that was all. It did not lead him to meditate upon his frailty as a creature of temperature, and upon man's frailty in general, able only to live within certain narrow limits of heat and cold; and from there on it did not lead him to the conjectural[3] field of immortality and man's place in the

1) undulation: 파동, 넘실거림, 물결 모양

2) chechaquo: 신참자, 신출내기

3) conjectural: 억측상의, 확정적이 아닌, 불확실한, 추측하기 좋아하는

universe. Fifty degrees below zero stood for a bite of frost that hurt and that must be guarded against by the use of mittens, ear-flaps, warm moccasins, and thick socks. Fifty degrees below zero was to him just precisely fifty degrees below zero. That there should be anything more to it than that was a thought that never entered his head.

As he turned to go on, he spat speculatively. There was a sharp, explosive crackle that startled him. He spat again. And again, in the air, before it could fall to the snow, the spittle crackled. He knew that at fifty below spittle crackled on the snow, but this spittle had crackled in the air. Undoubtedly it was colder than fifty below -- how much colder he did not know. But the temperature did not matter. He was bound for the old claim on the left fork of Henderson Creek, where the boys were already. They had come over across the divide from the Indian Creek country, while he had come the roundabout way[4] to take a look at the possibilities of getting out logs in the spring from the islands in the Yukon. He would be in to camp by six o'clock; a bit after dark, it was true, but the boys would be there, a fire would be going, and a hot supper would be ready. As for lunch, he pressed his hand against the protruding bundle under his jacket. It was also under his shirt, wrapped up in a handkerchief and lying against the naked skin. It was the only way to keep the biscuits from freezing. He smiled agreeably to himself as he thought of those biscuits, each cut open and sopped in bacon grease, and each enclosing a generous slice of fried bacon.

4) the roundabout way: 돌아서 가는 길, 우회적[간접적]인 방법

He plunged in among the big spruce trees. The trail was faint. A foot of snow had fallen since the last sled had passed over, and he was glad he was without a sled, travelling light. In fact, he carried nothing but the lunch wrapped in the handkerchief. He was surprised, however, at the cold. It certainly was cold, he concluded, as he rubbed his numb nose and cheek-bones with his mittened hand. He was a warm-whiskered man, but the hair on his face did not protect the high cheek-bones and the eager nose that thrust itself aggressively into the frosty air.

At the man's heels trotted a dog, a big native husky, the proper wolf-dog, gray-coated and without any visible or temperamental[5] difference from its brother, the wild wolf. The animal was depressed by the tremendous cold. It knew that it was no time for travelling. Its instinct told it a truer tale than was told to the man by the man's judgment. In reality, it was not merely colder than fifty below zero; it was colder than sixty below, than seventy below. It was seventy-five below zero. Since the freezing-point is thirty-two above zero, it meant that one hundred and seven degrees of frost obtained. The dog did not know anything about thermometers. Possibly in its brain there was no sharp consciousness of a condition of very cold such as was in the man's brain. But the brute had its instinct. It experienced a vague but menacing apprehension that subdued it and made it slink along at the man's heels, and that made it question eagerly every unwonted movement of the man as if expecting him to go into camp or to seek shelter somewhere and build a fire. The dog had learned fire, and it wanted fire, or else to burrow under the

---

5) temperamental: 기질의, 신경질적인, 변덕스러운, 까다로운

snow and cuddle its warmth away from the air.

The frozen moisture of its breathing had settled on its fur in a fine powder of frost, and especially were its jowls, muzzle, and eyelashes whitened by its crystalled breath. The man's red beard and mustache were likewise frosted, but more solidly, the deposit taking the form of ice and increasing with every warm, moist breath he exhaled. Also, the man was chewing tobacco, and the muzzle of ice held his lips so rigidly that he was unable to clear his chin when he expelled the juice. The result was that a crystal beard of the color and solidity of amber was increasing its length on his chin. If he fell down it would shatter itself, like glass, into brittle fragments. But he did not mind the appendage[6]. It was the penalty all tobacco-chewers paid in that country, and he had been out before in two cold snaps. They had not been so cold as this, he knew, but by the spirit thermometer at Sixty Mile he knew they had been registered at fifty below and at fifty-five.

He held on through the level stretch of woods for several miles, crossed a wide flat of niggerheads[7], and dropped down a bank to the frozen bed of a small stream. This was Henderson Creek, and he knew he was ten miles from the forks. He looked at his watch. It was ten o'clock. He was making four miles an hour, and he calculated that he would arrive at the forks at half-past twelve. He decided to celebrate that event by eating his lunch there.

---

6) appendage: 첨가[부가]물, [~의] 부속물[to · ·], 종속물

7) niggerhead: 색이 검은 씹는 담배, 니거헤드탄, 니거헤드

The dog dropped in again at his heels, with a tail drooping discouragement, as the man swung along the creek-bed. The furrow of the old sled-trail was plainly visible, but a dozen inches of snow covered the marks of the last runners. In a month no man had come up or down that silent creek. The man held steadily on. He was not much given to thinking, and just then particularly he had nothing to think about save that he would eat lunch at the forks and that at six o'clock he would be in camp with the boys. There was nobody to talk to; and, had there been, speech would have been impossible because of the ice-muzzle on his mouth. So he continued monotonously to chew tobacco and to increase the length of his amber beard.

Once in a while the thought reiterated itself that it was very cold and that he had never experienced such cold. As he walked along he rubbed his cheek-bones and nose with the back of his mittened hand. He did this automatically, now and again changing hands. But rub as he would, the instant he stopped his cheek-bones went numb, and the following instant the end of his nose went numb. He was sure to frost his cheeks; he knew that, and experienced a pang of regret that he had not devised a nose-strap of the sort Bud wore in cold snaps. Such a strap passed across the cheeks, as well, and saved them. But it didn't matter much, after all. What were frosted cheeks? A bit painful, that was all; they were never serious.

Empty as the man's mind was of thoughts, he was keenly observant, and he noticed the changes in the creek, the curves and bends and timber-jams, and always he sharply noted where he placed his feet. Once, coming around a bend, he shied abruptly, like a startled horse, curved away from the place where he had been walking, and retreated several paces back along the trail. The creek he knew was frozen clear to the bottom, -- no creek could contain water in that arctic winter, -- but he knew also that there were springs that bubbled out from the hillsides and ran along under the snow and on top the ice of the creek. He knew that the coldest snaps never froze these springs, and he knew likewise their danger. They were traps. They hid pools of water under the snow that might be three inches deep, or three feet. Sometimes a skin of ice half an inch thick covered them, and in turn was covered by the snow. Sometimes there were alternate layers of water and ice-skin, so that when one broke through he kept on breaking through for a while, sometimes wetting himself to the waist.

That was why he had shied in such panic. He had felt the give under his feet and heard the crackle of a snow-hidden ice-skin. And to get his feet wet in such a temperature meant trouble and danger. At the very least it meant delay, for he would be forced to stop and build a fire, and under its protection to bare his feet while he dried his socks and moccasins. He stood and studied the creek-bed and its banks, and decided that the flow of water came from the right. He reflected awhile, rubbing his nose and cheeks, then skirted to the left, stepping gingerly and testing the footing for each step. Once clear of the danger, he took a fresh chew of tobacco and swung along at his four-mile gait. In the course of the next two hours he came upon several similar traps. Usually the snow above the hidden pools had a sunken, candied appearance that advertised the danger. Once again, however, he had a close call; and once, suspecting danger, he compelled the dog to go on in front. The dog did not want to go. It hung back until the man shoved it forward, and then it went quickly across the white, unbroken surface. Suddenly it broke through, floundered to one side, and got away to firmer footing. It had wet its forefeet and legs, and almost immediately the water that clung to it turned to ice. It made quick efforts to lick the ice off its legs, then dropped down in the snow and began to bite out the ice that had formed between the toes. This was a matter of instinct. To permit the ice to remain would mean sore feet. It did not know this. It merely obeyed the mysterious prompting that arose from the deep crypts of its being. But the man knew, having achieved a judgment on the subject, and he removed the mitten from his right hand and helped tear out the ice-particles. He did not expose his fingers more than a minute, and was astonished at the swift numbness that smote them. It certainly was cold. He pulled on the mitten hastily, and beat the hand savagely across his chest.

At twelve o'clock the day was at its brightest. Yet the sun was too far south on its winter journey to clear the horizon. The bulge of the earth intervened between it and Henderson Creek, where the man walked under a clear sky at noon and cast no shadow. At half-past twelve, to the minute, he arrived at the forks of the creek. He was pleased at the speed he had made. If he kept it up, he would certainly be with the boys by six. He unbuttoned his jacket and shirt and drew forth his lunch. The action consumed no more than a quarter of a minute, yet in that brief moment the numbness laid hold of the exposed fingers. He did not put the mitten on, but, instead, struck the fingers a dozen sharp smashes against his leg. Then he sat down on a snow-covered log to eat. The sting that followed upon the striking of his fingers against his leg ceased so quickly that he was startled. He had had no chance to take a bite of biscuit. He struck the fingers repeatedly and returned them to the mitten, baring the other hand for the purpose of eating. He tried to take a mouthful, but the ice-muzzle prevented. He had forgotten to build a fire and thaw out. He chuckled at his foolishness, and as he chuckled he noted the numbness creeping into the exposed fingers. Also, he noted that the stinging which had first come to his toes when he sat down was already passing away. He wondered whether the toes were warm or numb. He moved them inside the moccasins and decided that they were numb.

He pulled the mitten on hurriedly and stood up. He was a bit frightened. He stamped up and down until the stinging returned into the feet. It certainly was cold, was his thought. That man from Sulphur Creek had spoken the truth when telling how cold it sometimes got in the country. And he had laughed at him at the time! That showed one must not be too sure of things. There was no mistake about it, it was cold. He strode up and down, stamping his feet and threshing his arms, until reassured by the returning warmth. Then he got out matches and proceeded to make a fire. From the undergrowth, where high water of the previous spring had lodged a supply of seasoned twigs, he got his fire-wood. Working carefully from a small beginning, he soon had a roaring fire, over which he thawed the ice from his face and in the protection of which he ate his biscuits. For the moment the cold of space was outwitted[8]. The dog took

8) outwitted: ~을 계략으로 앞서다, ~보다 한 수 위이다, ~보다 약다

satisfaction in the fire, stretching out close enough for warmth and far enough away to escape being singed.

When the man had finished, he filled his pipe and took his comfortable time over a smoke. Then he pulled on his mittens, settled the ear-flaps[9] of his cap firmly about his ears, and took the creek trail up the left fork. The dog was disappointed and yearned back toward the fire. This man did not know cold. Possibly all the generations of his ancestry had been ignorant of cold, of real cold, of cold one hundred and seven degrees below freezing-point. But the dog knew; all its ancestry knew, and it had inherited the knowledge. And it knew that it was not good to walk abroad in such fearful cold. It was the time to lie snug in a hole in the snow and wait for a curtain of cloud to be drawn across the face of outer space whence this cold came. On the other hand, there was no keen intimacy between the dog and the man. The one was the toil-slave of the other, and the only caresses it had ever received were the caresses of the whip-lash and of harsh and menacing throat-sounds that threatened the whip-lash. So the dog made no effort to communicate its apprehension to the man. It was not concerned in the welfare of the man; it was for its own sake that it yearned back toward the fire. But the man whistled, and spoke to it with the sound of whip-lashes, and the dog swung in at the man's heels and followed after.

The man took a chew of tobacco and proceeded to start a new amber beard. Also, his moist breath quickly powdered

---

9) ear-flaps: (모자에 달린 방한용) 귀마개, [의학] 귓바퀴

with white his mustache, eyebrows, and lashes. There did not seem to be so many springs on the left fork of the Henderson, and for half an hour the man saw no signs of any. And then it happened. At a place where there were no signs, where the soft, unbroken snow seemed to advertise solidity beneath, the man broke through. It was not deep. He wet himself halfway to the knees before he floundered out to the firm crust.

He was angry, and cursed his luck aloud. He had hoped to get into camp with the boys at six o'clock, and this would delay him an hour, for he would have to build a fire and dry out his foot-gear. This was imperative at that low temperature -- he knew that much; and he turned aside to the bank, which he climbed. On top, tangled in the underbrush about the trunks of several small spruce trees, was a high-water deposit of dry fire-wood -- sticks and twigs, principally, but also larger portions of seasoned branches and fine, dry, last-year's grasses. He threw down several large pieces on top of the snow. This served for a foundation and prevented the young flame from drowning itself in the snow it otherwise would melt. The flame he got by touching a match to a small shred of birch-bark that he took from his pocket. This burned even more readily than paper. Placing it on the foundation, he fed the young flame with wisps of dry grass and with the tiniest dry twigs.

He worked slowly and carefully, keenly aware of his danger. Gradually, as the flame grew stronger, he increased the size of the twigs with which he fed it. He squatted in the snow, pulling the twigs out from their entanglement in the brush and feeding directly to the flame. He knew there must be no failure. When it is seventy-five below zero, a man must not fail in his first attempt to build a fire -- that is, if his feet are wet. If his feet are dry, and he fails, he can run along the trail for half a mile and restore his circulation. But the circulation of wet and freezing feet cannot be restored by running when it is seventy-five below. No matter how fast he runs, the wet feet will freeze the harder.

All this the man knew. The old-timer on Sulphur Creek had told him about it the previous fall, and now he was appreciating the advice. Already all sensation had gone out of his feet. To build the fire he had been forced to remove his mittens, and the fingers had quickly gone numb. His pace of four miles an hour had kept his heart pumping blood to the surface of his body and to all the extremities. But the instant he stopped, the action of the pump eased down. The cold of space smote the unprotected tip of the planet, and he, being on that unprotected tip, received the full force of the blow. The blood of his body recoiled before it. The blood was alive, like the dog, and like the dog it wanted to hide away and cover itself up from the fearful cold. So long as he walked four miles an hour, he pumped that blood, willy-nilly, to the surface; but now it ebbed away and sank down into the recesses of his body. The extremities were the first to feel its absence. His wet feet froze the faster, and his exposed fingers numbed the faster, though they had not yet begun to freeze. Nose and cheeks were already freezing, while the skin of all his body chilled as it lost its blood.

But he was safe. Toes and nose and cheeks would be only touched by the frost, for the fire was beginning to burn with strength. He was feeding it with twigs the size of his finger. In another minute he would be able to feed it with branches the size of his wrist, and then he could remove his wet foot-gear, and, while it dried, he could keep his naked feet warm by the fire, rubbing them at first, of course, with snow. The fire was a success. He was safe. He remembered the advice of the old-timer on Sulphur Creek, and smiled. The old-timer had been very serious in laying down the law that no man must travel alone in the Klondike after fifty below. Well, here he was; he had had the accident; he was alone; and he had saved himself. Those old-timers[10] were rather womanish, some of them, he thought. All a man had to do was to keep his head, and he was all right. Any man who was a man could travel alone. But it was surprising, the rapidity with which his cheeks and nose were freezing. And he had not thought his fingers could go lifeless in so short a time. Lifeless they were, for he could scarcely make them move together to grip a twig, and they seemed remote from his body and from him. When he touched a twig, he had to look and see whether or not he had hold of it. The wires were pretty well down between him and his finger-ends.

All of which counted for little. There was the fire, snapping and crackling and promising life with every dancing flame. He started to untie his moccasins. They were coated with ice; the thick German socks were like sheaths of iron halfway to the knees; and the moccasin strings were like rods of steel all twisted and knotted as by some conflagration[11]. For a moment he tugged with his numb fingers, then, realizing the folly of it,

10) old-timers: 고참, 고풍(古風)의 사람, (특히 미) 노인

11) conflagration: 큰 화재, 돌발

he drew his sheath-knife[12].

But before he could cut the strings, it happened. It was his own fault or, rather, his mistake. He should not have built the fire under the spruce tree. He should have built it in the open. But it had been easier to pull the twigs from the brush and drop them directly on the fire. Now the tree under which he had done this carried a weight of snow on its boughs. No wind had blown for weeks, and each bough was fully freighted. Each time he had pulled a twig he had communicated a slight agitation to the tree -- an imperceptible agitation, so far as he was concerned, but an agitation sufficient to bring about the disaster. High up in the tree one bough capsized its load of snow. This fell on the boughs beneath, capsizing them. This process continued, spreading out and involving the whole tree. It grew like an avalanche, and it descended without warning upon the man and the fire, and the fire was blotted out! Where it had burned was a mantle of fresh and disordered snow.

The man was shocked. It was as though he had just heard his own sentence of death. For a moment he sat and stared at the spot where the fire had been. Then he grew very calm. Perhaps the old-timer on Sulphur Creek was right. If he had only had a trail-mate he would have been in no danger now. The trail-mate could have built the fire. Well, it was up to him to build the fire over again, and this second time there must be no failure. Even if he succeeded, he would most likely lose some toes. His feet must be badly frozen by now, and there would be some time

---

12) sheath-knife: (선원용의) 칼집 달린 나이프

before the second fire was ready.

Such were his thoughts, but he did not sit and think them. He was busy all the time they were passing through his mind. He made a new foundation for a fire, this time in the open, where no treacherous tree could blot it out. Next, he gathered dry grasses and tiny twigs from the high-water flotsam. He could not bring his fingers together to pull them out, but he was able to gather them by the handful. In this way he got many rotten twigs and bits of green moss that were undesirable, but it was the best he could do. He worked methodically, even collecting an armful of the larger branches to be used later when the fire gathered strength. And all the while the dog sat and watched him, a certain yearning wistfulness in its eyes, for it looked upon him as the fire-provider, and the fire was slow in coming.

When all was ready, the man reached in his pocket for a second piece of birch-bark. He knew the bark was there, and, though he could not feel it with his fingers, he could hear its crisp rustling as he fumbled for it. Try as he would, he could not clutch hold of it. And all the time, in his consciousness, was the knowledge that each instant his feet were freezing. This thought tended to put him in a panic, but he fought against it and kept calm. He pulled on his mittens with his teeth, and threshed his arms back and forth, beating his hands with all his might against his sides. He did this sitting down, and he stood up to do it; and all the while the dog sat in the snow, its wolf-brush of a tail curled around warmly over its forefeet, its sharp wolf-ears pricked forward intently as it watched the man. And the man, as he beat and threshed with his arms and hands, felt a great surge of envy as he regarded the creature that was warm and secure in its natural covering.

After a time he was aware of the first faraway signals of sensation in his beaten fingers. The faint tingling grew stronger till it evolved into a stinging ache that was excruciating[13], but which the man hailed with satisfaction. He stripped the mitten from his right hand and fetched forth the birch-bark. The exposed fingers were quickly going numb again. Next he brought out his bunch of sulphur[14] matches. But the tremendous cold had already driven the life out of his fingers. In his effort to separate one match from the others, the whole bunch fell in the snow. He tried to pick it out of the snow, but failed. The dead fingers could neither touch nor clutch. He was very careful. He drove the thought of his freezing feet, and nose, and cheeks, out of his mind, devoting his whole soul to the matches. He watched, using the sense of vision in place of that of touch, and when he saw his fingers on each side the bunch, he closed them -- that is, he willed to close them, for the wires were down, and the fingers did not obey. He pulled the mitten on the right hand, and beat it fiercely against his knee. Then, with both mittened hands, he scooped the bunch of matches, along with much snow, into his lap. Yet he was no better off.

After some manipulation he managed to get the bunch between the heels of his mittened hands. In this fashion he carried it to his mouth. The ice crackled and snapped when by

---

13) excruciating: 심한 고통을 주는, 몹시 괴롭히는, 괴로워 견딜 수 없는(agonizing)

14) sulphur: 유황의, 레몬색

a violent effort he opened his mouth. He drew the lower jaw in, curled the upper lip out of the way, and scraped the bunch with his upper teeth in order to separate a match. He succeeded in getting one, which he dropped on his lap. He was no better off. He could not pick it up. Then he devised a way. He picked it up in his teeth and scratched it on his leg. Twenty times he scratched before he succeeded in lighting it. As it flamed he held it with his teeth to the birch-bark. But the burning brimstone went up his nostrils and into his lungs, causing him to cough spasmodically. The match fell into the snow and went out.

The old-timer on Sulphur Creek was right, he thought in the moment of controlled despair that ensued: after fifty below, a man should travel with a partner. He beat his hands, but failed in exciting any sensation. Suddenly he bared both hands, removing the mittens with his teeth. He caught the whole bunch between the heels of his hands. His arm-muscles not being frozen enabled him to press the hand-heels tightly against the matches. Then he scratched the bunch along his leg. It flared into flame, seventy sulphur matches at once! There was no wind to blow them out. He kept his head to one side to escape the strangling fumes, and held the blazing bunch to the birch-bark. As he so held it, he became aware of sensation in his hand. His flesh was burning. He could smell it. Deep down below the surface he could feel it. The sensation developed into pain that grew acute. And still he endured it, holding the flame of the matches clumsily to the bark that would not light readily because his own burning hands were in the way, absorbing most of the flame.

At last, when he could endure no more, he jerked his hands

apart. The blazing matches fell sizzling into the snow, but the birch-bark was alight. He began laying dry grasses and the tiniest twigs on the flame. He could not pick and choose, for he had to lift the fuel between the heels of his hands. Small pieces of rotten wood and green moss clung to the twigs, and he bit them off as well as he could with his teeth. He cherished the flame carefully and awkwardly. It meant life, and it must not perish. The withdrawal of blood from the surface of his body now made him begin to shiver, and he grew more awkward. A large piece of green moss fell squarely on the little fire. He tried to poke it out with his fingers, but his shivering frame made him poke too far, and he disrupted the nucleus of the little fire, the burning grasses and tiny twigs separating and scattering. He tried to poke them together again, but in spite of the tenseness of the effort, his shivering got away with him, and the twigs were hopelessly scattered. Each twig gushed a puff of smoke and went out. The fire-provider had failed. As he looked apathetically[15] about him, his eyes chanced on the dog, sitting across the ruins of the fire from him, in the snow, making restless, hunching movements, slightly lifting one forefoot and then the other, shifting its weight back and forth on them with wistful eagerness.

The sight of the dog put a wild idea into his head. He remembered the tale of the man, caught in a blizzard, who killed a steer and crawled inside the carcass, and so was saved. He would kill the dog and bury his hands in the warm body until the numbness went out of them. Then he could build another

15) apathetically: 무관심하게, 냉담하게

fire. He spoke to the dog, calling it to him; but in his voice was a strange note of fear that frightened the animal, who had never known the man to speak in such way before. Something was the matter, and its suspicious nature sensed danger -- it knew not what danger, but somewhere, somehow, in its brain arose an apprehension of the man. It flattened its ears down at the sound of the man's voice, and its restless, hunching movements and the liftings and shiftings of its forefeet became more pronounced; but it would not come to the man. He got on his hands and knees and crawled toward the dog. This unusual posture again excited suspicion, and the animal sidled mincingly away.

The man sat up in the snow for a moment and struggled for calmness. Then he pulled on his mittens, by means of his teeth, and got upon his feet. He glanced down at first in order to assure himself that he was really standing up, for the absence of sensation in his feet left him unrelated to the earth. His erect position in itself started to drive the webs of suspicion from the dog's mind; and when he spoke peremptorily[16], with the sound of whip-lashes in his voice, the dog rendered its customary allegiance and came to him. As it came within reaching distance, the man lost his control. His arms flashed out to the dog, and he experienced genuine surprise when he discovered that his hands could not clutch, that there was neither bend nor feeling in the fingers. He had forgotten for the moment that they were frozen and that they were freezing more and more. All this happened quickly, and before the animal could get away, he encircled its body with his arms. He sat down in the snow, and in this

16) peremptorily: 단호하게, 독단적으로, 명령적으로

fashion held the dog, while it snarled and whined and struggled.

But it was all he could do, hold its body encircled in his arms and sit there. He realized that he could not kill the dog. There was no way to do it. With his helpess hands he could neither draw nor hold his sheath-knife nor throttle the animal. He released it, and it plunged wildly away, with tail between its legs, and still snarling. It halted forty feet away and surveyed him curiously, with ears sharply pricked forward. The man looked down at his hands in order to locate them, and found them hanging on the ends of his arms. It struck him as curious that one should have to use his eyes in order to find out where his hands were. He began threshing his arms back and forth, beating the mittened hands against his sides. He did this for five minutes, violently, and his heart pumped enough blood up to the surface to put a stop to his shivering. But no sensation was aroused in the hands. He had an impression that they hung like weights on the ends of his arms, but when he tried to run the impression down, he could not find it.

A certain fear of death, dull and oppressive, came to him. This fear quickly became poignant as he realized that it was no longer a mere matter of freezing his fingers and toes, or of losing his hands and feet, but that it was a matter of life and death with the chances against him. This threw him into a panic, and he turned and ran up the creek-bed along the old, dim trail. The dog joined in behind and kept up with him. He ran blindly, without intention, in fear such as he had never known in his life. Slowly, as he ploughed and floundered through the snow, he began to see things again, -- the banks of the creek, the old timber-jams, the leafless aspens[17], and the sky. The running made him feel better. He did not shiver. Maybe, if he ran on, his feet would thaw out; and, anyway, if he ran far enough, he would reach camp and the boys. Without doubt he would lose some fingers and toes and some of his face; but the boys would take care of him, and save the rest of him when he got there. And at the same time there was another thought in his mind that said he would never get to the camp and the boys; that it was too many miles away, that the freezing had too great a start on him, and that he would soon be stiff and dead. This thought he kept in the background and refused to consider. Sometimes it pushed itself forward and demanded to be heard, but he thrust it back and strove to think of other things.

It struck him as curious that he could run at all on feet so frozen that he could not feel them when they struck the earth and took the weight of his body. He seemed to himself to skim along above the surface, and to have no connection with the earth. Somewhere he had once seen a winged Mercury, and he wondered if Mercury felt as he felt when skimming over the earth.

His theory of running until he reached camp and the boys had one flaw in it: he lacked the endurance. Several times he stumbled, and finally he tottered, crumpled up, and fell. When he tried to rise, he failed. He must sit and rest, he decided, and next time he would merely walk and keep on going. As he sat and regained his breath, he noted that he was feeling quite warm

17) aspen: [식물] 아스펜, 포플러(quaking aspen), 당버들, 사시나무, 버드나뭇과의 일종

and comfortable. He was not shivering, and it even seemed that a warm glow had come to his chest and trunk. And yet, when he touched his nose or cheeks, there was no sensation. Running would not thaw them out. Nor would it thaw out his hands and feet. Then the thought came to him that the frozen portions of his body must be extending. He tried to keep this thought down, to forget it, to think of something else; he was aware of the panicky feeling that it caused, and he was afraid of the panic. But the thought asserted itself, and persisted, until it produced a vision of his body totally frozen. This was too much, and he made another wild run along the trail. Once he slowed down to a walk, but the thought of the freezing extending itself made him run again.

And all the time the dog ran with him, at his heels. When he fell down a second time, it curled its tail over its forefeet and sat in front of him, facing him, curiously eager and intent. The warmth and security of the animal angered him, and he cursed it till it flattened down its ears appeasingly[18]. This time the shivering came more quickly upon the man. He was losing in his battle with the frost. It was creeping into his body from all sides. The thought of it drove him on, but he ran no more than a hundred feet, when he staggered and pitched headlong[19]. It was his last panic. When he had recovered his breath and control, he sat up and entertained in his mind the conception of meeting death with dignity. However, the conception did not come to him in such terms. His idea of it was that he had been making

18) appeasingly: 매력적으로, 호소하듯이

19) pitched headlong: 거꾸로 곤두박이로 떨어지다

a fool of himself, running around like a chicken with its head cut off -- such was the simile that occurred to him. Well, he was bound to freeze anyway, and he might as well take it decently. With this new-found peace of mind came the first glimmerings of drowsiness. A good idea, he thought, to sleep off to death. It was like taking an anaesthetic[20]. Freezing was not so bad as people thought. There were lots worse ways to die.

He pictured the boys finding his body next day. Suddenly he found himself with them, coming along the trail and looking for himself. And, still with them, he came around a turn in the trail and found himself lying in the snow. He did not belong with himself any more, for even then he was out of himself, standing with the boys and looking at himself in the snow. It certainly was cold, was his thought. When he got back to the States he could tell the folks what real cold was. He drifted on from this to a vision of the old-timer on Sulphur Creek. He could see him quite clearly, warm and comfortable, and smoking a pipe.

"You were right, old hoss[21]; you were right," the man mumbled to the old-timer of Sulphur Creek.

Then the man drowsed off into what seemed to him the most comfortable and satisfying sleep he had ever known. The dog sat facing him and waiting. The brief day drew to a close in a long, slow twilight. There were no signs of a fire to be made, and, besides, never in the dog's experience had it known a man to

20) anaesthetic: 마취의, 마취제, 마취약

21) old hoss: 늙은 이, 노인네

sit like that in the snow and make no fire. As the twilight drew on, its eager yearning for the fire mastered it, and with a great lifting and shifting of forefeet, it whined softly, then flattened its ears down in anticipation of being chidden by the man. But the man remained silent. Later, the dog whined loudly. And still later it crept close to the man and caught the scent of death. This made the animal bristle and back away. A little longer it delayed, howling under the stars that leaped and danced and shone brightly in the cold sky. Then it turned and trotted up the trail in the direction of the camp it knew, where were the other food-providers and fire-providers.

ESSAYS IN CRITICISM

"The Kipling of the Klondike": Naturalism in London's Early Fiction

Earl J. Wilcox

The first period of Jack London's fiction clearly indicates the ways in which both his personal experiences and his reading shaped his outlook. Though London had been writing and sending his stories to publishers for some time, not until December, 1899, when Houghton Mifflin offered him a contract for his first volume of short stories, did he gain any recognition. The first collection, *The Son of the Wolf* (1900), outlined the plots, introduced the characters, and announced the themes that were later to give London a title of which he was proud. "The Kipling of the Klondike." The stories tell of man's attempts to survive the forces of nature, the threat of savages, and the competition with other fortune seekers in the north country. In *The God of His Fathers* (1901), London was eager to show that he could vary his themes, though keeping them essentially the same as in the first collection: the survival of the fittest, the deterministic orientation of the universe, and the superiority of the inevitable white man. In his first novel, *A Daughter of the Snows* (1902), London used his first opportunity to explore in some detail the ideas he had introduced in the short stories. When the novel proved an inept vehicle for London's talents at this point in his career, he turned again to the stories, exploring the same general theses in *Children of the Frost* (1902).

"The White Silence" introduced London's hero of the Yukon

and the Klondike, the Malemute Kid. The story also introduced the dominant philosophical and stylistic patterns that characterize not only the stories and the novel of this first period of London's career but of the whole range of his fiction. Undoubtedly London's most secure position in American letters rests on the quality of these early stories. For even the first one he shows his talent for developing a relationship between theme and character as he places man in the presence of the White Silence:

> The afternoon wore on, and with the awe, born out of the White Silence the voiceless travelers bent to their work. Nature has many tricks wherewith she convinces man of his finity, — the ceaseless flow of the tides, the fury of the storm, the shock of the earthquake, the long roll of heaven's artillery, — but the most tremendous, the most stupefying of all, is the passive phase of the White Silence. All movement ceases, the sky clears, the heavens are as brass; the slightest whisper seems sacrilege, and man becomes timid, affrighted at the sound of his own voice. Sole speck of life journeying across the ghostly wastes of a dead world he trembles at his audacity, realizes that his is a maggot's life, nothing more. Strange thoughts arise unsummoned, and the mystery of all things strives for utterance. And the fear of death, of God, of the universe, comes over him, — the hope of the Resurrection and the Life, the yearning for immortality, the vain striving of the imprisoned essence, — it is then, if ever, man walks alone with God.[1]

This description of environment is significant primarily because London's naturalistic heroes must cope with it in order

1) Jack London, *Best Short Stories of Jack London* (New York: Garden City Books, 1953), p. 13.

to survive. The inter-relationship between man and nature is of central importance in London's fiction, even as it had been in Crane's *Maggie* where the city overcomes Maggie. For as Darwinian "animals," the characters in London's northland stories learn that they must adapt to the environment or be subdued by it. This relationship is clearly outlined in the beginning of "In a Far Country."

> When a man journeys into a far country, he must be prepared to forget many of the things he has learned, and to acquire such customs as are inherent with existence in the new land; he must abandon the old ideals and the old gods, and oftentimes he must reverse the very codes by which his conduct has hitherto been shaped. To those who have the protean faculty of adaptability, the novelty of such change may even be a source of pleasure; but to those who happen to be hardened to the ruts in which they were created, the pressure of the altered environment is unbearable, and they chafe in body and in spirit under the new restrictions which they do not understand. This chafing is bound to act and react, producing divers evils and leading to various misfortunes. It were better for the man who cannot fit himself to the new groove to return to his own country; if he delay too long, he will surely die.[2]

As a prelude to an "inevitable" battle between the Red Man and the White Man in a later story in the same collection, a similar setting in all its naturalistic splendor is detailed:

> On every hand stretched the forest primeval, — the home of

2) Jack London, *The Call of the Wild, The Cruise of the Dazzler, And Other Stories of Adventure* (New York: Platt and Munk, 1960), p. 452.

> noisy comedy and silent tragedy. Here the struggle for survival continued to wage with all its ancient brutality. Briton and Russian were still to overlap in the Land of the Rainbow's End—and this was the very heart of it—nor had Yankee gold yet purchased its vast domain.
>
> The wolf-pack still clung to the flank of the cariboo-herd, singling out the weak and the big with calf, and pulling them down as remorselessly as were it a thousand, thousand generations into the past. The sparse aborigines still acknowledged the rule of their chiefs and medicine men, drove out bad spirits, burned their witches, fought their neighbors, and ate their enemies with a relish which spoke well of their bellies. But it was at the moment when the stone age was drawing to a close. Already, over unknown trails and chartless wildernesses, were the harbingers of the steel arriving,—fair-faced, blue-eyed, indomitable men, incarnations of the unrest of their race. By accident or design, single-handed and in twos and threes, they came from no one knew whither, and fought, or died, or passed on, no one knew whence.[3]

The Darwinian concept of survival of the fittest is carefully woven into this pattern of man's struggles. In no less than ten of the first twenty-five stories the survival motif dominates the action, and it is implicit in almost all of the others. Although in later stories and a novel London was to expand the survival thesis to include species generally, in these first stories the emphasis primarily is that of survival of the individual.

In "The White Silence" Malemute accompanies a man and his wife through the Yukon in an attempt to get to civilization before Spring. But the hostile environment overcomes Mason,

---

3) Jack London, *The God of His Fathers* (New York: McClure, Phillips, Co., 1902), pp. 1-2.

the traveler, in the form of a huge tree which falls on him. Nature plays the same trick on a group of travelers in "In a Far Country." Some of the voyageurs make the trip safely back to civilization, but two men from the "older" civilization remain behind and fail to survive because of their inability to adapt to the environment.

In these stories London makes clear that the "law of survival" permeates all levels of existence. For when Malemute's dogs weaken in their traces, the stronger dogs devour the weak. And when the dogs are unable to subsist on their own ration, they turn to men in order to survive. After Mason dies, Malemute tries to find food for himself and the woman, only to return to discover the dogs attacking. Darwinian survival is stated in its simplest terms.

> Bursting into the camp . . . (Malemute) saw the girl in the midst of the snarling pack, laying about her with an axe. The dogs had broken the iron rule of their masters and were rushing the grub. He joined the issue with his rifle reversed, and the hoary game of natural selection was played out with all the ruthlessness of its primeval environment. Rifle and axe went up and down, hit or missed with monotonous regularity; lithe bodies flashed, with wild eyes and dripping fangs; and man and beast fought for supremacy to the bitterest conclusion. Then the beaten brutes crept to the edge of the firelight, licking their wounds, voicing their misery to the stars.[4]

Indeed, only the fittest survive either nature's or man's attacks. The affinity between man and dog is no mere accidental

---

4) London, *Best Short Stories*, p. 7.

relationship to suggest that both obey laws of survival. In the evolutionary scheme of things both obey such laws because both are part of the evolutionary process. Man is merely a high-order animal, and his survival, his progress toward a higher state, is dependent upon his adaptability. In the northland, environmental and hereditary traits are more forcefully evident because of the heightened struggle. And under stress, man shows his latent animal traits — his atavism — and reverts to that state. The allusion to "son" in "The Son of the Wolf" is probably meant, therefore, to convey that Scruff Mackenzie, the protagonist, is a descendant of some earlier animal form, or simply that his survival indicates his animal nature. London describes Mackenzie as a true product of the wild:

> 'Scruff' Mackenzie bore the earmarks of a frontier birth and a frontier life. His face was stamped with twenty-five years of incessant struggle with Nature in her wildest moods,—the last two, the wildest and hardest of all, having been spent in groping for the gold which lies in the shadow of the Arctic Circle.[5]

The survival-oriented plot involves Mackenzie's desire to have Zarinska, an Indian maiden, for his wife. To win her he must fight Fox, the medicine man, who has been claiming that his black magic can subdue the white man's. Finally the two engage in physical battle in a fight for survival. The entire fight is a re-enactment of the survival motif:

> Time and again . . . (Mackenzie) was forced to the edge of the

5) Jack London, *The Son of the Wolf, Tales of the Far North* (New York: Arco Publications, 1962), p. 28.

> fire or the deep snow, and time and again, with the foot tactics of the pugilist, he worked back to the center. Not a voice was lifted in encouragement, while his antagonist was heartened with applause, suggestions, and warnings. *(Ibid, p. 45).*

And in the final stages of the struggle, when Mackenzie is winning, the true son of the wolf emerges:

> At first he felt compassion for his enemy; but this fled before the primal instinct of life, which in turn gave way to the lust of slaughter. The ten thousand years of culture fell from him, and he was a cave-dweller, doing battle for his female. *(Ibid, p. 45-46).*

The atavism in Mackenzie is yet a latent characteristic of the "civilized" man. Precisely the same theory is propounded in the death of the two survivors in "In a Far Country," for when at last they have been overcome by the White Silence (environment) their true nature is evident: "What with the Fear of the North, the mental strain, the ravages of the disease, they lost all semblance of humanity, taking on the appearance of wild beasts, hunted and desperate."[6] Thus the survival tendency is pictured as inherent, as animal instinct. The implicit materialism in this view of a biological assumption is the central idea also in "Jan, the Unrepentant" in the same collection. Having been found guilty of killing a man, Jan flees, and during the pursuit his instinct for survival seems to give him courage:

> Jan ran blindly, reckoning not of the way of his feet, for he was mastered by the verb "to live." To live! To exist! Buck

6) London, *Stories of Adventure*, p. 452.

> flashed gray through the air, but missed. The man struck madly at him, and stumbled. Then the white teeth of Bright closed on his mackinaw jacket, and he pitched into the snow. *To live! To exist!* He fought wildly as ever, the centre of a tossing heap of men and dogs. *(Ibid, p. 347).*

This ubiquitous survival thesis takes on protean forms in London's early stories. For examples, not only is man forced to do battle with nature, with animals, with other white men to survive, the Red Man also provides added challenge. Though the Red Man-White Man encounters are given trite portrayal in London's stories, the central significance is in providing for another dimension of the survival themes. In "God of His Fathers," whose setting we have noted earlier, the struggle is intensely dramatized in a familiar naturalistic pattern. Hay Stockard, a white man, hopes to live in the Yukon. But his arch-enemy, Baptise the Red (an Indian), will not let him, primarily because Baptise wants Stockard to admit that there is no God. An open struggle is precipitated by the appearance of Sturges Owen, a missionary priest. Stockard, married to an Indian girl who is now the mother of his child, and Baptise are continuing their debate when Owen arrives. Baptise refuses to let Owen preach to him, though he is willing for the priest to pass safely through the country. Owen is adamant: he will stay and preach to the "heathen." Though he despises Owen, Stockard vacillates between his desire to let the priest be killed and his inclination to help defend him against Baptise. It is Owen, the cowardly priest, whom London disparages, for in the battle — a futile one in which the wife, the child, and several others are killed — Owen muses on his materialistically-oriented impulse to live in the knowledge of the martyrdom he could achieve. There is little that is admirable in Owen's death; in fact, the story's ending seems to imply that the priest has been foolish in dying for a cause which apparently means very little to him except as it will bring him some personal glory.

The most original aspect of the struggle between the White Man and the Red Man as introduced in these first stories is London's belief in the superiority of the White, Anglo-Saxon race. This thesis, which is a dominate and pervasive one in all London's later fiction, is proclaimed as part of the survival theory. While not Darwinian in origin, the theory is at least Darwinistic, stressing the survival of the species as it adapts to its environment. Scruff Mackenzie, the son of the wolf, is the first character in London's fiction to voice the belief in white supremacy. After Mackenzie has won his mate, he proudly proclaims that his "people . . . are the mightiest of all the peoples, who rule all the lands . . . ."[7] And the corollary law of the wolf is "whoso taketh the life of one wolf, the forfeit shall ten of his people pay." *(Ibid.)*

While the theme is merely hinted at in Mackenzie's brief statement, London uses one entire story to focus on his concept. In "The Great Interrogation" Karen Sayther is London's spokesman for the "new" civilization, for the Anglo-Saxon. Ostensibly Mrs. Sayther has left a comfortable estate in the city to come to the Yukon on an unknown errand. The "interrogation" into which the citizens of the territory are drawn is in wondering why Karen has come. It is shortly revealed that before her sudden marriage to the late Colonel Sayther, Karen had been engaged to David Paine, the hero of the story. She

7) London, *The Son of the Wolf*, p. 44.

now lives with an Indian maiden and is caught in the matrix of deciding between the two ways of life. He recognizes that Karen has earlier deserted him for Colonel Sayther's money: the materialistic ideals of civilization were evident in the Colonel. Paine thinks of this, wondering, "What was he? A great, gross, material creature, deaf to song, blind to beauty, dead to the spirit. He was fat with laziness, and flabby-cheeked, and the round of his belly witnessed his gluttony—."[8] But Karen dismisses David's charges and pleads with him on the basis of their anthropological ties.

> Come, Dave, you must see. She is not your kind. There is no race affinity. She is an aborigine, sprung from the soil, yet close to the soil, and impossible to lift from the soil. Born savage, savage she will die. But we—you and I—the dominant, evolved race--the salt of the earth and the masters thereof! We are made for each other. The supreme call is of kind, and we are of kind. Reason and feeling dictate it. Your very instinct demands it. That you cannot deny. You cannot escape the generations behind you. Yours is an ancestry which has survived for a thousand centuries, and for a hundred thousand centuries, and your line must not stop here. It cannot. Your ancestry will not permit it. Instinct is stronger than the will. The race is mightier than you. Come, Dave, let us go. *(Ibid., pp. 56-57)*

David then considers the alternatives, civilization or the primitive North:

> His bleak life rose up and smote him,—the vain struggle with pitiless forces; the dreary years of frost and famine; the harsh and jarring contact with elemental life; the aching void which mere

---

8) London, *The God of His Fathers*, pp. 52-53.

> animal existence could not fill. And there, seduction by his side, whispering of brighter, warmer lands, of music, light, and joy, called the old times back again. He visioned it unconsciously. Faces rushed in upon him; glimpses of forgotten scenes, memories of merry hours; strains of song and trills of laughter —.
>
> "Come, Dave, Come," Karen said. "I have for both. The way is soft."
>
> She was in his arms, trembling, and he held her tightly. He rose to his feet . . . But the snarling of hungry dogs, and the shrill cries of Winapie bringing about peace between the combatants, came muffled to his ear through the heavy logs. And another scene flashed before him. A struggle in the forest,—a bald-face grizzly, broken-legged, terrible; the snarling of the dogs and the shrill cries of Winapie as she urged them to the attack; himself in the midst of the crush, breathless, panting, striving to hold off red death; broken-backed, entrail-ripped dogs howling in impotent anguish and desecrating the snow; the virgin white running scarlet with the blood of man and beast; the bear, ferocious, irresistible, crunching, crunching down to the core of his life. . . .*(Ibid., p. 57)*

While the final outcome of the story argues not for a victory for the "dominate, evolved race" (since David chooses not to return with Karen), London still asserts that the Anglo-Saxon species has evolved to its superiority through its struggle for survival. In a later story in *Children of the Frost,* written in this first period of his career also, London pictures Avery Von Brunt as he nears an Indian village with the same Anglo-Saxon consciousness: "He, alone, was full-blooded Saxon, and his blood was pounding fiercely through his veins to the traditions of his race. Clive and Hastings, Drake and Raleigh, Hengest and Horsa, walked with him."[9]

---

9) Jack London, *Children of the Frost* (London: Arco Publications, 1963), pp. 12-13.

But London is not content with asserting the white supremacy through the voice of his white men; he must also depict the Red Man's coming to the same conclusion. Thus the "Law of Life" for an old Indian chieftain, Koskoosh, is that a Darwinian biological concept explains the way of all flesh and the evils visited upon it. In a resigned mood of despair, Koskoosh laments his defeat:

> It was the law of all flesh. Nature was not kindly to the flesh. She had no concern for that concrete thing called the individual. Her interest lay in the species, the race. This was the deepest abstraction old Koskoosh's barbaric mind was capable of, but he grasped it firmly. He saw it exemplified in all life. The rise of the sap, the bursting greenness of the willow bud, the fall of the yellow leaf—in this alone was told the whole history. *(Ibid., p. 33)*

The "law" is, of course, the "natural" law of the white man's

---

Except for Taine's almost metaphorical assertion of the superiority of the French, no other naturalist has asserted a similar theory. Indeed, the American naturalists were wont to demonstrate that the human species was in no way superior to other species, that man was merely an animal of a higher order. London also preaches this simple biological theory time and time again. Thus his attempts to assert on the one hand a racial superiority and on the other an implicit atavism not only confuse his philosophy but also necessitate a stricter qualification of the degree of London' s affinity with the naturalistic movement. If London's use of the concept is to be considered naturalistic, one feels that he is on the periphery of the movement rather than in the mainstream. The only justification that can be made for inclusion of the motif here is on the basis of London's belief that the Anglo-Saxon race had evolved through centuries of struggle to become the dominate race. Aside from the fiction, see his statements in the *Kempton-Wace Letters* (p. 9, 54). See also Joan London's reports of the numerous occasions in which her father discussed his race views.

supremacy. Another grand old chieftain comes to precisely the same conclusion about natural selection. In "The League of Old Men," Imber tells a white man's court of his attempts to eradicate the white man before he destroyed Imber's civilization. In the end Imber's people are defeated, for it is the "Anglo-Saxon who have the custom of . . . giving the law to conquered peoples, and oft-times this law is harsh." *(Ibid., p. 143)* At last unable to fight because of his age, Imber has come to the city to tell his story and to acknowledge the "law." He laments, "I am very old, and very tired, and it being vain fighting the Law, as thou sayest. . . .I am come seeking the Law." *(Ibid., pp. 159-160)* The white man's law fuses again with the laws of nature in Imber's dim mind as he sits in rapturous contemplation of the inevitable forces that control his life:

> But Imber was dreaming. The square-browed judge likewise dreamed, and all his race rose up before him in a mighty phantasmagoria — his steel shod, mail clad race, the lawgiver and world-maker among the families of men. He saw it dawn red-flickering across the dark forests and sullen seas; he saw it blaze, bloody and red, to full and triumphant noon; and down the shaded slope he saw the blood-red sands dropping into night. And through it all he observed the Law, pitiless and potent, ever unswerving and ever ordaining, greater than the motes of men who fulfilled it or were crushed by it, even as it was greater than he, his heart speaking for softness. *(Ibid., p. 160)*

In these stories London asserts the Kiplingesque myth of the superior White Race, but he also adapts it to a naturalistic framework. For the survival thesis is clearly Darwinian in import. Too, the tone in which the survival and natural selection principles are adumbrated is obviously naturalistic. In "The Men of Forty Mile," for example, London explains that life in general is explainable in terms of a deterministic framework. In the story the same Scruff Mackenzie is a central figure in a brief struggle with another white man. It is the Malemute Kid, however, who glibly voices a naturalistic assumption in noting that men should understand that life itself is a gamble, a kind of game with no predictable outcome. Thus after attempting unsuccessfully to settle an argument between two men, the Kid concludes: "So you see we do not actually take away the privilege of fighting; and yet I don't believe they'll fight when they see the beauty of the scheme. Life's a game, and men the gamblers."[10] Furthermore, London adheres to the technique he has outlined before when in the same stories he depicts the Indians expressing the same kind of pessimism in reacting to a deterministic pattern of survival. Sitka Charley, the Indian hero who appears in many of the tales of this early period, tells of his taking a long journey with a white man and woman. Ostensibly, the story is about "The Grit of Woman," but it finally develops into a philosophical soliloquy in which Charley muses on the deterministic orientation of the universe. The plot, a typical one for London, concerns a white man's great love for his Indian squaw and their many years of hardship in the north. But the couple is finally to be defeated by nature, and the narrative centers around their demise, described in language reminiscent of the meaning of "The White Silence." In the story both the hero and his wife are overcome by their environment. But before the narrator dies, he asserts the pessimist's creed: life, which must be viewed materialistically, is

10) London, *Stories of Adventure*, p. 480.

futile and meaningless:

> Life is a strange thing. Much have I thought on it, and pondered long, yet daily the strangeness of it grows not less, but more. Why this longing for Life? It is a game which no man wins. To live is to toil hard, and to suffer sore, till Old Age creeps heavily upon us and we throw down our hands on the cold ashes of dead fires. It is hard to live. In pain the babe sucks his first breath, in pain the old man gasps his last, and all his days are full of trouble and sorrow; yet he goes down to the open arms of Death, stumbling, falling, with head turned backward, fighting to the last. And Death is kind. It is only Life, and the things of Life that hurt. Yet we love Life, and we hate Death.[11]

What is not accomplished in Charley's statement is captured in fuller measure in the clearest philosophical statement of determinism in the early stories. Like Malemute Kid's earlier declaration that life is a game, Fortune La Perle, the protagonist of "Which Make Men Remember", comes to the same pessimistic conclusion. Fortune, who is accused of murdering John Randolph, is befriended by Uri Bram. Uri hides Fortune from authorities, and while spending the many days waiting to come out of hiding, the outlaw meditates on his destiny. Obviously allegorizing the man's name for thematic impact, London portrays Fortune as feeling that Fortune's own account of how he came to murder Randolph is enunciated in classic deterministic terms.

---

11) London, *The God of His Fathers*, pp. 176-177. London's pessimism sprang from multiple sources, part of which was genuine and part of which was a literary device in imitation of Schopenhauer.

> All worked out, every bit of it, all parts fitting snug. Before I was born, like as not. I'll put the sack I never hope to get on it, before I was born. That's why. *(Ibid., p. 83)*

Finally, Uri and Fortune decide to draw cards to see who will shoot first in a duel through which Bram seeks to revenge his friend, Randolph. London, the naturalistic cynic, disparaging traditional Christian concepts, shows his cynicism in arranging the unusual denouement in which Bram seeks the revenge. The duel is set, with long ardent statements from Bram on the virtues of justice and on the virtues of his friend Randolph whose great name must be avenged. But Fortune's god is quite different from Bram's: "He did not know much concerning Uri's God, but he believed in Chance." And as they draw cards, Fortune feels that surely "Chance (will) not desert him now." The narrator (London) tells the reader, "Chance had been very good to him (Fortune) already . . . and if he tricked now he would have to pay for it afterward." *(Ibid., p. 84)* But Fortune loses the draw and is killed. As he dies, the fatalist succumbs amid London's refrain: "Fortune did not whirl, but gay San Francisco dimmed and faded; and as the sun-bright snow turned blacker and blacker, he breathed his last malediction on the Chance he had misplayed." *(Ibid., p. 85)*

The women in London's early stories constitute an integral part of the total view of life in the northland. Not insignificantly London' s first novel, also written during this period, centers around a woman. Because of the encompassing manner in which London explores the many avenues through which his naturalism can be expressed, he was wise not to discard the role of woman in these adventure tales. Importantly, then, a superior type of woman is needed to cope with the rigorous life demanded by the environment. A review of the tales already discussed indicates that the role of woman is a central one. In "The White Silence" the woman successfully fights off the pack until Malemute returns; in "The Son of the Wolf" Scruff's squaw is pictured as a sturdy and courageous woman; in "The God of His Fathers" the Indian wife of Stockard gladly dies for her white husband; in "The Great Interrogation" David Paine chooses to remain in the wilderness with his Indian maiden; and in "The Grit of Women" the courage and fidelity of women are emphasized. It may be noted parenthetically that London's alleged disdain for the Red Man is not borne out in a reading of these early stories. The Indian women, particularly, are consistently presented in a courageous and honorable light. Not unexpectedly, then, London advances a theory which also exalts the heroism of a white woman. In the "Priestly Prerogative" his first naturalistic "new woman" enters the scene. In the story, the "new woman" is Grace Bentham. Grace, the wife of Edwin Bentham, has come with her husband to the Yukon territory. Both had been reared in the city and thus are tenderfeet, until Grace sees that in order to survive she must take charge of the family affairs. Eventually, by Grace's clever maneuvering of their money, her buying of land, and her strict urging and directing Edwin to push farther north, the couple emerge wealthy. The "new woman" motif is announced in London's description of Grace's efficiency:

> This was the woman who urged and encouraged her husband in his Northland quest, who broke trail for him when no one was looking, and cried in secret over her weakling woman's body. So journeyed this strangely assorted couple down to old Fort Selkirk, then through fivescore miles of dismal wilderness to Stuart River.

> And when the short day left them, and the man lay down in the snow and blubbered, it was the woman who lashed him to the sled, bit her lips with the pain of her aching limbs, and helped the dog haul him to Malemute Kid's cabin.[12]

Her greatest energies are then directed in earning a fortune for them:

> This is what Grace Bentham proceeded to do. Arriving in Dawson with a few pounds of flour and several letters of introduction, she at once applied herself to the task of pushing her big baby to the fore. It was she who melted the stony heart and wrung credit from the rude barbarian who presided over the destiny of the P. C. Company . . . . It was she who studied maps, and catechised miners, and hammered geography and locations into his hollow head, till everybody marveled at his broad grasp of the country and knowledge of its conditions. . . .
>
> She did the work; he got the credit and reward. *(Ibid.)*

The "priestly prerogative" is made by a priest in the camp who discovers that Grace is in love with a close friend of the Benthams and plans to leave the Yukon country with him. The priest decides not to tell Edwin, assuring Grace that if she returns and remains faithful to Edwin her secret will always remain with her confessor. In general, the story epitomizes the materialistic aims which all the big fortune-seekers had in coming to the Yukon. Their lives, their hearts, and their souls are at stake in their desire to become rich and to "survive" on a larger scale than their neighbors. Yet the kind of survival which Jack London explores in these early stories was expressed

12) London, *The Son of the Wolf*, p. 99.

primarily in terms of animal instinct, with an occasional hint of race survival, both views stressing that the species was strengthened by the emergence of the winner. In the study of Grace Bentham, London indicates his early fascination with the strong, Amazon-like woman who became one of his dominate character types in later novels.

Henry S. Commager has well noted London's characteristic position in these early stories, as well as in much of the later fiction:

> Of all those who applied the doctrine of the survival of the fittest to human society, Jack London was the most enthusiastic and the most naive; it is suggestive that he was, also, the most widely read, at home and abroad. . . .London translated Darwin into the vernacular, presented it in a guise so romantic, boisterous, and extravagant that it proved irresistible; he wrote it up in dime novels and purveyed it as literature and philosophy. The stuff of his endless adventure stories was dredged up from his own fabulous career as newsboy, oyster pirate, tramp, sailor, prospector, and rancher; the philosophy was laid on like ornamental scrollwork on Eastlake buildings. London read Spencer and Haeckel and took the struggle for existence to be but a prophecy of his own struggle with the thugs of the San Francisco waterfront; he read Nietzsche and imagined himself a Superman. Science and philosophy conspired to explain his career and justify his fiction.[13]

To make these first stories superior in artistry, London buttressed both action and philosophical comment with a setting

13) Henry S. Commager, *The American Mind* (New Haven: Yale University Press, 1950), p. 110.

that complemented the tone and theme. Thus they achieve coherence and meaning despite Commager's claim that the philosophy is ornamental. What these stories portend is a pattern of naturalistic thought that permeates the greater part of all of Jack London's writing after 1902.

Answering the Call of the Wild

Daniel Dyer

I wouldn't read the classics, so my mother bought me comic books — not *Superman* or *Archie* (those I had to purchase with my own piddling allowance), but *Classics Illustrated*, a periodical which offered comic-book versions of major literary works. (This was, in fact, a public-relations coup by comics pub-lishers, who were in those days viewed by respon-sible parents, like mine, as the "corrupters of youth," an unsavory reputation from which prod-ucers of Saturday morning television programs now suffer. *Classics Illustrated* helped sanitize the image of comic books just as *Sesame Street* has helped legitimize television viewing.) Embracing the principle that any comic book was better than none, I accepted *Classics Illustrated* into my literary world (as did many of my coevals), thereby allowing myself to be coerced into a close encounter with "serious literature." The experi-ence was not all that unpleasant. Urged along by simplified dialogue, full-color illustrations, and (I discovered much later) bowdlerized texts, I read-and enjoyed!-such acclaimed works as *Ivanhoe*, *Les Miserables*, and *Romeo andJuliet*. (The editors of *Classics Illustrated* were somewhat liberal and eclec-tic in their tastes: listed with works of Shake-speare, Dumas, and Homer were other "masterpieces" like *Tom Brown's Schooldays*, *The Adventures of Kit Carson*, and *Wild Animals I Have Known*.)

Seeing me sprawled in a chair in contented company with *Hamlet*-never mind that it *looked* as if I were reading a comic book-my parents must have felt that curious glow of pleasure I now feel whenever I entice my own fourteen-year-old son into doing something which has even the most nebulous intellectual content. Of course, parents were just beginning to become sneaky in the 1950s. Responding to child psychologists who urged understanding and restraint, enlightened parents employed guile rather than violence with their offspring. Manufacturers and advertisers were quick to cooperate, and it was during my boyhood that such products as sweetened tooth-paste and children's orange-flavored aspirin began to appear-medicine-chest ana-logues of *Classics Illustrated.*

To this day I vividly remember my comic book *Call of the Wild*-from the front cover (Buck barks in the foreground, the frozen Yukon wilderness behind him), to the opening panel (Buck, blood dripping from his jaws, lunges at a wounded stag), to the final, mournful portrait of broken-hearted Buck-no longer a pet, but a beast, a creature of the wild-baying at the full moon. As I look at that comic book now, I am certain that I did not accept the gracious invitation printed at the bottom of the final page: "Now that you' ve read the '*Classics Illustrated*' edition, don't miss the added enjoyment of reading the original obtainable at your school or public library." Nor, I am sure, did I read the subsequent full-page biog-raphy of Jack London, which features such florid distortions as "He died a martyr to his craft and to truth as he knew it"-hyperbole acceptable in a comic book, I guess.

But I *did* read the *Classics Illustrated* versions of two of London's other novels, *The Sea-Wolf* and *White Fang*, never realizing at the time that this inchoate interest in Jack London would one day lead me on a transcontinental quest, from Harvard University's Widener Library (to locate long out-of-print works by London) to Dawson City, Yukon Territory, one of the principal settings of *The Call of the Wild*. And I would have been astounded had I known that this search would lead me directly to the roots of my family tree.

I don't like teaching what I don't know.

My distaste for doing so began the first days of my career in September 1966 when I discovered that I was not *exactly* a seventh-grade English teacher; I was, more precisely, a "core" teacher. Translation: I would teach English *and* American history.

In 1966, the dimensions of my knowledge of American history were not impressive. Oh, I knew a few things about the *Mayflower* and the Alamo. Pearl Harbor. That was about it. Nevertheless, I managed to fool my students for, oh, a week or so before their feral instinct informed them that I was a fake. (Once we passed the Pilgrims I was in serious trouble.)

Later in my career-especially in the heyday of elective English courses-I made an art of teach-ing subjects and topics about which I knew next to nothing. Could I teach a mini-course in film-making? Radio drama? Science fiction and fan-tasy? You bet.

In those days I was also an inveterate romantic; if called upon to defend myself ("How can you teach what you don't know?"), I had a knapsack stuffed with nifty replies: I was "learning along with the kids," "modeling effective strategies and behaviors," "demonstrating the rewards of life-long learning." But in realistic moments (i.e., on Friday afternoons) I was agonizingly aware I was a fraud, terrified to admit my ignorance with the frequency that truth demanded.

And so it was that I developed one principle that has impelled my career in its recent stages: Know everything you conceivably can about the subject at hand. Become a fanatic. A freak.

Accordingly, when our board of education recently adopted Ginn's *Exploring Literature* as the eighth-grade literature text, I promptly scanned the table of contents for potential problems. There were many (alas), the most serious being the novel which consumes the final eighty pages of the volume; it was *The Call of the Wild*, which I'd read only in its *Classics Illustrated* version. Twenty-five years earlier.

I should note that I was not *completelyi* gnorant of London: in high school I'd read Martin Eden (a book report); in college, *The Sea-Wolf* (for a course). And my memory of the comic-book *White Fang* remained unaccountably acute and complete. On the diskette of my brain I also found partial sectors of biographical information that I'd once "written to file" in high school English classes dur-ing sessions devoted to "To Build a Fire" or "The All-Gold Canyon." I knew I had much to do before acquiring even marginal competence with Jack London and his work.

I began my study in the same manner as a kid assigned an odious social studies report: I looked in the *World Book* encyclopedia. But I quickly pro-gressed to more respectable publications (like *Cliff's Notes* and *MasterPlots*). After reading the popular biographies (*Sailor on Horseback, Jack: A Biography of Jack London, and A Pictorial Life of Jack London*), I finally opened *The Call of the Wild.*

As I read, insights banged against my window-pane brain:

The vocabulary was extremely difficult. (In the short, four-line epigraph, I was brought up short by "brumal" [wintry]. The kids, I knew, would have problems with "nomadic," "chafing," and "ferine.") And beyond the epigraph, reading becomes no easier: on the first three pages alone appear such words as "veranda," "artesian well," "demesne," "imperiously," "kindred," "unwonted," "intimated," and "conveyance"-words not litter-ing the tongues of most junior-high schoolers.

London was fond of complex locutions which are unfamiliar to today's generation bred on tele-vision's pidgin English: "Buck multiplied himself, attacking from all sides, enveloping the herd in a whirlwind of menace, cutting out his victim as fast as it could rejoin its mates, wearing out the patience of creatures preyed upon, which is a lesser patience than that of the creatures preying." Yow! An impressive string of participial phrases, each trailing a prepositional phrase or two, or an adverb clause, or another participle, the whole thing finished off with a wham-bang adjective clause, slightly misplaced.

The settings were completely foreign to me. I knew nothing about the geography of the "sun-kissed Santa Clara Valley," even less about the Yukon wilderness. A confession: I thought the Yukon was part of Alaska, not a Canadian territory!

I had only vague notions about the historical context of the novel-the Klondike Gold Rush. I was certain only of this: lots of people wanted gold, so they rushed to the Klondike to get it.

The kids would need a lot of help with this novel. So would I.

A wisp of a memory: my father had known something-done something?-about the Gold Rush.

A phone call home revealed an unlikely coinci-dence: my great-grandfather, Addison Clark Dyer, had joined the stampede to the Klondike in 1898. Better yet: he'd kept a diary of his experiences, a diary my father had transcribed and photocopied ten years earlier. He'd sent me a copy-didn't I remember? (Oops.)

A frantic search through file drawers rescued the document from the clutter, and I eagerly read the words of my gold-seeking ancestor. The entries were, understandably, brief-after all, he was trav-eling one thousand miles by horseback through dense forests (from Spokane to Wrangell, Alaska); he was struggling across brutal mountain passes; he was shooting the Whitehorse Rapids on the Yukon River; he was laboring on his claim in frigid temperatures that sometimes dropped to sixty below. He was, in a word, busy.

Addison Clark Dyer spent a year working a claim on Bonanza Creek then returned to Walla Walla, Washington, where he used his modest "poke" to purchase the farm that only the Depression could wrest from the family.

Great-grandfather died before my father was born, so neither of us knew him, except through one faded photograph.., and through his diary, which he scrawled with the stub of a pencil

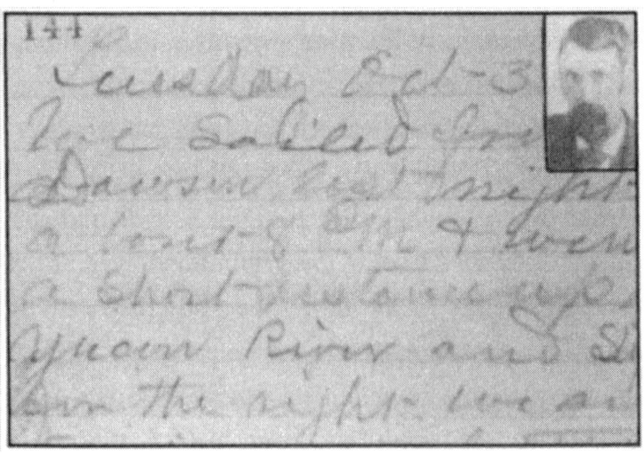

Addison Clark Oyer and a page from his diary

over campfires and woodstoves in the very country Jack London describes in *The Call of the Wild.*

I spent a year squirreling money away, then applied for a sabbatical leave (request granted!), thereby equipping myself with the time and money I would need to re-trace my great-grand-father's journey-and, coincidentally, to walk in the footsteps of Jack London.

My son and I substituted Alaska Airlines for horseback (a decision we did not ponder long) and arrived in Skagway, Alaska, not far from Dyea where Buck first hit the beach.

In 1898, Skagway was the busy seaport where the gold-seekers began their overland journey; now it's a tourist attraction and center for the Klondike Gold Rush National Historical Park. We rented a car (Avis had two on the lot, a dirty red one and a dirtier red one), and we set out to cross the White Pass on the Klondike Highway.

During Jack London's day the White Pass was a heartbreakingly difficult, barely passable way over the mountains. Klondike historian Pierre Berton asserts that no horse made it across alive, and it soon became known as the Dead Horse Trail.

In "Which Make Men Remember" (a story con-tained in *The God of His Fathers*, 1901) London describes the brutal conditions confronting those who crossed the White Pass:

> The horses died like mosquitoes in the first frost, and from Skaguay to [Lake] Bennett they rotted in heaps. They died at the Rocks, they were poisoned at the Summit, and they starved at the Lakes; they fell off the trail, what there was of it, or they went through it; in the river they drowned under their loads, or were smashed to pieces against the boul-ders; they snapped their

> legs in the crevices and broke their backs falling backwards with their packs; in the sloughs they sank from sight or smothered in the slime, and they were disembowelled in the bogs where the corduroy logs turned end up in the mud; men shot them, worked them to death, and when they were gone, went back to the beach and bought more. Some did not bother to shoot them-stripping their saddles off and the shoes and leaving them where they fell. Their hearts turned to stone-those which did not break-and they became beasts, these men on Dead Horse Trail.

Several years later the White Pass and Yukon Railroad traversed that rugged terrain, and now an asphalt highway provides glorious vistas to travelers who enjoy aesthetic pleasures that would have been inconceivable to my great-grandfather.

Just over the mountains is a string of lakes where the stampeders stopped to build boats to float the remaining 350 miles down the Yukon River to the goldfields. Most boats were of the homemade variety-equal in quality to what a random group of English teachers might constructso quite a few were destroyed in one of three perilous places along the river: Box Canyon, the Whitehorse Rapids, or Five Finger Rapids. Fortunately, the Mounties quickly took control of the river and required that all craft be piloted through the rapids by experienced whitewater men; a year after the rush began, there was regular steamboat service on the river.

At the confluence of the Klondike and Yukon rivers stands the little town of Dawson City, Yukon Territory, about one hundred miles east of the Alaska border and two hundred miles south of the Arctic Circle. It was here that most of the gold was dredged from two rich, gold-bearing tributaries of the Klondike, the Bonanza and El Dorado creeks. At the height of the rush in

1898, there were 30,000 people in Dawson. There was an opera house, newspaper, church, post office, bank, and an entire street known as Paradise Alley where lonely miners could purchase female "companionship." Dawson was called the Paris of the North.

Once the stampeders reached Dawson, they quickly found out the bad news: all the prime sites had been staked and claimed nearly a year before (poor communications and transportation prevented news from reaching the outside until it was too late), so there was nothing for most of them to do but work the claims of others to earn enough for a steamboat ticket home. About thirty miners became millionaires from the rush; the other 29,970 had a "learning experience."

The streets of Dawson City today (population 700) are dirt; many of the buildings-some crumbling, others in the process of restoration by Parks Canada-date to the early twentieth century. Across the Yukon River are the deteriorating remains of a few of the two hundred or so sternwheelers which once chugged up and down the river, sometimes consuming as much as a cord of wood per hour. Only three remain intact, all in dry dock. The only craft now operating on the river are the canoes and outboards of the Yukon denizens and a couple of launches which transport tourists to various historical spots along the river.

In the short Yukon summer, Dawson survives on a tourist economy. During our week there we saw many tour buses and countless RVs, many of which had been disgorged by the enormous cruise ships which call every day at Skagway. Dawson offers Gold Rush museums, old-time dance-hall entertainment in the restored opera house, tours of the gold-fields, gambling at Diamond-Tooth Gertie's (the only legal gambling spot in all of Canada), readings from the works of Klondike poet Robert W. Service... and from Jack London... and opportunities to pan for gold along the very creeks the stampeders worked in 1898.

We were surprised to see that gold mining continues unabated throughout the Dawson City area. Although most of the creeks have been dredged down to bedrock (the landscape appears to have been gouged by a giant claw), claims are still bought and sold, and *No Trepassing* signs are still enforced, if necessary, with firearms.

In the Mining Recorder's Office in Dawson, my son and I were able to identify the site of the claim once worked by my great-grandfather, and later, following a surveyor's map, we drove along a dusty mining road a few miles up Bonanza Creek and found the spot, which is now labeled 49 Gulch. Grandpa' s claim. Heavy machinery was still working there, and visitors were clearly not welcome, so we did little more than walk around, pick up a few rocks, take a few photographs.., .and imagine.

During his short time in the Yukon, the young Jack London (he was in his early twenties) did not do much "mucking for gold," although he did file a claim on the nearby Henderson Creek and did live for awhile in a remote cabin which was recently found and verified to have been his. (The "Jack London cabin," as it's known, has been divided in two: the lower half is in Dawson City, the upper in Oakland; at each location new "halves" have been combined with the old to give both Dawson and Oakland an entire cabin-the Wisdom of Solomon!)

Even though London did not find mining a lucrative endeavor, his experiences with miners, Indians, Mounties, and the vast Yukon wilderness would nourish his prolific and highly profitable literary career. It is said that Jack London extracted more wealth from the Klondike than any miner.

My journey to Dawson took me to many of the locations London describes in *The Call of the Wild.* Readers of the novel will recall that the dog Buck, stolen from sunny California where he lived a life of ease, is taken to Dyea, Alaska (Dyea, now abandoned, is two miles from Skagway; we drove to the site along the unimproved road which still connects the two). In Dyea, Buck becomes a sled dog, owned first by a couple of couriers who haul mail from Skagway to Dawson, then by a group of slovenly novices to the North (who, ignoring warnings that the spring thaw has begun, die under the Yukon River ice), and finally by John Thornton, for whom Buck finally feels "love" and to whom he manifests unquestioning devotion and obedience.

When Thornton is killed by Indians in the MacKenzie Mountains (east of Dawson; no public roads go there), Buck joins a wolf pack, returning to life in the wilderness where the instincts of his ancestors emerge from their long period of dormancy.

London never realized much profit from *The Call of the Wild*; in 1903, he sold it to the *Saturday Evening Post* for $750, then released all book rights to Macmillan for $2000. These figures must have seemed immense to a struggling writer in those days-but, in hindsight, London made one of literary history's great miscalculations: his heavily anthologized novel still can be found on the shelves of just about every bookstore in America and has never been out of print.

Publication of *The Call of the Wild* made London a celebrity; from then on he published anything he wanted *wherever* he wanted. His output was astonishing (fifty books in fifteen years), and he soon became the most popular and highest-paid author in the world. He built an ocean-going yacht and set out to circumnavigate the globe (he made it no farther than the Solomon Islands where illnesses forced him home). He designed and constructed a dream house in the Valley of the Moon near Glen Ellen, California (it burned to the ground the day before he was to occupy it). He supported Socialist causes (primarily the abolition of child labor, conservation of natural resources, and the establishment of old-age pensions). But mostly he wrote, averaging more than three volumes a year.

His work varied enormously in genre (and quality!). Between 1901 and 1916 he published volumes of short stories, memoirs, essays and monographs, allegories, plays, and, of course, novels. His long works of fiction displayed tremendous energy and a desire to experiment with subject and form: he wrote on such topics as the Klondike Gold Rush (*A Daughter of the Snows*), boxing (*The Game*), pre-historic man (*Before Adam*), marital relationships (*The Little Lady of the Big House*), outofbody experiences (*The Star Rover*), and dystopian futures (*The Scarlet Plague and The Iron Heel*); he collaborated with Anna Strunsky on an exchange of letters dealing with the subject of love (*The Kempton-WaceL etters*); he wrote an autobiographical novel (*Martin Eden*), traditional yarns set on the high seas (*The Mutiny of the Elsinore*), a novelization of a screenplay (*Hearts of Three*), adventures in the South Seas (*Adventure and Jerry of the Islands*), children's stories (*Tales of the Fish Patrol and The Cruise of' the Dazzler*); he wrote stories which urged wise use of the land (*The Valley of the Moon*), which excoriated unscrupulous businessmen (*Burning Daylight*), and which exposed corruption in athletics (*The Abysmal Brute*). And, of course, he wrote about dogs (*White Fang, Jerry of the Islands, and Michael, Brother of Jerry*).

I have read every one of his books.

Before my sabbatical year, I'd read only those works still easily available (*The Sea-Wolf, Martin Eden, White Fang*, and *The Call of the Wild*). Most of the others are now out of print-deservedly so, in many cases, I fear.

I found most of the volumes at nearby Kent State University library; others I ordered through my local public library's interlibrary loan. But the final seven I could find nowhere in the area.

During a trip to Boston to visit my brothers I located five of the seven in Harvard's Widener Library. (The remaining two were in special collections, unavailable to me.)

Desperate to read the last two (*Scorn of Women*, 1906, and *The Acorn-Planter*, 1916-both were plays originally published in very small runs), I phoned Russ Kingman, a London biographer who operates the Jack London Bookstore (Glen Ellen, California), which specializes in first editions of london's works and other London memorabilia. He did not have either of the two in stock, but, aware of my unfulfilled passion (he'd once experienced it himself), he graciously provided me with copies of both plays to read. Within hours of their arrival in the mail I'd finished them both. They were dreadful-almost laughably bad-but I'd read them!

Generally speaking, London's best-known works are also his best. *The Sea-Wolf, Martin Eden, The Call of the Wild*, and *White Fang* deserve the continuing attention and admiration they've received over the years. Of the lesser known novels, The Star Rover, one of his last (1915), should take its place alongside *The Sea-Wolfas* his greatest effort. *John Barleycorn* and *The Road* are interesting for the biographical bounties they yield. A hand-ful of short stories are among the best written by an American realist.

Unfortunately, most of the rest of the London canon is embarrassing to read nowadays. In his later work especially, he expresses white suprem-acist and macho sentiments which modern readers would find repugnant. His social idealism seems naive and simple-minded. Moreover, throughout his career he wrote about the same sorts of people (strong men of action; weak men who redeem themselves through physical exertion; women who share his passions for horseback riding, hiking, boxing, and intellectual debate); his characters are interchangeable--only the names are different. Finally, nearly all his work bears the mark of haste-not surprising, for he was, in fact, forced to write rapidly to keep up with the debts which troubled him throughout his life. Always eager to move on to the next project, he revised his work in a cursory manner, but editors and publishers didn't care: readers were hungry for anything by London.

Chronic ill health in his later years worsened the situation and must have made concentration difficult. Years of alcohol abuse, debilitating ill-nesses acquired in his trips to the tropics (yaws, dysentery, pellagra), and bizarre eating habits (he went through a period when he would consume only partially cooked or raw duck)-all combined to make miserable his waking hours. At night he slept very little, preferring to use his bed as an extension of his study (much of the night he read, edited manuscripts, and maintained his wide cor-respondence). He rose before dawn each morning and wrote fifteen hundred words before he would emerge from his study to begin another long day of strenuous mental and physical activity.

To relieve his agony, he began injecting himself with morphine. Finally, on November 22, 1916, fol-lowing an attack of uremia and a final injection, his poor body could stand no more. Jack London was dead at 40. Official cause of death was kidney failure, but, in fact, his lifestyle had been a form of slow suicide.

So now, I guess, I'm ready to do a better job with *The Call of the Wild.* I can show my slides of Skagway, Dyea, Dawson City, and London's home in Glen Ellen (now a California state park); I can describe my cruise on the Yukon River, summarize all of London's published work, read relevant pas-sages from my great-grandfather's diary, display my growing collection of first editions of London's work (and *Classics Illustrated*).

I can share with my students other London-iana I've acquired over the past year: an authentic London autograph, a mint sheet of the 25-cent postage stamp issued in his honor, videotapes of *The Call of the Wild* and *Jack London* (an awful film made during World War II displaying London's vile anti-Japanese sentiments, which were, at the time, shared by many Americans), tape recordings of 1940s radio broadcasts of *The Sea-Wolf* and *The Scarlet Plague*, a numbered reproduction of a watercolor of the Jack London Cabin (painted by Yukon artist, Jim Robb), a German translation of The Cruise of the Snark (*Die Fahrt der Snark*).

I can bake sourdough biscuits prepared from the authentic starter I bought in Whitehorse, Yukon; I can... well, I could continue for quite awhile, far beyond the limits of space and reader patience. But the point is made: I think I'm ready. Now just watch what will happen: the school board will adopt a new literature text. Nothing by London will be included. Featured instead will be works by authors whom I know only from *Classics Illustrated*. And I'll be forced by conscience and insecurity to embark on yet another crazed quest. To tell you the truth, I can hardly wait.

SOCIAL DARWINISM & THE CALL OF THE WILD:

The Anti-Semitism of Nazi Political Ecology

R. Mark Musser
M. Div.

Introduction

Some 100 years before the Nazis rose to power, German philosopher Arthur Schopenhauer (1788-1860) ominously wrote that "we owe the animals not mercy but justice, and the debt often remains unpaid in Europe, the continent that is permeated with *Foeter Judaicus* … it is obviously high time in Europe that Jewish views on nature were brought to an end … the unconscionable treatment of the animal world must, on account of its immorality, be expelled from Europe."[1] That such words became prophetic under the umbrella of a secular religion of nature that was Nazi Germany colored by an environmental totalitarian views during the 1930's and 40's, is a historical truth that has been underappreciated for too long a time. Borrowing from Tacitus, *Foeter Judaicus* means "the odor of the Jews." For Schopenhauer, this bad odor was Jewish animal cruelty. Furthermore, that Adolf Hitler could quote Schopenhauer verbatim[2] from the top of his head is no coincidence, and neither

1) Schopenhauer, *On Religion*, pp. 370-77.

2) *Hitler's Table Talk*, p. xxxvii.

is the fact that the Jews would find themselves shoved into cattle cars and sent to concentration camps set up like stockyards where they would often be treated like experimental animals. Hitler made sure that the Jews would pay for their animal cruelty by subjecting them to the same punishment that he assumed they were guilty of.

Unbeknownst to many, Adolf Hitler was especially green with regard to animal rights and vegetarianism. He was however less green, but not disinterested, when it came to other environmental issues like sustainable development, anti-industrialization, conservationism and the dreaded SS "blood and soil" get back to nature romantic agrarianism, things which many Nazis were deeply involved in well ahead of its time. Hitler's racism lauded German cultural and technocratic progress, but because his Aryanism was rooted in the Social Darwinian ecology of the 1800's, he always held a certain respect for romantic and environmental thinking, in spite of some of his inconsistencies on the issue. His environmentalism was of the chauvinistic kind rather than a feminine Mother Nature brand. It was R. Trevor-Roper, the editor of "Hitler's Table Talk: 1941-44," who strongly pointed out that Hitler's naturism was a "devouring whose cruelty justified his own: not a sociable pagan Nature of nymph-haunted woods and populates streams, but a romantic Wagnerian Nature of horrid Alps in whose intoxicating solitude he could best hatch his own equally violent and implacable interventions."[3] Nonetheless, because of Hitler's penchant for Nature, many Nazi leaders were in fact very attracted to green ideas and practices, and many German nvironmentalists heartily

3) Ibid., pp. xl-xli.

volunteered to "work for the *Fuhrer.*"

How Green Were the Nazis Debate

Not surprisingly, there is thus a highly controversial debate among a limited group of scholars over how green were the Nazis that goes all the way back to Dr. Daniel Gasman's book written in 1971 called "The Scientific Origins of the National Socialism." Gasman, an expert on fascist ideology, specifically wrote his book to save Charles Darwin from being smeared with Nazi blood. Whether or not Gasman was ultimately successful in this particular matter is of course open to great debate,[4] but the the upshot of his excellent work is that he implicates instead the father of German ecology, Ernst Haeckel (1834-1919). Gasman strongly argues that Haeckel was indeed the father of German Social Darwinism which inevitably led to the slippery slope of the holocaust. Worse is that his biological and ecological views were holistic, fascist, and Anti-Semitic all at the same time.

Since the book was written, the Nazi environmental debate has been slow to develop because Gasman deals primarily with the nature religion of Haeckel and National Socialism, not their environmental views or practices. However, the Nazi ecological debate became much more heated during the 1980's when British author Anna Bramwell' wrote "Blood and Soil: Walther Darre and Hitler's Green Party." Since Gasman mentions that the SS leaders Heinrich Himmler and his teacher, Richard Walther Darre, were heavily involved in naturist youth groups that can be traced back to Haeckel and his ecological followers,

---

4) See Richard Wiekart's *From Darwin to Hitler.*

Bramwell explores this connection in much more detail. Suprisingly, Bramwell shows herself somewhat sympathetic to Darre's romantic green agrarianism, which in those days was trumpted under the slogan "blood and soil." Along the way, she characterizies Darre as a misguided radical, but demonizes Himmler. She also contrasts Darre's more reasonable environmentalism with the more radical greens that made up a sizalbe portion of the Nazi Party.

Such suggestions of course sparked a firestorm of contoversy. Bramwell's book was thus countered by Raymond Dominick' s "The Environmental Movement in Germany: 1871-1971 Prophets and Pioneers" that strongly downplayed the Nazi connections to the early German green movement. Bramwell came back in 1989 with her "Ecology in the 20th Century: A History." In this book, she also manages to take a few swipes at Gasman along the way as she tries to place distance between Haeckel and Hitler. Luc Ferry, Simon Schama, Peter Staudenmaier, Janet Biehl and Michael Zimmermann kept the ecological fascist debate simmering throughout the 90's and early 2000's with their respective works, which was finally answered by a small collection of books written by environmental historians like "Animals in the Third Reich: Pets, Scapegoats, and the Holocaust," and "How Green Were the Nazis: Nature, Environment and Nation in the Third Reich?" and "The Green and the Brown: A History of Conservation in Nazi Germany," not to mention David Blackbourn's "The Conquest of Nature: Water, Landscape, and the Making of Modern Germany."

These later books do indeed admit a convergence between early German environmentalism and Nazism that is stunning with regard to how the Nazis promoted nationalistic ecological ideas. On the other hand, the environmental historians also strongly point out that the Nazis were unable to match in practice the green rhetoric they were espousing for a variety of reasons. Thus, while it may be true that from the perspective of modern environmental historians, the Nazis were not nearly as green as they said they were, it must also be kept in mind that there was one aspect of their nationalistic environmental campaign that was accomplished with brutal efficiency – the elimination of the Jews – which in the eyes of the Nazi leadership was the first necessary step, if not the most important. Only the turning tide of the war prevented the Nazis from finishing the job that Schopenhauer prophetically announced 100 years earlier. Here begins the lesson of a nationalistic racism and environmentalism that got hotwired together into an explosive political ecology that eventually dug a biological-ecological hole as deep as Auschwitz.

German Anti-Semitic Romanticism Rebels Against Genesis 1

While Henry David Thoreau, the first environmental hippy of America going back to the 1840 and 50's was blaming the immigrant Protestants and Puritans for despoiling the New England landscape, German romantics were blaming the invasive Jewish people for the same environmental degradation taking place all around their countryside as the Industrial Revolution, supposedly fueled by Jewish capital and banks, inexorably despoiled the forested landscape and sullied wildlife habitat with dirty cities and international commercial markets. Schopenhauer, an early proponent of what is today called animal rights, alleged that this was primarily a Jewish problem, "the fault lies with the Jewish view that regards the animal as something manufactured for man's use."[5] Schopenhauer even knew precisely which primary text was to blame, "these are the effects of Genesis 1 and generally of the whole Jewish way of looking at nature."[6] Such was the conclusion of one of Germany's most important genius's of the 1800's. Schopenhauer's disciple, the great musician Richard Wagner, parroted the same environmental complaints against both Jews and Christians. Wagner of course provided the musical background for the Nazis, and was highly esteemed by Hitler as well.

While Schopenhauer and Wagner of course did not anticipate the green sacrificial offering of the Jews in the gas chambers of places like Dachau where organic farms were planted nearby to feed Himmler's SS troops, the Nazis never asked them 'how' to expel the Jews from Europe. Schopenhauer and Wagner would have undoubtedly been aghast at how literally the Nazis fulfilled such anti-Semitic ambitions, but Hitler called Schopenhauer a genius. And no wonder, for he was one who saw through the alleged nature hating tendencies of the Jews whose religious views and political economic practices were informed by the Genesis 1 mandate to subdue and fill the earth, with marriage being designated as the very vehicle which would carry out this great divine purpose in the world. The Nazis, because of their Social Darwinian evolutionary views on nature, thus derogatively characterized this as the great problem of "the Eternal Jew."[7]

---

5) Schopenhauer, *On Religion*, pp. 370-77.

6) Ibid.

7) See especially the Nazi propaganda film called "The Eternal Jew."

The Jews were 'eternal' vagabonds, uprooted from Nature and destructive to local national populations with alien economic practices and politics.

The Nazi master race was considered to be the best precisely because they eschewed this Mosaic conquest of nature, something which Hitler called "Jewish nonsense."[8] According to Nazi ideology, the so-called 'eternal Jew' is the transcendent Jew who tries to live above Nature through economics and capitalism in the west, or through politics and communism in the east. In *Mein Kampf*, Hitler specifically called this process the pacification of Nature.[9] According to Hitler, the Jews try to pacify or tame Nature through international commerce and capitalism on the one hand, or by stressing universal political values like communistic equality on the other hand, both of which rebel against the stern rigid laws of Nature which cannot be overcome. Hitler strongly asserted that instead of overcoming nature, man must instead abide by her stern rigid laws.

However, in the creation story of Genesis, Adam and Eve were crowned as the king and queen of creation, and while it is true that nature was made for the glory of God, it was also made for man since he was made in the image of God as God's reflector in human form. This view on man and nature also strongly implies an autonomous utilitarian ecology. This of course has been the most hated ideological concept by environmental thinkers for some 200 years now, and it was especially the Protestant Reformation and the Enlightenment that emphasized this utilitarian view of nature that opened the

8) Hitler, *Mein Kampf*, p. 287.

9) Ibid.

door for the Industrial Revolution and free market capitalism, the two greatest forces of the modern world which has supposedly left the earth in ecological shambles. Here Nazi environmentalist Wilhelm Linnenkamper mockingly declared that the "First Commandment" of nature protection was the "merciless extermination of the utilitarian perspective."[10] Thus Linnenkamper ratchets up Schopenhauer's beastly recommendation that the Jewish views on nature should be expelled from Europe.

Earlier German romantics like Alexander Humboldt, Ernst Moritz Arndt, Heinrich Riehl, Ernst Haeckel, and others, slowly stoked the fires of this green environmental racist campaign throughout the 1800's. It was Humboldt who stressed a form of environmental determinism where the character of man is shaped by his own particular local environment. Here is seen one of the primary foundation stones upon which the idea of the German *volk* (people's collective community), romantically and holistically embedded into their own German landscape, was born. From this point on, the German folk peasants began to be idealized as the hearty indigenous natives of Germany. While Humboldt himself was no racist, Arndt and Riehl took such environmental ideas and fused it with German nationalism and Anti- Semitism. Arndt complained bitterly about the loss of the German forestland. Riehl intensified this nationalistic ecologism into a *volkish* environmentalism that would not be undone until the smoke cleared from the battlefields and gas chambers of World War II. Riehl loved German forests and wetlands,

---

10) HStAD NW 60 no. I603, p. 300 quoted by Frank Uekoetter, *The Green and the Brown*, p. 21

but hated tourists. He loathed international cosmopolitanism, urbanism, and the city life based on alienating market values where nature was reduced to a commodity. Worse of course is that he blamed the invasive Jews for all this.

With such pro nature anti-Semitic sentiments seething in the German background in the 1800's, it was Ernst Haeckel, a zoologist of all things, who opened the door wide open to path of Nazism when he propounded a holistic, racist Social Darwinism based on 'science' called Monism in those days. Haeckel was in fact the very man who coined the term 'ecology' in 1866. Thus Haeckel will help provide the Nazis the missing link between nationalism, socialism, ecology, race and nature protection. Haeckel took the Darwinian evolutionary theory about the origin of the species, and mutated it into a Romantic pseudo- scientific religious quest to recover and preserve that origin by trying to keep the races pure. In short, the Darwinian theory of the natural selection of the species mutated into eugenics where race became fused with species, so much so that the major concern was over preserving and protecting the original or indigenous German species from the disorderly mixing of the races. In other words, Haeckel took biological Darwinism, which stressed random change and variations through natural selection and mutation, and converted it into holistic Social Darwinism where the Germans of Europe were placed on the top of the indigenous Aryan totem pole. At this juncture, Darwinian evolutionary scientific theory gets inextricably tied up with German nationalism and racism where the myth of the German *volk* now becomes defended by science, rather than seen for what it really was – largely a movement of the occult with the lower peasant classes. Haeckel was thus advocating a crackpot *volkish* romantic nationalism and nature worship, all presented in contemporary scientific garb for modern intellectual consumption.

While Haeckel was certainly anti-Christian in his nature worship, even worse is that he was anti- Semitic as well. In fact, Haeckel bears the primary responsibility of bringing up the whole Jewish question as a biological problem. Unsurprisingly he discovered that the racial characteristics of the Jews were harmfully reactionary to the evolutionary laws of the natural world. Their transcendent view of man over nature made them resistant to evolutionary biological change, and hence had become a lesser race.[11]

While Hitler may have eschewed some of Haeckel's political views, he was certainly in hearty agreement with this particular belief. Like Riehl, Haeckel also decried the unnatural cosmopolitan Jews. The Jews were not properly related to nature from an ecological-biological Social Darwinian point of view. Their blood was not properly related to the evolutionary laws of nature, nor properly embedded in the German soil. Over time this Social Darwinist emphasis on returning back to the evolutionary laws of nature further mutated into an occultic *volkish* belief in 'blood and soil,' where the German *volk* assumed that they had a special mystical relationship to the German landscape through their blood. Thus well before the Nazis had even came to power, Haeckel and the Monists essentially argued for an early Nazi version of eugenics and the environment, which later became known as "blood and soil" under the SS leadership of Himmler and Darre.

---

11) Gasman, *The Scientific Origins of National Socialism*, p. 157.

Blood & Soil Totalitarian Environmentalism

By the time of the Nazi period, 'blood and soil' had become hardened into a romantic nationalistic green ideology where the German or Nordic master race would purify itself by returning back to the simplicity of the German landscape away from the alienating asphalt culture of the big cities and free market capitalism. Nazi ideologues used the slogan for many practical purposes, everything from getting Germans back to the farm, to calls for environmental sustainability and nature preservation, to emphasizing a buy local self-sufficient agricultural economics scheme, and including the upholding of traditional German values. Thus the slogan 'blood and soil' was a popular racial environmental slogan that the Nazis used throughout the 30's representing a whole cadre of various racial green ideas and practices. Borrowing from ancient Germanic mysticism that posited that German racial identity was essentially tied literally and metaphorically to the German landscape and then cleansed by Monist scientism, the slogan 'blood and soil' had thus become a rallying cry for a nationalistic racially charged ecologism, a dangerous politicized ecology that would spell disaster for the Jewish people in particular, and would have spelled disaster for the Christians had the Nazis won the war.

Even as early as 1927, the National Socialists Physician League declared "the primacy of national biology over national economy."[12] Thus the environmental department of keeping the German landscape healthy fit in perfectly with the racial

12) *Nationalsozialistische Monatshefte*, 2, (1931): 38, quoted by Proctor, *Racial Hygiene: Medicine Under the Nazis*, p. 64.

hygiene emphasis of the medical community. The Jews were thus a source of both medical and environmental pollution. In his memoirs, Albert Speer recalls the first time he heard Adolf Hitler speak in 1931. One of issues that Hitler talked about was how the modern industrialized civilized world was destroying the biological substance of the German people.[13] Though Hitler was careful at that early time to conceal his virulent anti-Semitism before such a crowd, this certainly meant for him that the Jews were polluting German neighborhoods, both culturally and environmentally. By 1938 Hitler declared that Germany must be cleansed of the parasitic Jewish enemy and that the "eternal values of blood and soil" must be raised to "the ruling laws of life."[14] In Hitler's speech, this meant above all the removal of Jewish international commercialism which had corrupted Germany.

National Socialists actually believed that they were most in tune with Nature precisely because they had adopted her holistic Social Darwinian laws, and environmentalism played an important role under this Nazi racist biology. Nazi biologist Walther Schoenichen went so far to say that National Socialism and environmental protection stand "in a tight connection because the *Fuhrer* wills a new German *volksgemeinschaft* (people's racial community) whose foundation is drawn from blood and soil, i.e., from the primordial forces of life and soul that are proper to our race, and from the nature-willed bond that subsists between us and the sod of the homeland."[15] Not to be outdone,

---

13) Speer, *Inside the Third Reich*, p. 15.

14) Hitler is here quoted in Domarus Zweiter Halbband 1934-38, p. 890 by Robert Pois, *National Socialism and the Religion of Nature*, p. 49.

15) Schoenichen, Walther. *Nature Protection in the Third Reich* (Berlin, 1934) quoted

but Schoenichen went on to say that "Adolf Hitler demands that man must understand the basic necessity of the rule of nature and must also grasp how much his existence is subjugated from above to these laws of eternal struggle and contest."[16] As such Schoenichen reminded his readers that "no technology, no rationalism can protect us, together with our civilization from going under, if we detach ourselves from the natural foundation of life." In 1930, Schoenichen bemoaned "the unscrupulous thirst for profit that holds nothing as holy or worthy of reverence except the welfare of the cash register."[17] In October 1933, he wrote that the German landscape must be cleansed of the "un-German spirit of commerce."[18] Such talk would of course ultimately target the Jews. Schoenichen even decided to carry out a study to investigate the evil roots of outdoor advertising," it would be a worthwhile cause for inquiry in how far this social-psychic disease is the result of an infection with Jewish poison."[19]

Thus by the time of the Nazi accession to power, the Nazi Party was widely represented by a whole host of differing aspects of the early German conservationist movement. The most powerful of them was Hermann Goering, the Nazi Reich

---

by Zimmermann in "Ecofasicsm: An Enduring Temptation," p. 7.

16) Ibid.

17) Schoenichen, Walther. Quoted in Dominick, "Nazis and Nature Conservationists," 514.

18) Schoenichen, Walther, "Das deutsche Volk muB gereinigt werden – Und die deutsche Landschaft?" *Naturshutz* 14, no. 11 (1933): 207, quoted by Charles Closmann, *How Green Were the Nazis?* p. 28.

19) Schoenichen, Walther, "*Biologie*," 76, quoted by Frank Uekoetter in *The Green and the Brown*, p. 38.

Forest Minister, a mountain climber, hunter, hiker, animal and forest lover. Goering was followed by the much more mystic homeopath Rudolf Hess, Hitler's secretary and Deputy Fuhrer who had several ecologists on his staff who emphasized the need for careful holistic environmental planning.[20] Dr. Alwin Seifert was perhaps the most thoroughgoing ecologically minded Nazi environmentalist, followed by Nazi biologist Walther Schoenichen. The highly praised Nazi civil engineer, Dr. Fritz Todt, appointed Inspector General for the German Roadways by Hitler, was not only a friend of Seifert's but also was sympathetic to ecological ideas and early environmental engineering experiments.

Hans Schwenkel was a conservationist professor, and Wiepking-Jurgensmann was a Nazi landscape planner who had the best laid plans designed for the occupied East during the height of the war. For the newly reclaimed land in the Eastern territories, he and Konrad Meyer essentially proposed all kinds of environmental schemes where a shaping of nature was respectfully pursued so that man, wildlife and plants could all live harmoniously together. Wilhelm Linenkamper represented the preservationist camp in helping to set aside nature preserves. Heinrich Himmler, the infamous SS leader, was obsessed with the Nazi 'blood and soil' agrarian peasant romanticism. He also was an animal lover and a strong nature mystic. He often involved himself in conservationism and became increasingly attracted to organic farming through the influence of Hess, Seifert and Darre. Darre was the very man who was instrumental in providing Hitler with a solid green

20) Bramwell, *Ecology in the 20th Century: A History*, p. 197.

front based on romantic agrarian ideals in the early 30's – the so-called green peasant farmer – who were not very happy with Jewish capitalists and banks. The 'boy scouts' of the Nazi Party, the Hitler Youth, cannot be ignored either, which grew out of the romantic naturist youth movement of the early 1900's based largely on Ludwig Klages Anti-Semitic *volkish* environmental diatribes.

Even the Nazi Party itself had a highly proportional slice of environmental conservationists within its own ranks. Whereas only 10% of the German population belonged to the Nazi Party, between 60 and 70% of the environmentalists in various conservationists groups were Nazi Party members. This is not to say that every German conservationist was a Nazi Party member or a Nazi sympathizer, or that every conservationist joined the Nazi party because of ideological convictions, but it is to say that generally speaking, there was a convergence between Nazis and environmental conservationists that cannot and should not be ignored no matter how disturbing this may be. This was largely accomplished by the fact that Rudolf Hess and Walther Schoenichen managed to get the various conservation groups placed under the auspices of the German Labor Front in 1934. The greens were thus adopted into the Nazi Party via the German Labor Front. Thus it seems that the present cozy relationship that exists between modern environmentalism and labor may in fact have been born in Nazi Germany. As such, when the Nazis seized power, environmentalism was surprisingly given a premier role between 1933-35. Between these years, right at the outset of the Nazi accession to power, the Nazis passed several pioneering pieces of ecologically minded legislation which were in fact the most progressive environmental laws found anywhere in the world at the time. In 1935, Nazi Germany was by far the greenest regime on the planet.

Nazi Environmental Laws & Practices

In November 1933, the Nazis passed a law for the protection of animals called the *Tierschutzrecht*. Previously, Hitler declared, "in the new Reich cruelty to animals should no longer exist."[21] Even before the passing of this particular law at the federal level, Herman Goering threatened to send violators of a similar law at a local level to concentration camps. As part of this 300 page law, the Nazis also forbid cruel experiments on animals, something which they had no reservations about with regard to live experimentation on Jews later on. Closely related to this is that the Nazis even devoted an entire chapter over to the Jewish barbarity of ritual slaughter, which of course had great repercussions with regard to celebrating the Passover. Thus even as early as 1933, the realization that love for animals does not mean a love for fellow man becomes strikingly apparent, especially if you were a Jew who believed in a false unnatural religion. Goering also used 'criminals' from concentration camps for weaponry testing instead of animals.[22] No doubt, most of those 'criminals' were Jews. That Hess, Himmler and Hitler were all vegetarians is also part of the historical record and fits in perfectly with their animal loving tendencies.

With such views about animals, in July 1934, following on the heels of the *Tierschutzrecht*, Goering helped draft the Nazi law for

---

21) Ferry, *The New Ecological Order*, p. 91.

22) Irving, *Goering*, p. 180.

limiting hunting called the *Das Reichsjagdgesetz*. As part of the provisions of the law, hunting with painful traps was outlawed. With further interest is that the law was expressly passed to protect wild animals and to educate the people to develop a love and understanding for nature and its creatures as important "cultural" assets. Here once again is seen the Nazi fusion between German culture, nature and animals in a very holistic understanding. That Hermann Goering was also an avid hunter is something which modern environmental historians try to use to demonstrate that he was not really serious about animal rights protection. They are quick to glibly post pictures of Georing standing over trophies that he had shot. What they fail to appreciate is that Hitler also chided Goering for the same alleged inconsistency, "first you protect the animals, then you shoot them dead."[23]

Even in 1942 at the height of the war, Hitler remarked that, "I have never fired at a hare in my life. I am neither poacher nor sportsman."[24] Regardless of such quibbling, Goering was in fact well known to be an animal lover even years after his death.

Beyond this is that Goering also became Germany's self appointed Reich Forestry Meister. In fact, under Goering's leadership, the Nazis also made a sharp break from forestry practices of the Weimar Republic by emphasizing a new environmentally sensitive model called *Dauerwald*. *Dauerwald* means 'eternal forest' and the German conservationists of the 20's had fought hard for this forestry concept during the Weimar Republic, but without success. It was the Nazis who granted

23) Klose, Hans "Wie das Reichnaturschutzgesetz wurde," 9-14, quoted by Dominick in *The Environmental Movement in Germany*, p. 107.

24) *Hitler's Table Talk*, midday September 2, 1942, p. 516.

the romantic environmentalists their wishes when they came to power in the early 1930's. Not surprisingly, along totalitarian lines, *Dauerwald* was mandated for all German forests, including private forest owners as well. In fact, thanks to the totalitarian nature of the Nazi rule, Germany has never looked at private forests the same. Indeed, during the Nazi rule, a private German forester might find himself in jail for cutting down a conifer tree under 50 years of age.

The main thrust of *Dauerwald* was not the scientific maximization of wood production for unlimited human consumption but the desire to make the forest ecosystem more healthy in the long run so that there would more sustainable yields in the future without destroying the forest. The modern lingo for this would of course be sustainable forestry. They also planned to curtail the ecological shock of clear cutting and to protect the overall forest canopy as much as possible. This was to be done by emphasizing single tree selection rather than clear-cutting and to refrain from cutting the youngest and oldest trees. The Nazi foresters were also very concerned about eradicating diseased trees, not to mention invasive species, both of which they deemed detrimental to the German landscape. Thus the forest ecosystem must be kept consistent with its local Aryan natural healthy environment, "ask the trees, they will teach you how to become National Socialists!"[25] Indeed in 1937, Nazi conservationist Hans Stadler complained that the Jewish logger

25) Modersohn, A.W., "Weltauschauung und beruflicher Einsatz," Deutsche Forst-Zeitung 8, no. 15 (1939) 602-03, quoted by Imort in "Eternal Forest – Eternal Volk: The Rhetoric and Reality of National Socialist Forest Policy," in *How Green Were the Nazis?*, p. 54.

capitalists had purchased and processed the "last of the strong oaks and the last of the beautiful walnut trees."[26]

The high water mark for nature conservationism in Nazi Germany came in June-July of 1935 with the passing of the RNG, the Reich Nature Protection Law called the *Reichnaturs-chutzgesetz*, chock full of social engineering ecological holistic schemes, called organic in those days. The RNG required comprehensive land use environmental planning called 'environmental effects reports' before new construction projects could be built. These were essentially early forms of what is today called environmental impact statements. They of course created a huge bureaucratic paper chase scheme. The Nazi environmental slogan on this was all-encompassing, "it shall be the whole landscape!" Here the thrust of environmental totalitarianism cannot be missed, which also demonstrates why the RNG is no footnote in environmental history, the first of its kind at the federal level, precisely because of its landscape planning provisions over already developed areas that went way beyond the typical conservationist and preservationist models of environmental thinking. In fact, so ahead of its time was that even many Nazi conservationists did not really know what to do with it. Nazi biologist Walther Schoenichen pointed this problem out by arguing that "the task of landscape preservation was to influence the human use of landscapes in a certain way."[27] In other words, the RNG legalized environmental social engineering

26) StAW Landratsamt Ebern no. 1336, Der Regierungsbeauftragte fur Naturschutz in Unterfranken to the Bezirksbeauftragten fur Naturschutz in Mainfranken, March 12, 1937, quoted by Uekoetter p. 38.

27) Uekoetter, p. 141.

schemes along totalitarian lines.

As a necessary part of this environmental scheming, the RNG allowed the expropriation of land without compensation. Here is seen why the Weimar Republic was not so keen about passing environmental laws to satisfy the romantics of the 1920's. How will they compensate private property owners for loss of using their property because of environmental restrictions? For Hitler and the Nazis, this was not a problem. Thus with regard to the RNG here, one is talking about a lot more than just preserving national parks and the like, ala Teddy Roosevelt and the early conservationist movement in America with the likes of Gifford Pinchot and company. Nazi environmental laws were holistic, organic, and thus totalitarian as well. They struck at the heart of freedom and private property. Once entire landscapes and ecosystems become the hallmark of nature preservation, private property of course falls by the wayside under the stress of social engineering environmental totalitarian schemes. Thus in Nazi Germany, nature protection, socialism, collectivism and emergency powers were all used to trump private property rights. More telling is that with concerns over private property rights waning, and with the ministries of the interior, education and justice fighting over the right to control the RNG, Hermann Goering seized it for himself, "Listen Herr Rust, what's happening with *Naturschutz*? I am the only one who pursues proper *Naturschutz*. Are you agreed that it goes over to my jurisdiction? (pause) Oh but I have the forests and the animals, so *Naturschutz* fits much better in my jurisdiction than yours ⋯ OK, you are agreed ⋯ Thanks."[28]

---

28) Dominick, p. 107.

Nonetheless, with the passage of the RNG the gap between the conservationists and the Nazis was bridged. The law was universally praised. German environmentalist Hans Klose, even though he was not a Nazi party member, still called the RNG the 'Magna Carta' of German nature protection and declared that previous regimes were unable to pass such a measure because "those essential political and worldview assumptions were lacking."[29] What they lacked of course was a holistic totalitarian view of the natural world at the political level which was succinctly summarized by Hitler himself, "from now on, one may consider that there is no gap between the organic and the inorganic world."[30] Thus trying to sever the gap between man and nature was the hallmark of the Nazi regime. Hitler and the Nazis wanted to cut man down to size and plunge him back in the natural world where he rightfully belongs, and the RNG was part of this naturist campaign against the Judeo-Christian worldview. Here, Nazi environmentalist Hans Schwenkel even went so far as to point out that the Mosaic Law contained no provisions for nature protection, "since the first book of Moses, the Jews do not know nature protection, since God has given to the children of Israel all plants and animals for their enjoyment."[31] In other words, the Jews do not protect nature but exploit it as a divine right of personal selfish enjoyment.

---

29) Klose, Hans, "Der Schutz der Landschaft nach 5 des Reichnaturgesetzes," 5, 7, quoted by Closmann, "Legalizing a Volksgemeinschaft," in *How Green Were the Nazis?*, p. 32.

30) *Hitler's Table Talk: 1941-44*, evening of October 24, 1941, p.66.

31) Schwenkel, Hans, "Im Zeichen des Reichsnaturschutzgesetzes," *Natur und Heimat*, 3, no.1 (January-March 1936):1, quoted by Charles Closmann in "Legalizing a Volksgemeinschaft," in *How Green Were the Nazis?*, p. 32.

At this juncture, environmental historians quickly point out that the Nazi leadership later betrayed their initial interest in environmentalism. In fact, the environmental blitzkrieg of 1933-35 seemed to have petered out by the later 30's in a great disappointment as the Nazi hierarchy began to sacrifice their own environmental laws to get ready for an all out war effort. The animal rights and anti-vivisection laws had to be redrafted several times and thus relaxed (thanks largely to the fact that Hitler's personal doctor warned him about the scientific fallout of such a draconian measure). The great eco-theorist philosopher Martin Heidegger, who emphasized an anti-humanistic 'let it be' authentic approach to nature, lost his enthusiasm for the Nazi Party by the mid to late 30's. *Dauerwald* forestry practices were given up and replaced with a 'close to nature' approach to logging because of a rebounding economy and the upcoming war.

The enforcement of the RNG turned out to be very lax as it was massively underfunded. However, that the Nazi socialist public works machine ran roughshod over the RNG rather than the capitalists is of course nothing short of ultimate poetic justice. In the later 30's, Martin Boorman and many others like him strongly opposed the more radical green Nazis like Hess and Seifert. Thus while it is certainly true that Nazi environmentalism was not nearly as far reaching as its own laws trumpeted, this should not be surprising since the Nazis were undoubtedly far more interested in using environmental laws to restrict Jews, capitalism and private property, not their own national socialist agenda. Even so, Nazi environmentalism continued as a strong rationale for what Germany was doing throughout the 30's and early 40's. The fact of the matter is that Nazi conservationists pioneered their way up into the higher echelons of federal authority, and as such, they accomplished much with little made available to them, all in a veritable wartime atmosphere from 1936 on. Like all pioneers, they did suffer deprivation, but that is precisely what one would expect. Nazi environmentalists did more with less than most modern greens give them credit for.

White Fang & Eco-Imperialism in the East

In fact, as the war in the East blazed through Poland, the Baltics, western Russia, and the Ukraine, wide open eco-imperial opportunities often replaced German environmental efforts at home. With no small interest is that Hitler's personal attorney, Dr. Hans Frick, was made the governor-general of conquered Poland. This is the very man who publicly attacked the Jews for their Passover ritual slaughter practices in 1930 before a group of animal lovers in Munich. After he finished his tirade, the assembly adopted a resolution which stated that "the time will come for the salvation of animals from the perverse persecution of retarded subhumans."[32] The prophetic insight of that animal lover's conference about the fate of the subhuman literally became a self-fulfilling prophecy once the Nazis seized power, especially in Poland, the very place where 'blood and soil' racial environmentalism and concentration camps would come together on a barbarous scale unimaginable at the time the resolution was made. In fact, environmental landscape planners were given what they called total 'planning freedom' in the East. Salivating at the opportunities, Landscape Planner Heinrich Frierich Wiepking Jurgensmann, who was the Chair of the Institute for

32) *Volkischer Beobachter*, April 9, 1930 quoted by Dominick, p. 92.

Landscape Design at the University of Berlin, proclaimed "a golden age for the German landscape and garden designer that will surpass everything that even the most enthusiastic among us had previously known."[33] The Nazis thus had all kinds of cockamamie eco-imperial sustainable development plans for the newly acquired territories in the East.

Cleaning out Jews and Slavs for the Aryan preservation of nature shows that the great campaign in Poland and Russia was also fought for ecological reasons as well, where a depopulated East could help rebuild the natural rural health of the German people. Thus by cleansing the land from both Jews and Slavs in the East, *Lebensraum* (ecological living & breathing space) could be enlarged greatly in order to get the Germans back to more natural romantic surroundings. To accomplish all this the Nazis had plans to Germanize the landscape by creating nature preservation areas, national parks, garden cities, and pioneer farms to return Germans back to more natural healthy living conditions to help relieve their own overpopulated country. In 1941, Seifert sermonized that "if the East is to become home for Germans from all over the Germany, and if it is to flourish and become as beautiful as the rest of the Reich, then it is not enough just to cleanse the towns of past Polish mismanagement and construct clean and pleasant villages. The entire landscape must be Germanized."[34] Here is seen the complete fusion

33) Wiepking-Jurgensmann, Heinrich Friedrich, "Der Deutsche Osten: Eine vordringliche Aufgabe fur unsere Studierenden," *Die Gartenkunst* 52, 1939, 193 quoted in Wolschke-Buhlman, "Violence as a Basis of National Socialist Landscape Planning," pp. 246-47.

34) Wolschke-Buhlman, "Violence as the Basis of National Socialist Landscape Planning" in *How Green Were the Nazis?*, p. 245.

between their ecological views and their nationalistic racial pride. They were one in the same.

In other words, in the eyes of the Nazis, to Germanize the landscape was to properly take care of it by creating nature reserves, national parks and green landscape development plans for its inhabitants, all with the help of a depopulation program of Jews and Slavs to help really bring it along. Hence Nazi biologist Walther Schoenichen had dreams of getting rid of both Jews and Poles out of the Bialowieza Forest in order to turn into a giant national park in the East, much bigger than what the Poles had already designated for the area. Herman Goering wanted to use much of the same area for a giant hunting reserve for German elk and bison. Hans Klose wanted to set aside nature reserves as far east as the Caucasus Mountains looming above the vast Russian steppe. Even Polish cities would be redone with beautiful gardens. Beautiful pastoral farms would replace the huts that were scattered across the eastern landscape. Small Polish farms with many families were even converted into much larger farms for just one German family. Nature reserves, green landscape plans, organic farms and concentration camps – it's all here in the most grisly set of circumstances imaginable.

Worse is that this was a big job suitable only for the fittest planners the Reich could muster. As a part of this huge construction plan German oak trees were planted in many Polish towns as symbols of the Germanization of the landscape where little tiny acorns were to grow into huge trees with deep roots in the soil. Pagan nature mystic Heinrich Himmler was the very man placed in charge of this huge utopian construction operation, one which both he and Hitler assumed would take more than a century to complete. Himmler had even planned to use industry in the conquered territories to fund his green program of turning Poland, Ukraine and western Russia into a beautiful environmentally sustainable countryside where animals and man could live harmoniously together. On October 17, 1941, when the *Wehrmacht* was within 20 miles of the gates of Moscow, Hitler proclaimed that the East "will be one day be one of the loveliest gardens in the world."[35] However, within a matter of weeks, this green plan came to a screeching halt when the *Wehrmacht* got bogged down in the mud of primitive Russian roads, and then later virtually froze to death in one of the most brutal winters in living memory.

In spite of these tragic setbacks Himmler later stated the following in an instructional letter sent to Dachau Concentration Camp and Ester-wegen, "I wish the SS and the police also will be exemplary in the love of nature. Within the course of a few years the property of the SS and the police must become paradises for animals and Nature."[36] Thus while the Poles were being herded around and shot at, and the Jews being crammed into dirty city ghettos, a place befitting of their nature hating tendencies, organic farms were feeding the SS. As such, landscape cleansing reached an explosive climax under National Socialism. Ultimately, the Jews were sacrificed, not on altars of stone as in ancient nature worship practices, but in such vast numbers that the modern scientific engineering of the day was pushed to its limits to keep up the with the body count. Thus in Poland and Russia, millions of people were sacrificed

35) *Hitler's Table Talk*, evening of October 17, 1941, p. 54.

36) Degregori, Thomas, "Environmentalism, Animal Rights Activism, and Eco-Nazism," April 1, 2001.

by the nature religion of the Nazis because they did not fit in with their Social Darwinian get back to nature scheme, and environmentalism played a significant role in this nationalistic ecocide.

More telling still is that in 1981, Albert Speer pointed out that Himmler was both backward and helplessly romantic.[37] The SS itself hated industry, and often tried to thwart his own efforts to modernize Germany. Moreover, Speer also clearly recognized that that an industrial empire that would be able to fund such a utopian project could not be built on slave labor. Worst of all is that Hitler was ordering Himmler to gas many of the very people who were supposed to build Himmler's industrial empire. Here is seen the ultimate in a contradiction of terms. How on earth can anyone build an industrial empire on the burnt ashes of places like Auschwitz? Slave labor and human sacrifice belong to the pre-industrial world of agriculture and nature worship, not to modern industrial states. Hence, one of the great lessons of Nazi Germany is not that technology and industry are evil in themselves, as many Nazis believed, but that technology and industry are dangerous tools in the hands of people who really do not believe in it. They will invariably use industry for wrongful purposes, like, gas Jews for example, in order to build a green utopia.

That the Nazis brought to its logical conclusion the 19th century environmental complaints of Schopenhauer, Wagner, Arndt, Riehl and Haeckel goes without saying. Jews and Slavs were considered unnatural. They ruined their natural landscape and hence were worthy of what they forced to

---

37) See *Infiltration* by Albert Speer.

suffer. Environmental degradation was used to justify the ethnic cleansing of people not properly suited to their natural surroundings. Landscape Planner Heinrich Friedrich Wiepking Jurgensmann handily summarized this Jewish-Slavic conundrum quite well, all with pictures in hand and full of commentary, "the landscape is always a form, an expression, and a characteristic of the *Volk* living within it. It can be gentle countenance of its spirit and soul, just as it can be the grimace of its soullessness and of human and spiritual depravity. In any case, it is the infallible, distinctive mark of what a people feels, thinks, creates, and does. It shows, divine creative power, or part of a destructive force. The German landscape – like the German people – differs in every way from those of the Poles and the Russians. The murders and atrocities of the Eastern peoples are engraved in a razor sharp manner, in the grimaces of their native landscapes."[38] In short, the Slavs were not properly related to nature and thus should be liquidated. Even much later in 1944, when the war was all but lost, the Nazis published for the *Wehrmacht* a special edition of Wilhlem Riehl's *Natural History of the German People*. The *Wehrmacht* needed to be reminded why they were there in the first place.

38) Wiepking-Jurgensmann, Heinrich Friedrich, "Die Landshaftsfibel, 1942, 13 quoted by Wolschke-Buhlman in, "Violence as a Basis of National Socialist Landscape Planning," in *How Green Were the Nazis?*, p. 251.

Conclusion

Thus while many modern environmentalists point out the Nazi regime was an ecological catastrophe because of all its wartime destruction, the Nazi leadership viewed things much differently. The war was not an end in itself, but a means to get Germans back to a more naturally healthy rural lifestyle, and depopulating the East was at the heart of the issue. Both Himmler and Hitler even had plans to make Germany vegan after the war, following Wagner's socialist scheme to cleanse Germany from the Jews by emphasizing a vegetarian diet.[39] The quest for *Lebensraum*, or 'living space' in the East, was far more than just imperialistic form of colonialism, it was also a mystical-ecological extension of 'blood and soil' outside of Germany's borders. It was in fact an eco-imperial plan that far exceeded the evils of the western powers in their drive for colonial expansionism. Such was the dark shade of green that characterized the holocaust, so dark in fact that the green nature of it all has been camouflaged and overlooked for many years now. Or as one German physicist acutely observed, "if you mix green with red, you will get brown."

39) Proctor, *The Nazi War on Cancer*, p. 139.

민경택

충남대학교 영어영문학과를 졸업하고 충남대학교에서 박사학위를 취득하였으며 현재 충남대학교 영어영문학과에서 교수로 재직 중이다. 미국 Clark University에서 방문교수를 마치고 한국현대영어영문학회 회장을 역임하고 현재 미국소설학회 감사와 한국현대영어영문학회 자문위원을 맡고 있다. 저서로 『비극적 세계에서 희망찾기-멜빌과 그린의 작품세계-』, 『미국소설 명장면 모음집』 (공저), 『모비딕 다시 읽기』 (공저), 『영화로 읽는 영미소설1-사랑이야기』 (공저), 역서로 『알파 미국문학사』 (공역), 『미국소설과 서술기법』 (공저) 등이 있다. 그리고 "But the Past Was Not Dead.": The Meaning of the Past in Hawthorne's Novels 등 영미소설에 관한 다수의 논문을 발표했다.

Jack London

THE CALL OF THE WILD

& Other Stories

WITH ESSAYS IN CRITICISM

초판 발행 _ 2018년 2월 28일

편 주 자 · 민 경 택
발 행 인 · 정 현 걸
발　　행 · 신 아 사
인　　쇄 · 토탈프로세스
주　　소 · 서울시 은평구 통일로 59길 4(2F)
전　　화 · 02)382-6411 · 팩스 02)382-6401
홈페이지 · www.shinasa.co.kr
E-MAIL · shinasa@daum.net
출판등록 · 1956년 1월 5일 (제9-52호)

ISBN 978-89-8396-264-5(93840)

정가 15,000원